TURN UP THE STROBE

THE KLF, THE JAMS, THE TIMELORDS
A HISTORY

IAN SHIRLEY

TURN UP THE STROBE

STROBE

THE KLF, THE JAMS, THE TIMELORDS A HISTORY

IAN SHIRLEY

CHERRY RED BOOKS

First published in Great Britain in 2017 by Cherry Red Books (a division of
Cherry Red Records), Power Road Studios, 114 Power Road, London W4 5PY.

A CIP Catalogue record for this book is available from the British Library.

ISBN: 978-1-909454-63-7

Design/Layout: Nathan Eighty (nathan.eighty@gmail.com)
Cover photograph by Dave Anderson
Back cover quote: Jimmy Cauty, Melody Maker, 16th February 1991.

CONTENTS

ACKNOWLEDGEMENTS

I would like to thank Richard Anderson at Cherry Red for being brave enough to commission this book when neither of us was sure if anyone would talk. Thankfully, many people were willing and I would like to thank the following, who were gracious enough to either be interviewed face to face or answer questions by email or otherwise: Azat Bello, James Brown, Patrick Buchanan, Chris Clunn, Nick Coler, Martin Collis, Ben Cull, Phil Harding, Kevin Foakes, Martin Glover (Youth), Dominic Glynn, Maxine Harvey, Nick Halkes, Mick Houghton, John Hollingsworth, Noddy Knowler, Clive Langer, Nigel Laybourne, Andrew Lee, Tom Langton-Lockton, Kris Needs, Neil McCormick, Rolo McGinty, Mark Manning (Z), Bernie Mirault, Adam Morris, Errol Nicholson, Nancy Noise, Richard Norris, David 'Yorkie' Palmer, Alex Paterson, Simon Patterson, Karel Post, Ed Sirrs, Andrew Swain and Lawrence Watson.

I would like to extend particular thanks to Andrew Lee and Yorkie (who, amongst other things, let me see that famous basement), as well as Nick Coler, who answered a number of detailed questions with good grace. Thanks also to the members of various KLF groups online, who were very gracious with their time in steering me not only towards online archive material but answering a number of nit-picking questions. I would also like to thank the John Peel Archive for access. There were also a significant number of people who contributed in some way or other to this book who wish to remain anonymous - I respect your wishes but would like to thank you as well. For those of you who *really* wanted to talk but felt that the time wasn't right, the door is still open...

Finally, in the fantasy world of my imagination it would be nice to think that I could end up having a kind of *Come Dine With Me* session with Drummond and Cauty, where they talk off the record to correct my mistakes as well as reflect on their past.

One thing I learned from The KLF - if you can dream it, it just might happen.

Ian Shirley
Transtreatham, 2017

INTRODUCTION

"I was working on it solid up to Xmas before I took a two-week break. That was fatal because, in the meantime, I had another idea to do something. There's a lot of Bill Drummond in it, a case of me trying to understand myself really. I've described it as a science fiction book because there'll no doubt be details in it that are perceived as lies by certain people. Calling it SF is like my get-out clause."
- Bill Drummond discussing unpublished novel,
Melody Maker April 1987

In an ideal world, this book would have been based on interviews with everybody who ever crossed the paths of Bill Drummond and Jimmy Cauty, as well as the main protagonists themselves. Sadly, both Drummond and Cauty declined to be interviewed for this book, and a number of their former associates who were contacted also did not want to speak. With regards to some friends and collaborators, I imagine there was some worry about the "million pound question", one which has dogged the steps of Drummond and Cauty ever since the 23rd August 1994 in that boathouse on Jura and has been the main focus of attention since then.

With the pair returning to active duty in 2017 there's been a lot of media interest in their legacy that, sadly, has given too much attention to the million pound question. This probably kept a few fish away from the Good Ship Shirley, worried that I might try to hook them for a quotes about all of that business up in Jura. To be clear, if you are interested in that side of the coin then this book is not for you, and you are directed to John Higgs' *Chaos, Magic and the Band Who Burned A Million Pounds*. This book is about the music, and won't be using a little philosophical kindling to build a theoretical fire. Of course, I cannot say that *Turn Up The Strobe* is chapter and verse on The KLF as I don't have the two protagonists serving up insights, information and perspective. Both have remained tight-lipped for twenty-three years and, although Drummond has leaked some information in his extensive writings, the only time they went on record was in an all too brief chapter on their activities for Richard King's excellent book on independent music, *How Soon Is Now?*

Thankfully, both Drummond and Cauty were interviewed on numerous occasions in the music press between 1987 and 1992, when The Justified Ancients of Mu Mu, The Timelords, The Orb, Space, and The KLF were active, and my extensive trawl through print and digital archives means they are very much present in the following pages. Drummond, in particular, probably filled more than one field of a donkey sanctuary with his ability to talk the hind legs off that particular breed of animal and spoke like Charlie Parker, with a wonderful inventive flow of words. Cauty was a bit more Miles Davis in his choice of verbal notes, restrained and measured but equally compelling.

Turn Up The Strobe starts before the key 1987-1994 period, taking a look at Drummond's membership of Big In Japan and his time spent running Zoo Records and managing Echo And The Bunnymen and The Teardrop Explodes. It also looks at his time as an A&R man at Warner Brothers, where he, conveniently, tried to turn Brilliant into a mainstream chart act in tandem with David Balfe. Brilliant, in its final incarnation, featured Jimmy Cauty in the line-up, and he, as you will see, also had some previous musical and artistic form.

This is, I feel, an honest and open look at a wonderful musical, visual and artistic legacy that remains one of the highlights of the late '80s and early '90s. One written with genuine affection for all involved, from Big In Japan to The KLF. That the music Drummond and Cauty recorded has remained deleted for a quarter of a century is something I hope they will put right. - everything they recorded should be legally available across multiple platforms, from the vinyl racks of the Rough Trade shops in London to the Apple servers that allow the world to surf amongst the musical pillars of iTunes. The KLF's music should be on streaming services too, filed alongside the Klaxons, Killing Joke, and even Kool And The Gang. Whilst their videos and music can be seen and heard on YouTube, like all great art it should be *properly curated* and is currently ill-served by a number of enthusiastic or mercenary bootleg CDs and records. After all, it's their music rather than the burning of paper that we should be celebrating as their legacy. No one would have been interested in the activities of The K Foundation and their other post KLF literary and artistic endeavours if they'd not recorded classics like *What Time Is Love?*, *3AM Eternal*, *Last Train To Trancentral* and *Justified And Ancient*. Indeed, The Orb's *A Huge Ever Growing Pulsating Brain That Rules From The Centre Of The Ultraworld* has also helped to make the world better place. It was the success of Bill Drummond and Jimmy Cauty in the music business that gave them the financial and artistic credibility to launch their post KLF careers.

Crucially, Bill Drummond and Jimmy Cauty did not work in a

vacuum, and the music they made was informed by what was going on at the time. In the late '80s, sampling was beginning to be part of the creative process, allowing artists to stitch together new clothes from older fabrics. When these new clothes began to look wonderful, record companies were only too happy to sell them to a new generation, despite the resulting conflict over copyright and compensation. And, lest we forget, the eventual success as The KLF was only possible due to the rise of Chicago, techno and acid house, and the adoption of *What Time Is Love?* as an underground trance anthem. The KLF story *could* have petered in 1989 after the undercooked *Kylie Said To Jason*, rather than expand outwards into the musical big bang that led to their becoming one of the biggest bands in the UK and Europe in 1991. But, I'm getting ahead of myself...

In closing, it's unfortunate that, whilst I managed to interview anonymous members of The Residents for one of my previous books, I was unable to speak to the members of The KLF, even though we live in the same city. There is also the famous storage unit crammed full of all manner of archive material that I didn't have access to, as well as lost interviews with those people who declined to participate in this project. So, what follows is not presented as the original version of The KLF story but my *remix* of that story.

Mr. Drummond and Mr. Cauty, I bow down and accept the contradiction.

Ian Shirley

OPENING SCENE: CAN YOU HEAR IT IN A SONG?

We are at the National Theatre in London on the South Bank. The Oliver Theatre, to be precise.

The stage is empty apart from a young man, well over six feet tall, wearing blue jeans turned up at the hem and a plaid shirt. He is holding a large hammer by the head in his right hand, arm limp at his side. The man is illuminated by a single white spotlight.

At this point, an older man runs onto the stage. This actor immediately conveys a feeling of drive, energy and power to the audience. He runs across to the younger man and grabs him by the shirt. Looking him directly in the eye, he begins to shout with great passion, "Bill, it has got to be heroic! Heroic! Do you understand me? IT HAS GOT TO BE HEROIC!"

Next, the lights dim and the older man runs from the stage, screaming the word "HEROIC!" as he departs. Out of the bowels of the stage a set emerges, and two characters perform part of the play *Illuminatus!*, first staged in the Liverpool Science Fiction Theatre in November 1976, then, after a brief run in Amsterdam, transferred to the National Theatre in London, where it ran at the Cottesloe in March 1977. Such was its success that it had another brief outing at London's Roundhouse too.

The man with the hammer remains on stage watching the action. He constructed the set that the actors are performing against with the very hammer that he holds in his hand. After a couple of minutes of dialogue the set and the actors begin to rotate and slowly vanish downwards into the bowels of the theatre, out of sight of the audience. Then, another set emerges from the depths. It is a white circular wall ten feet high, containing a large rectangular double glazed window with a mixing desk directly beneath it. There are speakers fixed to the wall either side of the rectangular glass window.

The man walks forward and places the hammer on the mixing desk. As he does so a young attractive man in his early twenties walks onto the stage wheeling two chairs that he sets in front of the mixing desk. They both sit down. The man we know as Bill sits on the left, and the attractive young man on the right.

13

There is movement beyond the window, and we can see that behind the glass is a recording studio containing a four-piece band. We cannot see them all, but the lead singer is prominent and stands behind a large professional microphone. We can also see the drummer sitting behind acoustic baffles directly behind him. The bass player is to his left and the guitarist stands to his right. The man, Bill, who no longer holds the hammer, presses a button just in front of the mixing desk and speaks into a microphone on his side of the glass. "OK lads," he states in a rich Scottish accent, "Let's go for a take. I want it to be legendary. Legendary, you hear me?"

After a brief interval the band begin to play a song called *The Pictures On My Wall*, and are about thirty seconds into the track when the attractive young man beside Bill the Scotsman reaches over, presses down the button of the intercom and interrupts the performance by speaking to the band, "Can you stop, please?"

The band stop playing, "What's the problem, Balfey?" the lead singer says in a thick Liverpool accent.

"You weren't together," states the attractive young Balfey.

"It sounded great to me," challenges the singer "What do *you* want Bill? Do you want us to be legendary or together?"

The Scotsman, whose full name is Bill Drummond, stands up and, pressing down the button, talks to the singer.

"Ian, I want you and the Bunnymen to be *LEGENDARY TOGETHER!* Do you understand me? LEGENDARY TOGETHER!"

ZOO DAYS

"There's nothing really original in Liverpool. There's not another Liverpool sound or anything. There will be soon, because there is definitely a lot of enthusiasm around, but it's just at the moment everyone seems to be so far behind London."

**- Member of The Yachts,
Melody Maker, October 1977**

"'I like mountaineering,' said Bill, 'with a hit record I could fund an expedition.'"

- New Musical Express, 1978

"When Mac (of the Bunnymen) walks down the street you know he is a star. That's another thing. The Zoo doesn't mind stars. As long as they are real stars."

**- Bill Drummond letter to Dave
McCullough, Sounds journalist,
August 1979**

"...and something Bill Drummond said when the Teardrops first started set him off laughing aloud, 'Don't ever take acid Copey,' Drummond had said, 'You're quite like that in any case and it would be just horrible!'"

**- Julian Cope, Melody Maker,
May 1984**

In an interview in 1986, Julian Cope revealed that he was writing a book about the early days of the Liverpool music scene. This Cope manuscript evolved into *Head-On,* a no holds barred classic published in 1994 to rave reviews and detailing not only the rise and disassembly of The Teardrop Explodes but, amongst other things, their rivalry with Echo And The Bunnymen.

As you might imagine, Cope was centre stage at all times - it was his book, after all - but what made *Head-On* so compulsive was the great supporting cast of characters. The Teardrop Explodes' keyboard player David Balfe, for example, fulfilled a kind of Iago role to the cotton-sock wearing Othello, and spent most of the time going through a revolving door as he fell in and out of Cope's affections. Another main protagonist in the book was Bill Drummond, who first stepped onto the stage of the Liverpool music scene after seeing The Clash perform at the famed Eric's club in Mathew Street on 5th May 1977.

A key factor behind the formation of what became Big In Japan was a Liverpool band called Deaf School, who had signed to Warner Brothers and released their debut album *2nd Honeymoon* in 1976, and were to follow it up with *Don't Stop The World* in 1977. Deaf School was an art school band shipwrecked by the emergence of punk rock, but had built up a strong following in Liverpool. "The reason Big In Japan started," states Clive Langer (aka Cliff Hanger), Deaf School's guitarist, "was because they were Deaf School's road crew. We'd gone to America and had left all of our equipment in Liverpool, so Phil Allen and Kevin Ward - who used to do our lights - they decided to start a band." Although Drummond was not a roadie, he was a friend and keen to get involved, and along with the Spitfire Boys, Big In Japan were one of the first punk bands in the Liverpool area.

The original line-up was a trio of Kevin Ward (bass/vocals), Phil Allen (drums) and Bill Drummond on guitar, and Big In Japan made their debut in May 1977 at a teacher training college called Bretton Hall in Wakefield, where they supported The Yachts, another Liverpool band sailing in waters that were to be marked on the nautical map as powerpop. Big In Japan played three songs they'd written the day before. "We also tried to do *Louie Louie*," Ward told a *Melody Maker* journalist in October 1977, "I knew the bassline and we thought that was enough. That was stupid. The guitarist was a total nutcase on stage. He's like Captain Sensible on guitar – just goes totally out of control. No one took it seriously, which was good." With no more material available, they also played a song called *Big In Japan* a second time. The nutcase on guitar – Drummond – later stated, "We went down a storm and realised we could get away with it."

The band soon recruited Jayne Casey to help out on vocals, becoming a four-piece before Ian Broudie became the fifth member, joining the line-up to add another guitar. At twenty-four years old, Drummond, whose CV already included a stint as a trawler fisherman, an art student and a set designer, was the elder statesman, making sure the band worked hard in the rehearsal room and taking care of important matters such as booking and driving the vans used to transport the band to gigs. When he returned from touring America with Deaf School, Langer went to see Big In Japan and, "I was quite excited by what they were doing, as it was a bit more relevant for that period than what Deaf School had become. So, when the opportunities arose, I would jump on stage with them." Langer was never officially a member of Big In Japan, "I was more like a friend, as I lived in the same flat as Kevin and would see them all the time, and if Deaf School weren't working I would hang around with them."

Langer saw Big In Japan many times during these early days and recalls that, "right at the beginning they were quite shambolic. It depends on what period you're talking about, I think. The Big In Japan I knew was Stage One, with Phil on drums and Kevin as the lead singer really, and Jayne was, I think, doing bits and pieces. Bill was there, and Ian as far as I can remember. They were good but a bit shambolic. Bill was always good live because he was one hundred and ten percent all thrown in. They couldn't play very well initially, but then they got better and better quite quickly. It was those punk days when anyone could do it, and if you're not that good it doesn't matter."

Big In Japan was soon a fixture at Eric's as a support act, and then as a headliner, and built up a small but dedicated following inspired by their music, look and set list. "We were known as the Liverpool punk band," Drummond told Mark Cooper for his book *Liverpool Explodes!* in 1982, "but we weren't really punk, we were show band punk. We didn't have the idealism that the younger people had. I wanted to have hit singles." Whether or not songs like *Suicide A Go Go*, *Taxi* and *Big In Japan* were potential hit singles wasn't put to the test with a major label, although *Melody Maker* were prescient in describing the band as a, "conceptual art attack" rather than as a punk or new wave band.

True to the emerging DIY spirit of the time, the first time Big In Japan appeared on plastic was on the first single that Eric's issued on its own eponymous label in November 1977. By this time Roger Eagle, who ran the club, was also their manager, and for economic purposes the 7", called *Religion Brutality And A Dance Beat* and featuring the track *Big In Japan*, was split with The Yachts, who contributed *Do The Chud* under another name – The Chuddie Nuddies – as they'd just issued their debut single, *Suffice To Say,* on the Stiff label.

Amazingly, Drummond didn't play on *Big In Japan* as he was on holiday in Brittany in August when the band went into the studio, and Clive Langer was drafted in to play his parts. "When I got back and heard about this, and that it was going to be our first single, I was…. I was going to say 'devastated' but that would be too strong a word," Drummond later wrote in 2006, "but disappointed isn't the right one either." He must have been upset - he was a founder member of the band, and for Eagle to record the song without him would have been frustrating. As for being drafted in at short notice, Clive Langer recalls, "It was, 'Bill can't make it - do you want to play?' OK... (sings) Big in Japan! Big in Japan! - It was not very hard to learn. Bill wasn't there, so I stepped in." As for Drummond, Langer remembers, "He didn't seem to be bothered really. We didn't fall out about it. I would not have done it if he wouldn't have been OK about it."

The single was reviewed in the music press, with Ian Birch in the *Melody Maker* stating, "It's conceptual art school mayhem, with vocalist Jane howling out 'Big In Japan' and winding up in some ludicrous chopstick percussion." As for the emerging fanzines, one named *Chainsaw* stated that, "The Chuddy Nuddies is the good one. It's a bit Stranglers-ish - lots of organ, not very much guitar. As for Big In Japan... well the tune is alright but the vocals... it's so high pitched squeaky and shrill it sounds like someone's killing a vicar. It's so bad I'm getting to like it."

A copy of the split single was actually sent to John Peel by Noddy Knowler, who'd first met Peel in the summer of 1975 when the Radio One DJ was booked to play a gig at Liverpool University's Carnatic Halls of Residence in Mossley Hill. Knowler, along with his partner David Kay, was a DJ himself with the Radio Doom Mobile Good Guys Disco, and was also booked to play that date, arranging in the process for Peel to use their equipment to play his records. After the gig, a grateful Peel told Knowler that if he was ever down in London he should pop into the BBC and sit in the studio when he was broadcasting his show, which was, at that time, called *Top Gear*. Knowler, along with his girlfriend, later took up this invitation, and also went out to dinner with Peel, "and someone from Virgin records who might or not have been Richard Branson, but I can't remember." With regards to the Eric's single, Knowler was used as a go-between and wrote to Peel, "Please find enclosed a copy of the first release on the Eric's label. Double A side by all accounts. Prefer the BIG IN JAPAN side myself."

Musically, Drummond was right in describing Big In Japan as a punk show band - a track like *Cindy And The Barbie Dolls* worked well with Casey's strong theatrical presentation, whereas *SCUM (Society For Cutting Up Men)* drew inspiration from the assassination attempt on artist Andy Warhol. "Well, that's been dropped from the set now," Drummond told a fanzine writer some time in 1978, "We're doing about ten new songs and there wasn't really room for it." As one of the songwriters, Drummond also fielded a question about why Big In Japan songs were observational narratives rather than dealing in subjects like boredom, oppression, unemployment and teenage angst, which were becoming the stock in trade of many punk and new wave bands. "I don't know. It's never occurred to me when I've been writing songs. I mean, do I have to mention Liverpool Football Club to convince you that we prefer our heritage to a televised culture?"

One young, hardcore Big In Japan fan was David 'Yorkie' Palmer (later of Space), who saw the band at Eric's on a number of occasions. "I can never express to people how great Big In Japan were," he told me, "Jayne won't have it, Ian (Broudie) won't have it, Bill won't have it. It was just their band to them, but to me, as a young kid and as a fan, it was astonishing, just the subjects of their songs. I was into Warhol and Burroughs and they covered both of them. I'd found a band that liked the same things that I liked and wrote songs about it."

Palmer not only saw Big In Japan at Eric's but also travelled to a number of gigs outside the Liverpool area, including one in Stockport. Here he saw how Casey dealt with a crowd, "It was packed in there, and there was some lad at the front giving it "Get your tits out!" to Jayne (who had marvelous tits), but I just remember she grabbed hold of this lad's hair and she was doing *Cindy And The Barbie Dolls* and singing "Oh Oh Oh Cindy" and swinging his head around, the poor fellah. It must have really hurt, but she just locked onto him for the rest of the song. That's a nice memory - you just did not fuck with Jayne."

It was Palmer who later coined the famous description of Big In Japan as a "supergroup in reverse," as many of them went on to greater things. But at that time they were struggling to get a contract and win fans outside their hardcore support. "There were things like the Probe Records petition to get them to split up," laughs Palmer today. "People thought they were just a fucking joke. But, being Big In Japan and being Bill, the first people to sign the petition were them."

This petition was instigated by a short-lived band called The Nova Mob, whose membership included two young lads called Pete Wylie and Julian Cope. "We were dedicated to making Big In Japan split up," Cope later told Mark Cooper in 1982, "We wanted to get a petition of fourteen hundred filled, and then they'd have to split up. Drummond insisted on fourteen thousand, so we said, OK. We had all these petitions up in Probe Records and places, but a lot of people thought it would be undiplomatic to sign. Big In Japan all signed it - with gusto! Phil Allen signed it because the rest of them had just kicked him out of the band. We only got about seven signatures!"

Although there was talk of a month of gigs in London, the recording of demos and a possible deal with Jet Records that eventually fell through, this didn't translate into a recording contract with an established record company. By 1978 there had also been line-up changes, with Budgie (Peter Clarke) joining on drums, and when new bass player

Holly Johnson missed a week of rehearsals he was replaced by Dave Balfe, who'd already been through the ranks of a few bands. But, by the summer of 1978 Big In Japan were approaching the end of the road.

After the Stockport gig, having missed the last train back to Liverpool, Palmer was given a lift by the band and recalls one of them asking Budgie, "'How can you join The Slits? You've got a penis.' Budgie is sitting there looking really dejected because everyone was having a go, and in hindsight now I know that everyone was having a go because they were on the verge of calling it a day. He was going to play with The Slits and they thought, 'You won't get the job, you're not good enough.' And then he did. Then he joined the Banshees and is one of the best drummers to come from that era."

Big In Japan split up after their last gig at Eric's on 26th August 1978, and Casey was quick to form Pink Military Stands Alone. But after a live EP they took their time in making their next musical statement. "In the last year we've been very quiet and stayed out of things, but it's been a planned things really," Casey told the *New Musical Express* in 1980, "we didn't want to play much - we weren't ready for it, we were working towards something. Now, we're ready to make a brilliant LP."

As for Bill Drummond, he planned to set up a record label called Bill's Records, specifically to issue a single by Big In Japan. He struck a deal with Noddy Knowler, who, in April 1978, had moved from Radio Doom to run a two-track studio that was part of the Merseyside Visual Communications Unit (MVCU), based upstairs at 90-92 Whitechapel in Liverpool. The MVCU traded under the name Open Eye, and also ran a gallery and a cafe. Knowler had been brought in to record local bands, had already upgraded the studio from two to four tracks and, as time progressed, began producing a number of bands from Liverpool and the surrounding area, including Big In Japan.

According to Knowler, "When I met Bill Drummond they were in the middle of splitting up," but this meeting led to his helming a number of tracks in the MVCU studio to go on the proposed EP. "It was funny because it was almost a posthumous recording," Knowler recalls today. He remembers laying down three tracks - *Cindy And The Barbie Dolls*, *Nothing Special* and *Match Of The Day* – and, as for how things went, "It was a four track studio, so we recorded the backing track – the drums, the bass and guitar – as a stereo pair then we overdubbed the vocals on the third track and the lead guitar on the fourth track. That was standard procedure."

With the band splitting up after the recording and a final gig at Eric's, the now former Big In Japan bass player David Balfe asked Drummond if he could get involved with the label; "Drummond was six years older than me and he'd done a lot," Balfe stated a couple of years later, "and there was me, this weird kid who'd come over from the fields a month before." But Drummond agreed, and the name Bill's Records was discarded before the eventual name for this new independent label was settled on - Zoo Records. According to Knowler, however, the first single was basically an MVCU record, "because we paid for everything. We recorded the A-side – the B-side tracks they already had in the can so their contribution was those - the two A-side tracks and all the costs were MVCU," As for the label name, "Bill had thought of the name Zoo and I went along with it."

In November 1978, Zoo issued the resulting four track Big In Japan EP, *From Y To Z And Never Again*. The tracks - *Nothing Special, Cindy And The Barbie Dolls, Suicide A Go Go* and *Taxi* - were recorded between 1977 and 1978 and featured the various line-ups of the band, from the Y-Z of their career. The arresting, fold-out sleeve clearly thanked the MVCU, "for putting up the money to make this record," and, musically, it was an excellent, short sharp overview of the band, and a fitting vinyl tombstone.

When it came to John Peel, Knowler now took Bill Drummond down to London with him to personally hand-deliver a copy. "That was my second visit to John, and by then his show was on in the evening – ten o'clock. He said it looked very good, but he couldn't play it until he'd reviewed it." What Peel meant by this was to actually play the record and establish the exact timings of the tracks and make sure there was no swearing on it - this was, after all, the BBC. Knowler and Drummond actually sat in the studio as Peel was broadcasting his show, and Knowler remembers Peel spinning around on his chair to say something to them and knocking the arm of the turntable, so that the record being broadcast actually jumped live on air.

Ironically, when Peel did listen to the Big In Japan EP the record must have jumped on one or more of the tracks as he had to request another copy due to a faulty pressing. "There isn't really any need to pay for it, since it's merely a replacement," replied Knowler - at this time, there was no Zoo postal address, only the MVCU's on the letterhead. Peel must have commented that he found *Cindy And The Barbie Dolls*, with Casey's sped up helium vocals acting as a strange counterpoint to Ian Broudie's singing, not to his taste, as Knowler - who had produced the track at MVCU in August 1978 - was quick to defend it:

"You should give *Cindy And The Barbie Dolls* another listen - it really is the best track on the EP! I know the 'pinky and perky' vocals are a bit off-putting at first, but after a couple of listens they just add to the absurdity of the whole thing. I feel that the overall effect follows in the true traditions of The Bonzos and The Mothers! English comedy music at its best! (I know that The Mothers isn't English comedy music but I feel that *Cindy* is very much a cross between The Bonzos and Zappa's Mothers as Ruben & the Jets)."

Crucially, the EP received positive reviews; "Another independent worthy of a basinful of anyone's airwaves. Actually, it's mainly the great *Taxi* track that makes the whole thing value for money, particularly Jayne's vocals and the climax after five minutes, fading out on a drum sound as full as a bull's bum," wrote Danny Baker in the *New Musical Express,* whilst Andy Courtney at *Sounds* declared it, "Excellent material carelessly handled in the studios, but there are redemptions. *Nothing Special* is outstanding: a self-effacing someday superstar settles for pop defeat, and possibly a goatskin hankie from Jackie O's wardrobe."

Of course, whilst there was a strong market for the *From Y To Z And Never Again* EP in Liverpool, Drummond later related how, as there was no independent national distribution network at the time, to shift units on the back of good reviews like this they drove to record shops around the county in David Balfe's father's car. Knowler recalls that, when he took Drummond down to Peel to hand him a copy of the EP, they'd also gone around trying to get places like Rough Trade to take copies at the same time.

The positive reaction to the EP in the music press led to a reunion of sorts, via the offer of a Peel session. Whether Peel or his producer John Waters contacted Drummond, Knowler, MVCU, Zoo or somebody else in the band is unknown, but on 12th February 1979 a line-up of Jayne Casey, Holly Johnson, Ian Broudie and Budgie laid down three tracks - *Suicide High Life, Goodbye* and *Don't Bomb China Now* - which were broadcast on 6th March 1979. Notable by his absence was Bill Drummond, who bookended his Big In Japan career by not taking part in their last recording session. Maybe he was spending a day at the Zoo with David Balfe.

The posthumous EP sold around six thousand copies, and at this stage Knowler recalls that Drummond and Balfe strolled off with the label, which really could have been the genesis of the MVCU's own imprint. "We should have registered the name really, but Colin Wilkinson who was in charge of MVCU wasn't bothered. He said to me, 'What's in a name? It's what's in a group that counts.'" Subsequently, The MVCU established their own Open Eye label, whose first release was *Street To Street - A Liverpool Compilation,* an album which not only featured the Knowler-produced Big In Japan track *Match Of The Day* but had sleevenotes penned by John Peel. He described the track as, "a little gem that reasserts the strength of the twangy guitar in a perverse little theme that would have made John Barry spit with impotent rage fifteen years ago."

With regards to Zoo, Drummond later stated that he wanted the second single to feature Pete Burns, who worked at Probe Records, displayed a unique dress sense and was one of the dominant personalities on the small Liverpool scene. He'd already been in a short lived band - The Mystery Girls - with Julian Cope and Pete Wylie, and was in the process of forming a band called Nightmares In Wax, but the plan didn't bear fruit. Instead, Zoo's second single was Those Naughty Lumps' *Iggy Pop's Jacket*, released in February 1979. By this time, Drummond and Balfe's car journeys had forged a partnership with emerging independent distributors like Rough Trade, Lightning and Bonaparte, who handled a single that was either fully or partially funded by the band.

Crucially, Drummond wrote to John Peel, not only to promote this second single in the Zoo catalogue but also the third by a new band called The Teardrop Explodes, whose recording and pressing he'd financed with a bank loan. "Both bands are from Liverpool," he wrote, "Those Naughty Lumps have been about for over a year, delighting many with their shambolic sets. The Teardrop Explodes have only been together since just before Christmas and are everybody's favourite not so serious, serious band around here. They are doing a spot for Granada TV this Thursday night. If you are interested I can send you info and tapes of both bands. Thanks." The TV appearance in question was on *What's On,* presented by Tony Wilson, where the band performed the B-side of that third Zoo single, *Camera Camera.*

The Teardrop Explodes emerged out of a group of young men who gravitated towards Eric's, had seen bands like The Sex Pistols, The Clash and The Damned and began turning threats of forming their own bands into reality. As well as conversations in Eric's, on the top of the buses that went in and out of the city centre and over cups of tea at the Armadillo Tea Rooms, one of the most important factors in the emergence of the Teardrops was a basement in the Fairfield area of Liverpool. So, let's rewind the tape a little.

"There was this lad I saw walking up and down the road with a bass guitar and he looked cool and I was into punk and that," recalls David Palmer, "I remember the first time I plucked up the courage to shout across the road, 'Are you going to see The Adverts at the Malford Hall tonight?' He said, 'Oh, no' - *very polite* in fact - and walked over towards me and said, 'I'm going to see Pere Ubu at Eric's.' I'd not heard of Eric's before, and I'd never heard of Pere Ubu. After subsequent conversations he lent me Pere Ubu records - they were his favourite band - on the original labels, and on *pain of death* if I scratched them or whatever. We started talking and he came around a couple of times."

This meeting with Julian Cope was before Palmer had been to

Eric's and seen Big In Japan, but was at a time when Cope was beginning to fold and unfold a number of bands together and, eventually, turning to the practicalities of actually making music. "He started this band called The Shallow Madness and asked if they could rehearse in our cellar," recalls Palmer. "I said, 'I'll ask my mum,' and she said, 'No.' I must have mentioned it a few times and he asked a few times and for some reason she relented. She said, 'We'll try it.' We had to run a lead down from upstairs before we got the electricity sorted, then they started rehearsing there as The Shallow Madness."

The Shallow Madness was the last stop on a list of many bands Cope journeyed through to reach his final destination with The Teardrop Explodes. In fact, he broke up The Shallow Madness one morning at the Armadillo Tea Rooms and formed the Teardrop Explodes the same afternoon with the same line-up - Paul Simpson on keyboards and Mick Finker on guitar - but with Gary Dwyer replacing Dave Pickett on drums. Cope played bass and sang. Palmer: "From then on it was my mum putting up with this band making a racket downstairs, because there was no soundproofing until, to make it easier for her, we brought lots of boxes home and did the room out as best we could and put up heavy curtains and things like that. Then Julian said, 'We've got some friends who have got a band, could they rehearse here as well? They haven't got a drummer, they've got a drum machine.' That's how the Bunnymen ended up rehearsing here. So, the Teardrops would rehearse two to three times a week and the Bunnymen would rehearse two to three times a week, but they would rehearse of an evening because they were quieter."

Ian McCullough had been part of the original Shallow Madness, but clashes with Cope saw him leave to play guitar and sing in this new band. Over time this arrangement worked well for both bands, and Gladys Palmer, who charged them a small fee for the use of her cellar, managed to put up with the noise. This did, on occasion, lead to problems with the neighbors, and even visits from the local constabulary. "We'd get that knock on the door, 'Yes officer?'" recalls Palmer, "I'd have to shout down to the Bunnymen, 'Could you put the keyboard on?' I had to *pretend* to be the keyboard player just so I could say, 'I am in this band,' that we were trying to do something rather than saying, 'Well, we let this band play here.' Palmer watched both bands rehearse and get tighter and tighter as musical units.

The Teardrop Explodes took their music out of Gladys Palmer's basement and onto a stage for the first time on 15th November 1978, when they played at Eric's with support from those other denizens of the cellar, Echo And The Bunnymen, who comprised of Ian McCullough (vocals/guitar), Will Sergeant (guitar), Les Peterson (bass) and Echo the drum machine. Bill Drummond and David Balfe saw them and were quick to ask the Teardrops to record. "We had a single out after two gigs," Cope later Dave McCullough of *Sounds* in August 1979, "That's what Zoo are all about."

This was indeed what Zoo was all about, and after seeing the band rehearse in the Palmer's cellar Drummond took the Teardrops into MVCU on 1st December 1978 to record their first EP, with himself and Balfe acting as producers and engineers. Three tracks ended up on the record - *Sleeping Gas*, *Camera Camera* and *Kirkby Workers Dream Fades* - and unlike the Big In Japan and the Those Naughty Lumps records, which had been housed in fold-out unglued sleeves, the Teardrops' 7" came in a traditional picture sleeve, although the artwork for the front was on the rear of the sleeve and the artwork for the rear was on the front. Whether this was the intention of Zoo and the band remains unclear. Was it a printing error? Whatever the case, The Teardrop Explodes were on their way.

One of the most arresting scenes in *Head-On* sees Cope walking into the one room Zoo Records office in the Chicago building in Liverpool's Whitechapel area, where Drummond was surrounded by army surplus camouflage scrim netting. Cope had been assiduously visiting and shopping at various army surplus stores to dress himself, and even stated in an early interview with the *Melody Maker* that, "we're heavily into army gear, I've got seventeen pairs of army pants all hanging up, and we've even got a jeep," so he probably thought the netting was for The Teardrop Explodes. But Drummond, somewhat sheepishly, admitted it was for Echo And The Bunnymen, who were about to go out on their first headlining UK tour. Cope was so upset that he ran upstairs and cried. Drummond stated in an interview in 1981 that it *was* intended for the Bunnymen, telling the *Melody Maker*, "We knew they played fantastic music but they were so static. Bill Butt (who was to do their lighting) and I were walking down the road saying, 'what can we do with them?' when I saw this camouflage netting in a fashion shop. I thought, that's it. I strung it up in my office and when they saw it they wanted it straight away."

At that time, Drummond was being pragmatic. Like The Teardrop Explodes' debut 7", the first single by Echo And The Bunnymen, *The Pictures On My Wall/Read It In Books*, received rave reviews in the music press. *Sounds* even made it single of the week - "this Liverpudlian trio will astonish all of us who looked upon that city's music scene as some sort of deranged Disneyland with a cutting vengeance." Drummond must have purred like a cat when another writer described it as, "The first piece of seven inch perfection from the excellent Liverpool Zoo label, who are at the core of a Liverpool movement that threatens quite rightly to dominate the last few month of the last year of the decade." Drummond initially described Mac and the boys to John Peel as "That weird and little known Liverpool Group Echo And The Bunnymen. It's a grower. The B-side maybe should've been the A, It's the toe tapper."

The Bunnymen were not to remain "little known" for long, as Seymour Stein soon wanted to sign them to Sire records. "I told him that we wanted to be like modern day pirates," Bill Drummond told the *Melody Maker* in 1981, "and he was saying, 'Pirates, pirates, whadya mean pirates? Like Douglas Fairbanks?' I don't think he understood, really, and besides, there wasn't a pirate shop nearby." In fact, Stein almost had to hoist the financial Jolly Roger as Drummond later revealed that, after offering a deal to the Bunnymen via Zoo, Stein discovered that he has reached the limit of his expenditure for new acts. He got around this by approaching Rob Dickens at Warner Brothers publishing and convinced him to sign the Bunnymen through a new label set up for this specific purpose. Amazingly, Dickens already had a connection to Zoo as he'd produced one of the tracks on the Big In Japan EP - *Suicide A Go Go* - as a demo at a London studio in November 1977. Dickens had been connected to Deaf School, who were, in turn, connected to Big In Japan.

"He kind of patched up the first album," recalls Clive Langer, "as we'd fallen out with (original producer) Muff Winwood, and then we did the second album with him. He was not only our publisher, but quite a good friend. He fancied himself as a producer. He was not experienced, so when we worked with him we were all having our say. He would have known Kevin and Phil from the Deaf School days already, so they could have approached him. It wasn't like I had to introduce them as they already knew each other." Thus, Dickens, in his day-to-day role of looking after publishing at Warner Brothers, had already done a deal to bring Zoo into the fold for publishing. As he already knew Drummond from Big In Japan and had something of a working relationship with him he needed little or no persuading from Stein, who, to be fair, buttered Dickens up, telling him that he was the best A&R man in the UK. Thus Echo And The Bunnymen ended up on the Korova label, which was established specifically for them, although it did later host a number of other acts.

Drummond brokered this deal in order to give the Bunnymen every chance of mainstream success. After all, it seemed at this time quite a stretch for a small independent label to fund the recording of albums for their artists and then find the money required to market them through advertising and tour support. Although Manchester's Factory Records issued the debut LP by Joy Division in June 1979 and Rough Trade were also starting to drop long playing anchors by artists like Stiff

Little Fingers and Cabaret Voltaire, it was initially thought that they would sell in small numbers and storm the emerging Independent Charts, rather than the national charts. It was also easier, cheaper and less risky for small labels to issue a number of singles.

So, when Julian Cope caught Drummond scrim-handed he was working hard to prepare the Bunnymen visually for first their major UK tour. Later that night, after Cope had dried his tears and gone home, Drummond popped round to see him. "I'm sorry Julian. I should have told you. I do feel really bad," Cope recalls in *Head-On*, "It's just… well it seemed perfect for the Bunnymen. And… well, we couldn't have afforded it for the Teardrops anyway. You know. I wanted it to be right." Cope went on to describe it as typical Zoo bullshit - "He just liked the idea and had to do it now" - but took great succor from Drummond's closing line. "Then he said I was more talented than them, but he could direct them because they were not so willful and they let him get more involved." Cope saw this as one of the important markers in his career. He *was* more talented than the Bunnymen, and Bill Drummond recognised that.

The picture of Drummond that emerges from *Head-On,* even through the prism of Cope's prose, is of a man devoted to the bands on his label. In August 1979, Cope, when asked to describe his label boss in an early Teardrop Explodes feature, stated that "Bill is a loveable blundering idiot. I remember we went to his place one day and he answered the door with the words 'I am a turd' written on his forehead in brown crayon. His wife had done it while he was asleep and he didn't know it was there! That's him all over, you know. Loveable." Lest we forget, at this time Echo And The Bunnymen and The Teardrop Explodes were beginning to establish themselves as recording and touring artists - Drummond and Balfe not only ran Zoo Records but now managed both bands, putting them on something in the region of £30 a week each.

Bill Drummond was not a passive manager. When Echo And The Bunnymen played a gig at Gaetano's restaurant in Manchester in July 1979, he performed a short two-minute skit entitled *Danger Quentin There's A Dog Behind You* before the trio hit the stage. He was accompanied by the Teardrops' Paul Simpson, who was asked to provide some strange sounds whilst Drummond also played guitar and related the story to the audience. He also went out on the road with the bands, although David Palmer recalls it could be a bit worrying with him at the wheel of a van, "I remember going to a gig with the Teardrops once and, God, I have never been so terrified in my life. It was Bill driving, and going over Snake Pass it was bad enough going. It was a sheer drop and it was terrifying as he was quite a manic driver, but coming back it was pissing down and you were on that side of the road where it really was a sheer drop, with Bill, this manic figure, driving and Gary (Dwyer) telling tales of this legendary character called the Ithampothicus. It was pure gothic horror. Maniac at the wheel and someone telling you about this thing on the moors, and it was just wonderful."

Whilst Drummond was working hard, with the money from their advance, to make Echo And The Bunnymen the biggest, most legendary band in the UK, the same also applied to The Teardrop Explodes. He'd produced their first two singles - *Sleeping Gas* and *Bouncing Babies* - with David Balfe, and issued them on Zoo, but the third, *Treason*, was turned over to former Deaf School guitarist Clive Langer, who'd not only gone solo but was moving into production. "Everything was connected," recalls Langer, "Bill was managing them and I knew Bill well, and obviously they respected me a bit because I'd made three albums with Deaf School by that point and done the early Madness stuff, so they just thought, 'What would Clive be like?' I suppose." Clive was very good indeed, and crucially re-arranged *Treason* in the studio, taking the "just a story" lyrical coda at the end and turning it one of the main hooks throughout the song.

Zoo gave *Treason* a strong push upon release in March 1980, and even linked up with Malicious Damage in London for some cross promotion. "When the second Killing Joke single came out - *Wardance and Pssyche* - Scott (Picring) was doing promotions for Rough Trade," recalls Adam Morris of Malicious Damage, "and we did a deal where they did a mailout and we shared the cost with Zoo Records in Liverpool. It was the Teardrop Explodes' *Treason* and Killing Joke's *Wardance* in the same mailer. That's how I first got to know Scott, as we packed all of the mailers together." Scott Piering was already working hard to promote early singles on Rough Trade, and was quick to jump into the debate about plugging when Radio One abandoned their strict playlist format in August 1980, "We have never pushed for playlisting, but I think records like Spizz Energi's *Where's Captain Kirk* or The Mo-Dettes' *White Mice*, which were pushed by independent pluggers employed by their managements, would have benefitted greatly from being on the playlist. The Joy Division single (*Love Will Tear Us Apart*), for example, was playlisted automatically because of its high chart position, and that is the way we like it to happen – much in the same way as The Specials' *Gangsters* happened. In general, I see all kinds of signposts marking the coming of age of the independents, and this move by the BBC is one of them."

Treason became Zoo's best-selling single to date, shifting in the region of sixteen thousand copies, which was strong sales indeed for a small indie label at the time. Even then, major labels were not sure about signing the band due to their hybrid nature. As Julian Cope told the *New Musical Express* in April 1980, "You get people who are heavily into bands like Joy Division coming along to our gigs, probably expecting something similar, and then finding us too commercial. Then you have all the pop people who don't even bother to come to see us 'cause we're bracketed away as a weird band."

By this time, Bill Drummond had already established a personal relationship with Tony Wilson and Factory Records, and in August 1979 he agreed that his bands would take part in The Leigh Rock and Music Festival, a festival located between Liverpool and Manchester which was also billed as Zoo Meets Factory Half-Way. "Zoo Records and Factory Records bring you the flesh that brought you the vinyl..." stated the poster generated by Factory, which received its own catalogue number, FAC 15. One of the bands on the bill was Orchestral Manoeuvres In The Dark, whose debut single, *Electricity*, had been issued by Factory in May 1979. Amazingly, as they were a Liverpool act, this could have been a Zoo release. "Orchestral Manoeuvres In the Dark had a studio around the corner on Button Street, opposite Probe, and had a manager who took this song into Zoo," recalls David Palmer. "It was definitely a single, a brilliant single called *Electricity*, and Bill wasn't there - it was Dave who listened to it, took it out of the cassette player, walked to the door and threw it down the stairs and told him to get out of the office with his 'rinky dink' music. He went straight to Factory, who released it in a beautifully designed Peter Saville black embossed sleeve and the rest is history." Whilst OMD went on to score worldwide hits, to be fair to David Balfe *everyone* on the Liverpool scene at the time just thought OMD were simply not cool, which may have been the reason he reacted so theatrically to hearing an early version of what later became a hit single.

As for the lack of record company interest in The Teardrop Explodes, to solve this problem Bill Drummond used Zoo money to fund the recording of an album. This was a major expense for a small independent label, although matters were helped by a cash injection they received from Seymour Stein, who licensed Zoo's sixth single, *Touch* by Lori and The Chameleons. "Lori and the Chameleons arrived at the Zoo's turquoise office a couple of months ago with a neat attaché case full of cassettes and told us it contained 'future pop'" ran the Zoo press release. "They are from the Allerton district of Liverpool, have yet to play outside a living room, and like melodrama, songs that break your heart, and the future."

In fact, whilst Lori Lartey - "a bird we used to watch walking down the street" - was the vocalist, the band's other members, Andrew Newton and Douglas Stewart, were actually David Balfe (on keyboards) and Bill Drummond (on guitar), with Tim Whittaker from Deaf School on drums. Musically, *Touch* was "rinky dink" too, and a very well-crafted early electro-pop single. "Balfe and I thought it sounded brilliant,"

Drummond later related in his book *17*, "Even revolutionary. We thought it sounded exactly how pop music should sound. Fragile, mysterious, beautiful, sexy."

Reviews were of the no-nonsense variety. "This is a hit single," gushed Dave McCullough in *Sounds*, "I bet you *Touch* is this summer's Jilted John trash culture success." It was probably after reading this review and buying a copy of the single that Stein agreed and paid Zoo in the region of £4,000 to license it. The re-released version on Korova was made single of the week by Dave Lee Travis, who played it every day for a week on his Radio One show, but the record only reached number seventy in the charts before falling back to earth. But Warner Brothers did take up the option of another single, and Drummond and Balfe spent three days at Rockfield Studios in Wales crafting what they thought was perfection. "We thought we had made the greatest pop record ever," Drummond again related in his book *17*. Sadly, *The Lonely Spy*, a story about Lori's lover being gunned down by the KGB in Red Square, got the short end of the cold war and failed to sell.

However, some of the money received for the licensing of the first Lori and The Chameleons single went towards funding those Teardrop Explodes album sessions, although it has also been stated that Bill Drummond secured additional funding by remortgaging his house. Clearly, he was as fully behind The Teardrop Explodes, who did not have a major label deal, as he was Echo And The Bunnymen, who did. A month at Rockfield was block booked, the first two weeks turned over to recording the first Bunnymen LP and the second fortnight to Teardrops sessions. The gamble paid off - eventually, The Teardrop Explodes were signed to Mercury/Phonogram, who, I imagine, paid back their recording costs as well as covering additional sessions to complete the LP.

Drummond and Balfe - as The Chameleons - worked hard producing the Bunnymen's debut LP. Drummond was very much in synch with the band, sharing a vision of not only how they should present themselves on stage but also how their records should sound, and according to David Palmer this extended to backing himself and the band when some early sessions had apparently not yielded the required results.

"Quite early, when they got Pete De Freitas in (on drums), they got a producer (Pat Moran) who'd produced Iggy Pop's *Soldier* LP, because they all loved The Stooges. They went and recorded with him, but when they got it back at the Zoo offices it just sounded a bit straight ahead rock, sort of New York Dolls and Stooges - probably what you'd expect someone like that to do. There were a couple of other attempts, and I think that was when Dave and Bill decided to produce the first LP themselves, because not only did they have a vision of how the Bunnymen should sound but it tied in with the way the Bunnymen saw themselves as well, and I think that was quite important. They were quite visionary in that sense - they were on the side of the band rather that what current trend was selling or what a label would dictate. (The label) could have said, 'No, we want this kind of Americanised Bunnymen thing,' but they stood their ground and thought they could achieve something greater, or to use one of Bill's phrases, 'more legendary.'"

The resulting LP, *Crocodiles,* was soon being played by John Peel, who privately allocated stars (and timings) to each track. *Pride, The Pictures On My Wall, All That Jazz* and *Happy Death Men* all received his highest accolade - three stars - and every other track received two. In the music press the LP received gushing reviews too. "The Bunnymen have dug an admirable first burrow. Merseybeat with spiked waters is worth getting addicted to," stated the *Melody Maker,* and the *New Musical Express* went even further, declaring that "*Crocodile*s is destined to be one of the contemporary rock albums of the year". Better still, the production was praised - Adrian Thrills stated that, "a lot of the credit could also go to the production team of - no, not Martin Hannett! - Chameleons Bill Drummond and Dave Balfe and Original Mirrors guitarist Ian Brodie. The three men at the controls create a sound full of body and depth without the aid of convoluted studio trickery." For the record, Ian Broudie, former Big in Japan guitarist, had produced the second single - *Rescue* - which was included on the LP, which went top twenty in the UK charts.

Bill Drummond was very much on a mission with the Bunnymen. Whilst Dave Balfe went through his revolving door phase of membership with The Teardrop Explodes, Drummond was present when the Bunnymen did their first UK and American tours, as he was when the Teardrops made it across the Atlantic later on. There was just something about the Bunnymen that had the critics - especially in the *New Musical Express* and *Sounds* - fondling them with praise. Apart from the music - and their stage lighting and camouflage netting - it was the growing quote-ability of lead singer Ian McCulloch, who was not only happy to tackle questions about what was being hailed as new Scouse psychedelia but also to be quite blunt as to what drove him on. "Yeah… ego. It's all kind of gratifying your ego. We want to do things that are valid; good songs, that mean something sincere. But egos always at the back of it." McCulloch was also quick to slap down any accusations that the Bunnymen had 'sold out' to a major label. "For a start, Zoo wanted us to do it," he told *Melody Maker* in October 1979, "If we hadn't signed we wouldn't be doing this tour and have all these lights and things. It's just a job, right? Would you criticise a bloke who works for Ford for not making his own car?"

Although Zoo had received positive press and reviews and had two of Liverpool's best bands under their wing - as well as the less highly regarded Expelaires - Drummond still had to perform the behind the scenes chores associated with running a small label and managing artists, from running the office, booking studios, pressing records and printing sleeves to handling expenses, sorting out bookings, driving vans and going out on tour. Neil McCormick worked for the *Hot Press* magazine in Ireland and interviewed both the Bunnymen and the Teardrops around this time, as well as wangling a support slot for his band Yeah Yeah when the Teardrops did a short tour of Ireland around 1980. He saw Drummond up close at this time, "He was obviously only in his twenties, but he seemed old to us as we were just kids. But he was this enthusiastic, Scotsman, very talkative and generous with his time in talking to a young musician like me."

As for the Teardrops' tour of Ireland, "I do vividly remember him behind the mixing desk in McConnagall's, where we supported the Teardrops, watching them and watching their whole show. He was a fan as much as a manager, and that's all well and good as a lot of managers disappear during the show because they've seen it maybe six hundred times already, but he was there absorbing every detail as I remember." Also absorbing every detail at this show was independent publicist Mick Houghton, who'd been assigned to the band by Mercury.

McCormick recalls that, "Julian Cope did this incredible show, and got really angry with the audience and had a kind of breakdown halfway through the set as he thought they weren't paying enough attention, and he had a rant. He stopped the band from playing and threw down his microphone and said, "We are all in this together! There should not be a barrier between us!" He went on, and when they were silent and he'd got their attention he built the band back up and they got back into the groove." McCormick remembers being very impressed by this, although when Cope did *exactly* the same thing at the next gig he asked Houghton if Cope did that every night. "How *else* do you become a legend?" was the reply.

Drummond (and Balfe when he was not on tour or in the studio) was learning on the job, but one of the key things he did for the Echo And The Bunnymen and The Teardrop Explodes was to hook them up with major labels. This gave both bands financial backing and access to big business machinery when it came to press, publicity and distribution. These were the things that Big In Japan never had, and so obtaining them for bands he was managing was vital to their forward momentum. No-one knew then that small independent labels like Factory, Rough Trade, Mute and even the growing sinews of Beggars Banquet, who'd scored massive success with Gary Numan, were not only going to be in the game for the long term but, through artists like Joy Division, New Order, The Smiths and Depeche Mode, would release million selling albums and singles that would be plugged onto radio playlists and into the charts by people like Scott Piering.

Ironically, despite the critical momentum behind the Bunnymen, it was The Teardrop Explodes who got into the singles charts first. Their first major label 7" was *When I Dream*, which had just about made a dent in the top fifty upon release in September 1980, but when *Reward* was issued in January 1981 it went top ten, and by the time *Treason (It's Just A Story)* was reissued and went top twenty in May 1981 everything had changed. Suddenly, Cope and the latest incarnation of the Teardrops, as well as Drummond and Balfe (who was having his cake and eating it when allowed) were having to deal with *Top Of The Pops* and other TV appearances, promotional videos, headline tours of the UK and Europe and dates in America as well as interviews in the serious music press and more glossy teen pop fodder.

Although he managed both bands, as Cope began to climb up the fire escape in the sky Drummond began to devote more creative energy to the Bunnymen. Although they'd yet to score a hit single outside of the independent charts, he worked hard to ensure that they stood out from other bands, and strived to put his ideas into practice. By January 1981 he'd smoked £20,000 out of Warner Brothers for an Echo And The Bunnymen feature film based around a one-off concert in Buxton, Derbyshire. *Shine So Hard* was intended to show the Bunnymen at work and play, and Bill Butt was the producer. "Bill Drummond and myself knew it was time to have a Bunnymen video, but none of us wanted a straight promotion thing and we'd already considered a film," Butt told the music press at this time, "The idea of a mystery gig seemed to tie in with the film and could relate to the Bunnymen because they do seem to be a band that are looking for things, in a way, finding new directions."

Drummond was originally going to direct the film, but this was turned over to John Smith, with Pat Duval acting as cameraman. Of course, on the set Drummond was more than happy to share his vision with the *Melody Maker,* "It's going to be much more like a classy feature film than a normal promo movie. You know, if we had them walking through the woods or something you'd immediately think it was a Rough Trade band or something, whereas this is the sort of film that maybe Bowie would make." Bowie would make? Drummond really was beginning to roll forward with his sound and vision now.

With sessions for the Bunnymen's second album approaching, Drummond also saw the film as a kind of closing of the first act of the band's career, "Really, this show will be the last time we use the camouflage netting on stage and the same lighting design, so in all its something of a momentous occasion." As well as the film there were also plans for a spin-off book and an EP, but in the end, although a thirty minute cut of the film was shown at the ICA in London and some footage was deployed for promotional purposes, *Shine So Hard* didn't receive a general theatrical release and only the EP saw the light of day.

At one point before the Buxton concert, Drummond turned up at the hotel in climbing gear. Whether he'd scaled a convenient crag remains unknown, although he was a fan of the great outdoors and his attire was very much in keeping with the fact that he had formed a company called Atlas Adventures with Bill Butt. "One of the things we want to do is swim the channel," he told a bemused journalist, "We plan on having an adventure every two years, each time in a separate continent. Once you realise that you can do anything you want to then there's no stopping you. When you're seventeen you think you're going to do everything - jump out of a plane in a parachute (what else?), climb Everest etc, but then you don't. We're going to put this right with Atlas Adventures."

Rather than spread themselves too thin, by April 1981 Zoo Records was being wound down as Drummond began to concentrate upon management and Balfe - whilst retaining a hand in Zoo Publishing - dedicated himself to The Teardrop Explodes. Indeed, the last single issued by the label had been the original version of *Treason* in March 1980, and it would not be until January 1982 that a final Zoo single would be issued by The Wild Swans.

Upon planning to move down to London in 1981, Drummond was accused of turning his back on the Liverpool scene, but was quick to defend his corner, "Well, I'm not from Liverpool for a start. And secondly it's just not financially sane to stop here. If I manage a band you have to become big. I want to take on the world, not play the cult game. To be big and still be good is to me the real challenge." That was the sort of quote that Ian McCullogh would have been proud of.

It was through the medium of the Bunnymen that Drummond intended to rule the world. By this time the growing drug consumption of Julian Cope had contributed to a souring in relations between Zoo management and The Teardrop Explodes, brought about - possibly - by the fact that Cope found it hard to square the circle of David Balfe being both a collaborator and his co-manager. But, as well as backing Cope's Scott Walker compilation, *Fire Escape In The Sky – The Godlike Genius Of Scott Walker*, in 1981 and releasing it on Zoo, Drummond did convince Cope to buy into his vision of what became Club Zoo, located at the Pyramid Club in Liverpool, where the Teardrops played every day for a number of weeks. Drummond was probably helping out Roger Eagle, who owned the building, but the Teardrops' performances ranged from the erratic to the brilliant. "It was wonderful," recalls David Palmer, who was there many a night, "just the variety and the fact that the Teardrops had to play every night. The sets would never be the same and *Sleeping* Gas might be the single length or it might be forty minutes long." There were also priceless moments when Balfe whispered something into Cope's ear and left the stage and the singer announced, "Dave needs to take a shit."

At this time, the Teardrops were gearing up to issue their second LP, whose producer Clive Langer recalls how hands-on Drummond was at this point. "I was always kind of surprised and excited by what he was doing because he was kind of like an outlaw, and a successful one as well, which was great. I always liked his attitude. I liked it when he came into the studio when we were working with the Teardrops and told us whatever he thought. He was exciting to be around and excitable. He is excitable and fun to be with really. Unpredictable. Out of the norm, which makes things much more interesting."

How unpredictable and interesting was best illustrated when Drummond related to the *Guardian* newspaper in 2016 how the Teardrops' second LP was named by his old mentor Ken Campbell. At the time, Campbell had returned to Liverpool to become artistic director at the Everyman Theatre, and Drummond took Balfe to see him and get some guidance as to what to do with this increasingly dissolute band.

"Give me £100 and I will tell you." was the reply. The pair got the money together and the answer was "Wilder!"

"What do you mean, Ken?"

"I mean Wilder! That is what you need your band to be. Wilder!"

Not only was the second Teardrops LP, released in 1981, called *Wilder*, but the subsequent unreeling of the band suggests they also took Campbell at his word! Drummond summed them up perfectly when talking to Mark Cooper around this time, "I see the Teardrops as a battered Second World War bomber heading back home across the Channel; they're losing and gaining height, circling around and dodging fire but keeping going, chugging away. And they'll always make it back – to a fanfare, with the crowds cheering and the home fires burning."

By this time David Balfe was back in the bomber with Julian Cope, and in one interview he explained that the split between him and the singer was due to his partner in crime at Zoo Records. "One of the things that led to a lot of the bitterness between Julian and I when we split was that Bill, much to my annoyance, had this big thing to *sell Julian*, and he started getting the solo interviews and everything, and I really believed it was a heavy group, as much as the Bunnymen." As they spiraled towards the recording of their third LP, the Teardrops grew too heavy, and

Drummond would sell on their management to their tour manager, and focus on the Bunnymen alone.

In many respects, the influence of Bill Drummond was vital in presenting the Bunnymen to the world through the sleeves for their singles and albums. Whilst McCullogh's hedgehog hairstyle was his own invention, Drummond had a big say in the photo shoots for album sleeves, which became miniature Atlas Adventures - from forests to arctic wastes - that subsequently inspired other bands to be equally wide-angled in their own album covers. Of course, the route to being 'legendary' and 'heroic' was, on occasion, smoothed by dog food.

"The band said that it absolutely stank," David Palmer laughs when recalling the photo shoot for the cover of the Bunnymen's second LP, 1981's *Heaven Up Here*. The sleeve showed the band on a beach with seagulls flying above their heads, but "to get all of the gulls they had to throw loads of (Pedigree) Chum (dog food) into the water. It was a long shoot, and they said it just stank. Thankfully you don't get that impression off the sleeve, you just get the birds hovering around."

The final single issued on Zoo, in January 1982, also had a Bunnymen connection. Sometime in 1981, Palmer's mum allowed another band to start rehearsing in her cellar - The Wild Swans had been formed by former Teardrops member Paul Simpson, who now switched to lead vocals whilst Jed Kelly provided a mesmerising guitar counterpoint. At one point, Mrs. Palmer wanted to throw them out as she thought they smelled, but her son discovered that the problem was not their personal hygiene but a dead rat that was decomposing beneath the bottom step of the stairs leading down into the basement. Palmer also recalls that one of the benefits of The Wild Swans rehearsing in the cellar was that original drummer Justin Staveley would occasionally do a bit of gardening. "I remember him saying once, 'They're all arguing about which bit is which and which bit is what and which bit goes where and I've just played the same drumbeat to every fucking song we've just done and no one has noticed.' So he just started pruning our roses."

Bunnymen drummer Peter De Freitas was a big fan of the band and funded and produced their debut single. The record featured London-based Rolo McGinty on bass, who'd been recommended by Julian Cope and would travel up for rehearsals, gigs in the area and this recording session. "It was recorded in this big dining room which had endless reverb in it, a real swimming pool sound," McGinty recalls today of the time working at Pink Studios. "Working with Pete was really good because underneath it he was a real pro." The only problem was that he somehow misplaced the master tapes, and so the final mixes of both sides of *The Revolutionary Spirit/God Forbid* were in mono. "It would have sounded more like a plush radio production, but actually it was fine as it was," states McGinty. Indeed it was, and even in mono the single was one of the best records to be released in the post punk period. In agreeing to release it as a 12", Drummond gave Zoo a final release that was a fitting finale, and although The Wild Swans were not as successful as the Bunnymen and The Teardrop Explodes, Simpson and Kelly went on to enjoy commercial and critical success as The Lotus Eaters.

As for Zoo, this was the end of the road. "I would imagine the Bunnymen and The Teardrop Explodes would have really, really taken a hell of a lot of anyone's time, so that probably had something to do with it," states McGinty, who went on to form The Woodentops. The parting shot from Zoo came in 1982, with the release of a compilation LP entitled *From The Shores Of Lake Placid,* which brought together a number of rare and unreleased tracks from bands on the Zoo roster, including David Balfe's Turquoise Swimming Pools.

Ian McCulloch and co toured hard to support their third LP, *Porcupine,* in 1983, playing UK, European and American dates, but, most interestingly, in July 1983 the band played three gigs in the Outer Hebrides. The jaunt was planned by Drummond, who told the *New Musical Express* it was, "a chance to see my favourite group in my favourite part of the world." He confessed that it was a ludicrous thing to do from a financial perspective, but it did generate some excellent publicity for the band in the music press. "More vaguely, Drummond hopes the islands and highlands will influence the group in some positive, semi spiritual way," wrote Paul Du Noyer, who accompanied them on this trip for the *New Musical Express.* "A group like The Jam, he theorises, aspire to a housing estate outlook, and Wham, for example, reflect the inner city, but the Bunnymen, in Drummond's eyes, are tapping 'more glorious' sources - hence the exotic settings that have become a feature of their LP sleeves and videos." Also, as Drummond later related in his own writings, he had, at this time, a theory about the mystical powers of a Rabbit God called Echo, and even planned an early Bunnymen tour based on drawing rabbit ears on a map. Whilst in the Outer Hebridies there was also the small matter of delving into leylines, and a midnight visit to the mystical stone circle of Callanish. "Once at the site, manager Drummond lay prostrate at the circle's centre, absorbing quantities of magical vibration and damp peat," wrote Du Noyer, "Scoff if you will - but at that moment his protégé, Mac McCulloch, was back at the hotel being inspired to whomp a belligerent Scotsman, following a heated argument about socks and politics. Obviously, we were meddling with powerful forces."

By this time Drummond needed all the energy he could muster. He was not only managing the Bunnymen but had begun working as an independent A&R man for Warner Brothers Records in London.

THE WHIPPETS FROM NOWHERE

"A band is a shared delusion. If one person is on their own with a tape they have made they are one possibly deluded person, people might not like it and it's hard for you. But if you have a gang it's a shared delusion, and you can make the dream come true."

- Rolo McGinty

"We play music from behind the kitchen sink"
- Cressida Bowyer, the (Totnes)
Times, March 1979

As well as producing bands like Big in Japan in cities like Liverpool, punk inspired bands to form in the provinces. As records and reports in the music press began to seep out, The Sex Pistols embarked on the *Anarchy* tour, and played in Devon on the 21st December 1976.

"I saw that the Sex Pistols were playing in Plymouth, so we thought, 'Let's go,'" recalls Martin Cottis, who was around eighteen at the time. "We were terrified as all we'd seen down there was the stuff in *The Sun* (newspaper) and that they were all animals. So we went and got a haircut and it was amazing. Not the Sex Pistols so much, but I think it was the Clash. They stood in as somebody had dropped out. It was that first tour when they were being banned all over the place - if you look, historically one of the few places they didn't get banned was Plymouth."

The gig led to the formation of the first punk band in Totnes. Tom Langton-Lockton was also at the gig, but recalls that seeing The Stranglers in Plymouth was more of an inspiration to him. "Maybe I was the first punk in Totnes," he recalls, "I just went mad and started telling everybody about it and just got really excited. There was someone doing some music that might be to do with who we were, rather than this ludicrous pompous rock. We just formed a band." This became Slammers Knobb, and, "We tried to find someone to sing, and this guy, he was insane - he used to come around and whittle his warts off with a Stanley knife. We had to lock him in the garden shed because he was so worrying."

One early singer was nicknamed Smiler. A friend of Langton-Lockton, he sang at a gig the band secured at a Sixth Form disco early in 1977. "We'd learned *Twist And Shout* and this Smiler guy came down to sing," recalls Martin Cottis, "and all we knew was that, so we played it for half an hour. Smiler ran out of words in about five minutes, so he was just rolling around on the floor. He was from London so he was already a bit ahead of us. He had spikey hair and looked the part, and he had a bottle of whiskey and he was rolling around the floor just telling everybody to 'Fuck off!' Most people left, but a few didn't, and from there on it was nothing matters. We can do this."

Song-writing sessions and rehearsals were held in an old barn owned by Martin Cottis' parents on the moors, where another local band, Furious Pig, also rehearsed. "They were all good musicians, so I was trying to pick up on them," recalls Cottis. As for Slammers Knobb, "as a keyboard player I didn't know what fucking key they were playing in or anything. It was no good me looking at the shapes of their hands on the guitars and copying it. I had to keep stopping and saying, 'What key are you in?'"

Cottis also had a job working in the local record shop Zounds, which became a meeting point. Langton-Lockton and drummer Simon Patterson would come down and he would play them the latest records from the slowly emerging punk scene – records by bands like The Damned, The Clash, The Stranglers and the Sex Pistols - as they were issued in 1977, and that summer Slammers Knobb managed to secure a gig in the village of Diptford.

"We were asked to play on the 7th June 1977, the Queens Silver Jubilee celebrations," recalls Patterson, "and we were called Slammers Knobb, but they refused to call us that as they thought it was disgusting. Very embarrassingly we were billed as Simon Patterson and the Swingers, which was completely against what we were standing for, but at least we did it. It would have been me, Tom and Martin but I can't recall who the vocalist was as we had a number of different ones."

Once Slammers Knobb had a set list together, they had no problem securing gigs. "Because Martin worked in a music shop and the owners also had a club called Woods in Plymouth," recalls Langton-Lockton, "We got to play there supporting bands, and got introduced to what the Plymouth punk scene was like. It was a bit more savvy, a bit more like London, but it was still much sillier. There was a band called The Bums who were quite pivotal in Plymouth, and they went on to become Department K.". As well as at Woods, the band also played on a regular basis at another venue in Plymouth called The Metro. They even supported 999 at a gig at Dartington College of Arts near their native Totnes. In fact, Totnes was quite an artistic haven at this time as there was a constant influx of students who came to study in Dartington, to this small but ancient market town.

As for the musical art of Slammers Knobb at this time...... they entered the regional *Melody Maker* Rock and Folk festival held in Bristol between the 18th and 19th February 1978 and performed a song called *Monica Shoves It.*

Eventually, the problem of a permanent lead vocalist was solved when a seventeen year old named Cressida Bowyer, who had also seen The Sex Pistols, took over around July 1978. "She was good, and brought something new to it," states Cottis. "We started looking and listening to Siouxsie much more, and Lene Lovich and people who were doing the same sort of stuff." Indeed, by this time the first Siouxsie And The Banshees single, *Hong Kong Garden,* had charted, as had Lovich with *Lucky Number*. Bassist Ben Cull remembers the band getting a gig at Routes in Exeter as late replacement for Lene Lovich, who couldn't make it. "It was a great gig, which ended with me being breathalysed in the grey minivan on the way back with all our equipment!"

After a couple more months and more gigs, it was decided that a name change was in order. "Slammers Knobb was a bit of an embarrassing name," states Patterson, "so in about September 1978 we changed to The Whippets From Nowhere. To be honest with you I really liked that as I was a bit of a Bowie fan, so it was like The Spiders From Mars. Tom was always putting on this kind of Yorkshire accent and talking about 'T'Whippets' so we thought let's be The Whippets From Nowhere. We were probably all stoned and having a giggle."

By that point, the line-up of The Whippets From Nowhere was Cressida Bowyer on vocals, Tom Langton-Lockton on guitar, Simon Patterson on drums, Martin Cottis on keyboards and Ben Cull on bass, and, like Big In Japan, they also had a song based on their name. Around this time they recorded their first session at a Studio in Torquay, intending to send it off to record companies in London.

One of those who saw the band at this time was Jimmy Cauty, who was also from Totnes. "He was a few years older than us, but super cool," recalls Cottis. "He got himself expelled from school early, so he had that kudos, and you would see him driving round and about town on a motorbike with a sidecar, but he'd taken off the sidecar and put an armchair on instead. It was cool." So was Cauty, who everybody knew had drawn a poster based on *The Lord Of The Rings*, which had become a bestseller in the Athena poster shop chain.

Born in 1956, Jimmy Cauty would have been around twenty two at this time. He'd not only drawn a best-selling poster for Athena when he was seventeen but had done further posters for the chain, as well as the artwork for the 1977 LP *The King Of Elfland's Daughter,* a concept album by former Steeleye Span members Bob Johnson and Peter Knight and based on the 1924 book of the same name by Lord Dunsany, who was a literary influence on fantasy writers like J.R.R. Tolkein and H.P. Lovecraft

"The connection with Jimmy went right back to when we were The Whippets in Devon," recalls Patterson, "We were asked to play at a place called The Castle down in Bigbury On Sea - at the party one of the friends of this guy was Jimmy Cauty, who came down from London. I think he made quite a lot of money with the *Lord Of The Rings* poster, and he had this mythical band called The Tets. He also had this huge PA system which we used, and a Bedford ambulance, which he painted and let me use for the band. It was amazing, and I was driving around Devon in it. So he was one of our mentors."

The Whippets took their music seriously, and around this time they all adopted stage names, with Cressida becoming Cleve Snippett, Cottis becoming Spider Cottis, Langton-Lockton becoming Seamus Android, Patterson becoming Spöön *Fazer*, and Cull becoming Bush Punes! Thoughts turned to trying to secure a recording contract and to this end another demo was recorded with somebody who had a small studio on Dartmoor. "Tom and Simon had met him in a music shop in Plymouth," recalls Cottis, "We were there for a couple of days I think, and he was phasing everything and putting weird stuff all over it." Patterson also recalls this rather strange session, "whenever something went wrong he would say the aliens were doing something. It was all on Dartmoor. Totnes is very close to Dartmoor so it was all a bit spooky!"

The important thing was that the band had some of their music on tape, and The Whippets From Nowhere began to send out demos to record companies in London with a view to securing a deal. Like many bands, they received letters back from companies like Chrysalis, letting them down easy - "Whilst we feel there is some potential within the material, we feel at this present time we are not the company to be able to assist you in furthering your recording career." Virgin Records also replied, "Many thanks for your tape, which you find enclosed. Unfortunately, it is not really the type of material we are looking for at the moment, but anyway, thanks for your interest."

But there *was* some positive interest, from Hansa Records. "There was this guy called Danny Morgan, and he came down to Totnes to see us," recalls Patterson, "he had a fur coat. It was all very exciting that this guy had come down from London to see us, and we thought we were going to make it and spent all of our dole cheques on the day. We thought we had made it." Although Morgan left without waving a contract under their noses, he did encourage The Whippets to move up to London to further their career, and the band began to plan the move.

On the cusp of this exodus, another opportunity presented itself early in 1979 when the band passed an audition to appear on *Southwest Showcase,* a programme to be broadcast by Westward TV. "We have had such an overwhelming response, and the standard of entries has been so uniformly high, that in reaching this stage you are without doubt one of the foremost acts in the Southwest," gushed a letter that also offered to cover their expenses. The series was to showcase performers from Cornwall, North Devon, South Devon, Dorset and Somerset, and the filming would take place in Plymouth on the 5th and 6th March 1979.

This upcoming exposure on TV quickly led to some local press coverage, "We have already an offer from Hansa Recordings, the people who recorded Boney M, but we turned them down because it wasn't what we wanted," Cottis told one local reporter, "They wanted to turn us into a disco band which isn't our line at all." Langton-Lockton was quick to tell another paper, "in fact we're a bit too different and the record companies have been a bit too scared to take us up." As for the band's plans to move to London, Cressida stated that, "If we can get a following there, we can prove to the companies that people want something different." Cottis confirmed their ambition, "Now we're going to London we'll see if we can make the big time and play to support ourselves."

Jimmy Cauty, already in London, was one of those who gave The Whippets some advice about moving. This didn't involve finding a flat that the band could rent, but rather somewhere they could squat for free. Squatting was something Cauty was already doing, along with other people from Totnes and the Devon area, like Plume, who'd been a student at the art college. Martin Cottis: "I packed in the record shop and Tom, Cressida and I came up and stayed with Plume in her squat. That was the plan; you could do that then - find a squat. Plume was a bit older, she was at the college (in Dartington) and there was a lot of mixing going on."

Bowyer, Cottis and Langton-Lockton were soon introduced to an Australian, Dale McCrae, who was seen as the king of the squatters around the Brixton and Clapham area and had a communal house called BACTERIA. "He showed us how to open up a house and squat in it and look after it," recalls Cottis, "we were all signing on, but it takes six weeks for any money to come through. He was showing us how to get down to New Covent Garden and scavenge vegetables." Once they found a house, Patterson and Cull soon followed. "They'd found a house in Iveley Road, a big house but there was no roof," recalls Patterson, "so it was really hardcore squatting, which was OK because we were all from the country anyway and I was brought up on a farm. Martin was brought up in a farmhouse so we were all used to living like that. And we were young!"

As they'd come to London to make a new start, it was decided that The Whippets From Nowhere would change their name to The 39 Steppes. "I remember the night at the Australian hippies' house when we picked the name," Cottis recalls, "and again invented a whole scenario about it and what it all meant. It was basically because I'd just read that book and really liked it. We spelt it as in the Russian Steppes to give it a bit of class."

The band worked hard to make connections, and soon met Charlie Gillett and his partner Gordon Nelky. At this time Gillett had ended his radio programme, *Honky Tonk*, on Radio London and was involved with Oval records. He'd steered Lene Lovich to Stiff Records, and not only had good ears but was willing to help young bands he liked. They also contacted Nicky Morgan at Hansa, who put them into a studio run by Radio Luxembourg with Simon Napier-Bell, where they recorded three demos.

The 39 Steppes began to play gigs, including one supporting Neil Innes at the Timeout Election Night Special at The Venue in Victoria on 3rd May 1979. The band had a brush with rock royalty that evening when Pete Townshend came in and used the toilet in their dressing room, and so did Jimmy Cauty, who did their sound. Indeed, Cauty was helping the band quite a lot, as Patterson recalls, "One of the weirdest things is that our roadies were Jimmy Cauty and Allanah Curry from the Thompson Twins when we were in London. They were enthusiastically helping this avant-garde band." The Thompson Twins were yet to form, but Curry had moved to the UK from New Zealand and was starting her musical career – she would perform a one-off gig in 1979 as The Unfuckables, who included Jimmy Cauty in the line-up.

Although they'd made a good contact in Charlie Gillett, who began to champion the band, Patterson believes that, in retrospect, the name change was counter-productive, "The same week that we were on TV in Devon as The Whippets From Nowhere we were doing gigs in London as The 39 Steppes. That is not good branding." The band performed *Computers Past And Present* on *Southwest Showcase*, broadcast on April 27th 1979, and came second behind a folk singer from Cornwall. Just seven days later they were evicted from Iveley Road by Court Order at a hearing in London.

Nevertheless, things did seem to be moving in the right direction - Hansa was still interested and a gig at the Rock Garden received a positive review in the *Record Mirror* in June 1979, "We're 39 Steppes and this is *The Perfect Omlette*," cries leading lady Cressida, and they're off." One of the telling phrases in this review came at the beginning, "If 39 Steppes channelled some of the piss take they gave me at the 'interview' into their stage act they could have a lot of potential."

The 39 Steppes were very much a gang sharing the delusion, but Martin Cottis believes their attitude might have not helped them at times. "We went to see a lot of record companies", he recalls, "I remember going to see A&M. Someone had arranged that and then, us being foul rude and abusive, they basically told us to get out. Virgin Records - these people would turn up and later you would find out it was a guy called Jumbo who was Richard Branson's number two. He was really nice to us and took us out for a meal, and again we were rude and abusive. They probably thought we were OK, but they're not going through that." When asked about this, Simon Patterson told me, "I think there was an arrogance. I was the drummer and I was told to shut up as drummers are always told to shut up."

The band did have a manager in Cressida's uncle, who wrote for the BBC TV show *Playaway,* but, whilst he did the best he could, rather than sending out photos to project their image he deployed a picture of them drawn by his daughter that probably didn't really have the desired impact. Ironically, the band had a very strong image, with Cressida, Langton-Lockton and Patterson often wearing aviator suits which gave off a semi-Devo vibe. They were also one of the first bands to shave the sides of their heads, which was another strong visual motif.

Sadly, The 39 Steppes couldn't secure a record deal, and eventually drifted apart. "We got evicted from our house and we had no money," recalls Patterson, "we were on the dole and then we ended up in two separate squats which were really primitive. Tom, Cressida and I ended up in one between Clapham North and Brixton and it had no floorboards. It had electricity but no running water. It was a derelict house, basically. Within six months we split up."

"We all carried on in our own ways," recalls Cottis, who was recommended as a keyboard player to Lene Lovich by Charlie Gillett. "I remember the phone call to Lene that Charlie arranged. She said, 'You can obviously play but have you got a beard?' I said, 'No.' She said, 'You're in.' There was that kind of attitude." Sadly, Cottis was unable to take the job.

As for Simon Patterson, he went on holiday to Greece and decided, "I'm fed up with living in a squat. It was pretty grim. I think we were splitting up really, and I decided to go back to Devon. I was going to stay in Devon and do electronic drum music. That was in my head and I bought Dave Simmons' first early drum synthesiser, probably borrowing money off my dad. I had a very good Tama drum kit and did quite a bit of stand in drumming for groups in Devon, then got this electronic drum kit." Spöön Fazer, as a solo artist, was born.

Out of the ashes of The 39 Steppes a new band formed. Big Hair was a trio of Cressida (vocals/bass), Martin Cottis (keyboards) and Tom Langton-Lockton (guitar/vocals). With Cressida and Langton-Lockton now being a couple, at times it could be a bit of a roller coaster. "When they were good they were brilliant," Cottis recalls, "They were young, so when they were sparking they were great, and Tom would be writing the music and Cressida would be doing the lyrics." Often using pick-up drummers, Big Hair began to play live and there was a bit of a buzz about the band. Charlie Gillett again helped out, funding some demos and putting them in touch with Fresh Records, who asked the band to record a single for them. The A-side was to be a cover version of the famous Sandie Shaw song *Puppet On A String.*

"Why did we do that?" asks Langton-Lockton today, "That was my idea. I thought it was going to get us a contract. I just thought it was the logical thing to do." The single was recorded by Ed Sirrs. "I had a tape machine and some gear at home, but almost zero experience or expertise," he recalls today, "I wasn't in the demo studio business - I'd never tried to record anyone else - so I guess it was a cost-effective, suitably lo-fi solution for Big Hair. They had a clear idea of what they wanted - very unadorned - speed was of the essence. They weren't into revising/repeating/finessing - bosh-bosh. I seem to recall they were a bit unhappy about my use of echo and stuff."

"It was in his front room," recalls Cottis "It was great!" Indeed it was, and both *Puppet On A String* and the B-side, *Lies,* on which Langton-Lockton sang, were excellent tracks full of panache and energy. The band must have been happy with the results Ed Sirrs obtained as, according to Cottis, "We did four or five other tracks as well, although that may have been a week later. That was Charlie (Gillett) again saying 'Do more'. I guess he must have paid for it."

At this time, Fresh Records were a small independent label who, like many others, were living hand to mouth. Although they'd issued some excellent singles by bands like UK Decay, The Dark and Family Fodder, there was no money in the kitty for things like tour support and extensive advertising. When it came to trying to promote *Puppet On A String,* "we asked the guy at Fresh for some money for publicity," recalls Cottis. "He gave us a tenner to go and buy some spray paint, so we did. I can't remember whose decision it was, but we wouldn't just do walls, we'd go to all of the music press and spray their front doors."

According to Langton-Lockton, it was Cottis who sprayed "BIG HAIR" on the door at the offices of the *New Musical Express,* whilst he took care of *Sounds. Melody Maker* and *Record Mirror* probably got the same treatment. But there was a reaction. "We got a call from the Fresh guy and he said, 'You have to go down to the *NME* now and apologise, because they're livid and threatening to sue and ruin the record company, and I can't take it,'" recalls Cottis, "So we did and we had to wait outside his (the Editor's) office. We walked in and he took our single and he broke it and threw it in the bin and said he was never going to touch anything any of us ever did again, and that we were lucky that he wasn't going to touch Fresh."

Despite the *New Musical Express* being set against them, *Puppet On A String* had potential - the type of record that could have been a surprise independent and mainstream hit. DJ Paul Burnette played it on Radio One as a bit of a joke, and John Peel also dropped his needle onto the record on air. This could have driven sales, but according to Cottis what hurt the record even more than the *New Musical Express* fatwa was poor distribution. "Because I'd worked (temporarily) in Harrods and joined another punk band, Perfect Crime, there I was hanging out a lot in Chelsea and Earls Court and drinking," recalls Cottis, "I met this rather posh girl who was working as a distributor for a massive record company about the time that *Puppet On a String* was released and she said, 'We just can't get it. We were getting all of this demand from all of these shops saying, 'Have you got it?' It's fucked up. It's impossible to get it. I keep trying.'" Perhaps Fresh didn't press enough, or just suffered with poor distribution. The label went bankrupt in 1982, by which time Big Hair was also no more.

According to Cottis and Langton-Lockton there was serious interest amongst larger record companies about signing the band. "We had this amazing drummer from Furious Pig who filled in when we did a gig in Dingwalls, and every record company you could think of wanted to sign us, we were the thing that was happening," states Langton-Lockton. However, the band had already started to drift apart due to personal differences.

Tangential to this, Simon Patterson had launched a career as a solo artist, returned to Devon in late 1979 and begun to explore electronic music. He recalls, "I remember getting really upset actually. I walked into Zounds and saw this record and I knew what it would sound like - it was Tubeway Army's *Are Friends Electric?* and from the cover I knew what it would sound like. I was so pissed off, but I loved it as well." Patterson did his first solo performance as Spöön Fazer at Totnes Civic Hall around Christmas 1979 - he wore a red fluorescent suit and, with his electronic drums and kitchen spoons, sang and recited poetry. By the end of the night there had also been a Whippets From Nowhere reunion gig of sorts, minus Ben Cull.

One of the people at the gig invited Patterson to play at a Christmas office party in London, which led to the offer of a job that allowed him to move back to London and start his Spöön *Fazer* career in earnest. He began performing at venues like the Blitz Club and Richard Strange's Caberet Futura in Soho. "My boss offered to be my manager but I said, "No." But I borrowed the money (from him) to put out my first EP, and the deal was that I would re-contact him after a year and if I'd not made it I would work again to pay the debt." There had also been another offer to fund the single, "Tom Bailey offered to put out my first single. He also asked me to be the drummer of the Thompson Twins when they went to a threesome and I said, "No." Mad really."

Patterson remained in contact with Jimmy Cauty, and at one time was a temporary member of The Tets. "They had this group called The Tets - The Tetrahedrons, so that pyramid, the KLF pyramid, has always been there – and, I don't know if they did any gigs (before then), but we did one eventually and I was asked to be the drummer - we played at the Friern Barnet mental hospital, where I also did a solo performance as Spöön Fazer." The line-up of The Tets for this gig was Sid Holmes on vocals, his partner Gilly on backing vocals, a chap called John on banjo, Patterson on drums and Jimmy Cauty on guitar. As for what they played, Patterson recalls one track called *Wigging Out With The Zooty Love Pecks*, "This was the bands anthem!" For a while, Cauty also had a band called Evil Baby, who played a support gig with The 39 Steppes in June 1979.

When it came to recording his EP, *Music 2 Live 2*, for Project Records, Patterson hired Lodge Studios in Hertfordshire for a day and went down with Cressida and Langton-Lockton, who were in Big Hair at the time. The studio was run by Robert Godfrey, who was in a band called The Enid and, as well as producing, also contributed some electronics to the track *Motorway Amberline*. As for the sleeve design, Patterson recalls, "I guess I must have hung around a lot at Jimmy's place, told him I was doing this and asked would he do a cover for me. He kindly said, 'Yes,' so the first Spöön Fazer EP had cover art by Jimmy Cauty."

Although a thousand copies of the EP were pressed and Patterson had distribution through Rough Trade, it sold slowly. As per his agreement, he had to go back to work to pay off the money he owed, but he continued to perform as Spöön Fazer, and would record another EP in 1981, issued on Illuminated Records and called *Sunset*. "One of the legendary tracks was *Ballad Of Insect Man* - I used to do it solo, and even did it at a gig at a place called Fungus Park in Brixton opposite the dole office. I eventually recorded it and Jimmy played bass and Wasp (synthesiser) on it - I believe that was his first recording. He's never said it wasn't! He was a great mentor and friend."

The demise of Big Hair saw Langton-Lockton form another band called Circus Circus, and then later Ecologist. Meanwhile, Martin Cottis moved from keyboards to drums and joined Cressida and Jimmy Cauty in a new band that was to be called Angels One 5.

"I think that's where we came closest," states Cottis. "It was Jimmy's band, him and Cressida, and they asked me (to drum). They needed a bass player, and I'd been playing with some people in Camden and they had a really good bass player called John (Cook). He was so funky in a way that we hadn't discovered."

Angels One 5 set about rehearsing a set of songs and soon sent a demo to John Peel. "I can remember sending the tapes off, and we weren't called Angels One 5 at that point," recalls Cottis. "I think on a whim I put Heavy Shopping on it, and then he wrote back to say that he really liked the name and we went in and did it (a Peel Session). Jimmy didn't like Heavy Shopping, so by the time we got there we were Angels One 5."

The Angels One 5 session was recorded on 1st July 1981, broadcast on the 8th July and comprised of four tracks, *Accident In Studio 4*, *Living For The Future*, *Cut And Dried* and *Workface*. Sounding like a cross between The Slits and The Magic Band, with elements of The Banshees and guitar lines reminiscent of John McGeogh, these were excellent songs. *Living For The Future* was particularly compelling.

At this point the band began to play live and hustle for their break, which came in the form of a large open-air concert under unusual circumstances. On April 10-12th 1981, the Brixton riots took place, and when the dust had settled it was decided to hold a Reconciliation Concert. As they were seen as a Brixton band, Angels One 5 were asked to take part. "We were the only white band," laughs Cottis today, "I just remember this hail of missiles and abuse coming from these black kids. Cressida was bravely standing there trying to give a speech, a kind of hope not hate speech, and it wasn't really working. Afterwards, I got surrounded by all these kids. They were going, 'You fucking bastards, you were in that band - what were you doing?' I said I was the drummer and one of them went 'Oh, that was quite good actually.'"

There was a lot of anger in the black community at this time over discrimination and the police's stop and search tactics, and this had been part of the spark that had set off the riots. The last thing a large black audience wanted was to hear was a white new wave act, however poppy some of their songs sounded. "You can't blame them," laughs Cottis, "but we did get a nice letter from the organisers and Councillors saying 'Thank you for being so brave.'"

They were also being brave in going out and trying to find a record label. Cottis recalls, "We were all off doing the thing, trying to get the contract, and I got very close with this guy who was with CBS, whose offices were in Soho. He really liked what we were doing. We were doing a version of *America* from *West Side Story* - he really liked that and said that we should do more covers. I said I'd liked that David Essex song *Rock On*, and he went, 'I know David really well!' The usual bollocks. But I was getting quite excited about it and going back to Jimmy saying we could do this, the moneys there and he's keen. But Jimmy went 'No, we'll go with these people.'"

These people were a small independent label called Galaxy Records, who were based in Essex and had just started up. Whether Cauty knew the label owner or had a connection with them is unknown, but it was decided that Angels One 5 would record their debut single for them. The A-side, *Countdown*, was recorded at G.R.A.M. studio in Harwich, Essex, where the label was based, but, when it came to the B-side, the band were unhappy with the recording so "we used the old recording (we'd made) that we were much happier with."

Galaxy Records only issued five or six singles, ranging from the heavy metal of T34 to a single by Private Collection, produced by Chester Kamem (who was to work with Roxy Music and Pink Floyd). They were, in effect, one of many small independent labels that were full of good intentions but underfunded, and when their records didn't sell they soon went bust as their initial capital investment dried up. Similarly, as there were so many independent bands around during this period, Angels One 5 were struggling to make an impact, even after issuing a single and recording a Peel session. According to Cottis, they did tour as support for Fad Gadget, but they basically needed a break and a deal with a bigger label, as shown by a letter that Cauty wrote to John Peel during this period;

> This is our single - *Cut And Dried* and *Countdown*, out now on Galaxy Records. *Cut And Dried* sounds the way it does because the record company remixed it without telling us. The A15 mix is available on tape only. *Countdown* was produced by us.
>
> We're playing at Coventry Polytechnic on 24th Nov - could you announce this on the air please.
>
> Can we do another session for you? We have a lot of new material, and have added two more girls to the group - Plume saxophone and Fish trombone - The Horns Of Dilemma.

The letter was signed "Jimmy Cauty", although to confirm that Angels One 5 were a democracy, the rest of the band's names were added afterwards.

By this time, the band had indeed expanded its line-up, and at the Coventry gig, where Spöön Fazer was also on the bill, Cottis recalls that Jerry Dammers from The Specials came up to him after the show to tell him how great he thought the band were, especially with the horn section. As for how Cauty behaved on stage, Cottis recalls, "He was very shy. Cressida would be bouncing around on stage, and there was a lot to look at with the horn section. I had a massive ceiling fan in front of the drum kit with wings on it that I thought made the drum kit look like a biplane that I was flying."

Sadly this was not the case with Angels One 5, and although they could secure live work they just didn't land the contract that would have sustained them. "Again, it just fizzled out," states Cottis, "I remember turning up at rehearsals and thinking, "I don't really feel like it." Jimmy was thinking ahead because he was so determined that this was what he was going to do. He used to practice on his own so relentlessly, we were a bit in awe over how hard he was working. He did stuff with John Cook for a while, and then he joined Brilliant with Youth."

IT COULD HAVE BEEN A BRILLIANT CAREER

"The record company have been trying to turn us into dancers. I mean, I like dancing but we're not Five Star!"
- Youth speaking to Melody Maker, 1986

"The two follow-up singles aren't so good. I'm reminded of those fine Ze records of 1981, namely Material's 'Bustin' Out' and 'Wheel Me Out' by Was (Not Was). Their power-trip collision of lurex dance-stomp and gung-ho hysteria have since been imitated but never surpassed. Brilliant's 'Love Is War' is a nice try, Jimi's predilection for half-hour guitar squalls curtailed to about four seconds on June's orders."
- New Musical Express, November 1985

Killing Joke was one of the most important bands to emerge out of the post punk period. Featuring Jaz Coleman (vocals/keyboards), 'Big' Paul Fergusson (drums) Geordie Wallace (guitar) and Martin Glover, aka Youth, on bass, they secured an early breakthrough when their debut *Turn To Red* 10" EP was issued by the small Malicious Damage label in 1979 and a copy was dropped off at the BBC one Monday. The following morning John Peel rang to ask their manager a question: was this band The Stranglers in disguise? When told that Killing Joke were a new band he played the entire EP on Tuesday, Wednesday and Thursday, leading to massive interest from major labels.

With the blessing of Malicious Damage, Killing Joke ended up signing to EG, who also ran a management company that looked after King Crimson and Brian Eno, among others. Like Bauhaus, Killing Joke had an edge on other bands as a compelling live act, and managed to capture the genie of their musical chemistry on early singles, their eponymous, 1980 long playing debut, *Killing Joke*, and its follow up, *What's THIS For?* (1981). Things were moving forward at such a pace it seemed to be just a matter of time before the band broke through internationally, especially when plans were made to record their third LP in Germany with legendary producer Conny Plank.

Fast forward five years and things had changed. Like the Clash, who now only revolved around the twin planets of Joe Strummer and Paul Simonon, Killing Joke had shed members, and only Coleman and Geordie were left standing from the original line-up when the band unleashed their 6th album, *Brighter Than A Thousand Suns*, in 1986. In truth, it was not that bright, and in a frank interview with *Melody Maker* Coleman brutally dissected the undercooked LP, stating that Paul Fergusson's drumming was so bad that he'd had to erase all of his parts and have them redone in two days by Jimmy Copley, "who's played with Jeff Beck." The same applied to the basslines laid down by Paul Raven. "Geordie did them, because he's brilliant." Ironically, when Youth had his acid meltdown in 1981 and was finding it somewhat challenging to play on sessions for W*hat's THIS For?*, Geordie tried to teach him what to play, but when Coleman suggested that Geordie record the bass parts to save time the guitarist had refused as he saw it as "Cheating." It seems that, a few albums down the line, this kind of division of labour was no longer a problem for the guitarist. As for his interview, striking a *magnanimous* note Coleman went on to say, "Raven was really someone to take over Youth's place, except he lacked Youth's charisma, I have to admit in retrospect. He doesn't work hard, he stands there and he still doesn't have the charisma to carry it off – that's one of the sad facts of life I'm afraid."

Youth had taken his bass and charisma out of the band in 1982, after the Conny Plank produced *Revelations,* intent on treading a rather different path, and eventually formed a band called Brilliant. Their first single, *That's What Good Friends Are For/Push*, was a clunky beginning, moving towards more funky and electro territory without finding the right groove. More Numan than New York, but the band began to move around the live circuit. "I had cachet coming out of Killing Joke," Youth recalls today, "we had an agent, we were getting gigs and Metropolis and people like that were promoting us. Bands like Southern Death Cult did their first gig supporting us and we could pull a crowd."

In 1982, the band – by now a five piece - recorded a Peel session, and one track, *Colours*, was remixed to become their next single. It was issued as a 12" in 1983, and funded by Mark Risk, who ran a clothes shop on Portobello Road and put the record out on his own Risk records. As the original track had been recorded for the BBC, Youth was quick to send a white label test pressing to John Peel for airplay, and shared information on the current position of Brilliant: "The band are, I'm afraid, very poor and are struggling to keep our heads above the sludge at the moment. But we are endeavoring to persevere.'"

Indeed they were, and musically they were on the right track - *Colours* was an excellent single, more successfully incorporating elements of soul and dance which had their nexus in New York and were slowly fanning out across the clubs of the world. Indeed, despite their near poverty, to serve up the sound that Youth was hearing in his head Brilliant, at one point, expanded to an eight-piece, meaning there was even less money to go around after gigs. "I thought, we'll really indulge ourselves here with two drummers and two bass players," Youth laughs today. "I got June (Lawrence) in and her sister Sandra as backing singers, and I thought that we'd get more of an authentic black sound." Money was too tight to mention, and organisation could also be somewhat haphazard - Brilliant once turned up for a gig in Liverpool a week late as they'd got the dates mixed up. They were allowed to play, but with no advance warning they played to the proverbial man and his dog.

One of the few people most likely at that gig was journalist Kris Needs, who admits that he "was kind of road manager and publicist as I was living in the middle of all these comings and goings." This not only referred to the band's turnover of personnel but also the fact that he ended up moving into the same flat as Youth, which became "Brilliant HQ". Needs very much had his ear to the ground, and, like Youth and his old school friend Alex Paterson, began to fall under the spell of Kiss FM tapes that were seeping in from America. "Anyone going to New York had strict instructions to come back with cassettes of what they were playing on the radio. There were guys like Shep Pettibone, who was playing these remixes and master mixes at noon, so you could walk down the street in New York hearing *Thriller* by Michael Jackson turned upside down and *Blue Monday* by New Order all going on for half an hour with all manner of effects, like Bugs Bunny. It was a big influence on The Clash as well, and this heavily informed what Mick Jones did with Big Audio Dynamite."

Of course, whilst New Order scored big with *Blue Monday* in 1983 and recorded the follow-up, *Confusion*, with New York dance producer Arthur Baker, Big Audio Dynamite didn't release their debut LP until 1985, and top twenty singles chart success wouldn't follow until 1986. So in tapping into the energy of this new music, Brilliant were ahead of the curve - could that translate into success?

One man thought so. After the demise of The Teardrop Explodes, David Balfe had moved into management, with Strawberry Switchblade - the Glasgow duo of Rose McDowell and Jill Bryson - being his first clients. After hearing sessions recorded for John Peel and Kid Jensen on Radio One, Balfe was initially interested in signing them to Zoo Publishing, but ended up co-producing their first single, *Trees And Flowers*, with Bill Drummond and taking over their management. Now living in London,

Balfe had become friends with Madness, and arranged for Mark Bedford and Woody Woodgate to play bass and drums on the session, whilst Roddy Frame from Aztec Camera played guitar and Nicky Holland of Fun Boy Three played piano. Oboe and French horn were also added to what was a gem of a debut single, and Balfe arranged for it to be released on Bunnyman Will Sergeant's 92 Happy Customers label in 1983, with a view to this being a stepping stone to a major label deal. Indeed, Strawberry Switchblade were soon snapped up by Warner Brothers, and, with the wind back in his sails, Balfe established a new record label called Food in March 1984 and signed Brilliant.

"The starter on Food's menu is a new single by the group Brilliant," gushed a press release around this time. This was *Soul Murder*, which was sent out to journalists with a lavish four page glossy A4 promotional fold-out that really banged the drum for the band and put their first two singles into the past: "Brilliant have moved on, they are gradually developing a niche for themselves, lodged between the anarchic, roots punk ethic and streetwise New York funk. There's a smattering of dub for good measure."

At that point a crystal ball was deployed to map out a possible future that not only included gigs in the UK but the storming of America - "New York gets the message. Six maybe more, dates. A homecoming of sorts to an audience who are already primed." As you might imagine, there were also two eye-catching pictures of the band - six members at this point - that pushed attractive singer June Montana front and centre.

August 1984 was penciled in as the possible date the debut Brilliant LP - "A landmark?" – would be released to the world, but sadly *Soul Murder* and a subsequent single, *Wait For It/Cut Price*, failed to sell and help fulfill these prophecies. August 1984 came and went without Brilliant releasing the LP, although David Balfe was now managing the band, and as early as June 1984 was trying to get them a deal with Warner Brothers. This move was only logical - Balfe was still connected to Bill Drummond, who, by this time, had signed to Warner Brothers himself as an independent A&R man. "They were a close knit team," Youth recalls of the Drummond and Balfe axis, "who worked together a lot, and I was happy with that as they were coming up with some good ideas."

Youth was also full of good ideas, and, amongst the revolving door of players who appeared on stage and record, added a new guitarist to Brilliant named Jimmy Cauty. "Jimmy, at first, was our sound guy," Youth recalls, "He was doing sound and he was a friend of (John) Chester's. Then one day our guitarist let us down and I said to Jimmy, 'Can you play?' He said, 'Yeah.' And he sounded just like Jimi Hendrix with a fuzzbox! I said, 'OK you're in the band now.' So he joined."

Kris Needs recalls that this line-up of Brilliant was, "absolute chaos on the road. Rehearsals were actually better than the gigs, and they were coming up with something that was really new but slightly ahead of its time, because acid house had yet to break." Of course, dope was in full flower, and Needs lovingly describes Brilliant at this time as "this gaggle of giggling stoners. I do remember going to a gig in Brighton, and we had the proverbial transit with everybody sitting in the back on cushions. Unusually, I'd managed to bag a seat in the front, and we got to Brighton and I opened the back door and you couldn't even see inside because of all the smoke. There was a lot of funny stuff, a lot of laughing. Jimmy was not an extrovert, he was quite quiet, smiling to himself a lot of the time. I don't know if he saw this band as a commercial proposition or if he ever wanted that."

But things would soon change and Brilliant *would* be seen as a commercial proposition – by Bill Drummond.

For Rob Dickens, who in 1983 became Chairman of Warner Music UK, offering Bill Drummond a job as an A&R man must have been a no-brainer. Drummond had unearthed Echo And The Bunnymen and The Teardrop Explodes, both of whom, from 1979 onwards, never seemed to be out of the music papers, and, rather than allow both bands to be stifled by the confines of his small independent label, had been both visionary and practical enough to move them on to major labels. Indeed, it was Dickens himself who signed the Bunnymen to Warner Brothers through the mechanism of the Korova sub-label, and early albums and singles had done very well. The Teardrop Explodes, meanwhile, had signed to Mercury and enjoyed massive chart success there. Drummond had taken up the reins of management for both bands and helped them widen their touring circles, and Dickens could see he had a nose for talent and that it would be a great business decision to bring him into the fold at Warner Brothers.

Did Dickens ask Drummond if the story was true that it was he who decided to add those famous trumpets to *Reward*?... One imagines that he was wined and dined and a deal was agreed which was acceptable to both parties - he received a three-year contract, would work out of the London office and was allowed to continue as Echo And The Bunnymen's manager. This was a canny move by both parties as the Bunnymen were signed to Korova, over which Drummond was given some control, and he would work hard to expand their commercial success. This was good news for Dickens and the Warner Brothers bottom line.

Rather than move down to London itself, Drummond and his family relocated to Aylesbury in Buckinghamshire, where his wife's parents lived, and commuted to the office. He soon got to work looking for talent that would either be issued through the main Warners Brothers label or via Korova, which was now his own personal fiefdom. Drummond has written that his Warners period was less than satisfactory. He worked with a number of bands who were either already signed to the label or actually signed by himself, such as Ellery Bop, a band with Jamie Farrell and Kev Connolley at its core who hailed from Liverpool and had once served as roadies for The Teardrop Explodes. They'd issued a number of singles on their own Base Ideas label from 1981 onwards, and in a 1982 interview with the *Melody Maker* described major label A&R men with derision, "They're all called Nigel and they wear bomber jackets and I bet they vote SDP (the forerunner of the Liberal Democrats). And they all seem to get sacked every ten months. How can you take people like that seriously?" But Bill Drummond was someone they knew and could take seriously. Sadly, though, they only issued one single on Korova, 1985's *Torn Apart*, before falling apart.

Drummond has written that his office at Warner Brothers contained his father's old desk and a piano. "There was no cassette player," he wrote in *17*, "I never listened to any cassettes that anybody sent in. If anyone came by and wanted me to listen to their stuff I asked them to play it on the piano." Although he had the pleasure of hearing Jimmy Ruffin play *What Becomes Of The Broken Hearted?* on this piano, he could not function fully as an A&R man without listening to music in his office or on the premises.

Luckily, by 1984 John Hollingsworth moved into the office next to his. Hollingsworth had been head hunted from independent label Cherry Red, and had the delicious job of keeping his ear to the ground and letting Seymour Stein and Max Hole know what was going on in the busy and exciting British independent music scene. He came from Liverpool too, so when it came to Drummond, "we sort of knew each other vaguely from the old days in Liverpool, with him in Big In Japan and stuff." He recalls, "We became better friends because we were of a similar age, and I had a big sound system in my office, so he was always in my office playing stuff and having meetings with the Bunnymen or whoever else he was meeting." It later got to the point where Drummond would add an extension to his phone and sit on Hollingsworth's sofa to hold some conversations, although there were times when this wasn't possible as Andy Eldritch, of the Sisters of Mercy, might be there sleeping off the effects of a night out.

By 1984 the Bunnymen were gearing up to issue their fourth LP, *Ocean Rain,* and Drummond worked hard to ensure that it received the necessary promotional push. Typically, he came up with the ambitious strapline, "The greatest album ever made" which ran across the bottom of adverts in the music press. It was a wonderful and ballsy piece of bombast that could have provoked a backlash if the album had been undercooked, but *Ocean Rain* was a masterpiece, and not only did the first single, *The Killing Moon*, go top ten but the album reached number four in the charts upon release in May 1984.

To coincide with the release of the album and subsequent tour, Drummond staged another unique Bunnymen event. "The Crystal Day will occur on Saturday May 12th," wrote Mick Houghton in his press release, "and, among other delights, includes a bicycle race, a return trip on the Mersey ferry, a visit to the Anglican cathedral - with a recital by the Cathedral Boys' Choir – and, as the culmination of the day, a performance by Echo And The Bunnymen and their guests at Liverpool's King George's Hall in the evening." Once again, Drummond was showcasing the Bunnymen in a unique setting that not only set them apart but also generated more column inches in the music press than their rivals. That said, the cycling route drawn by Drummond to resemble the ears of Echo the bunny did not coincide with any streets and was partially underwater!

According to Hollingsworth, Drummond was equally unique when dealing with the executive in charge of video production at Warner Brothers. He wanted Anton Corbijn to direct the video for *Seven Seas,* which was to be the third single taken from the *Ocean Rain* album. Whilst Corbijn was known as one of the best photographers in the music press, and had created iconic images of everyone from Joy Division to U2, as well as the Bunnymen, he had, at this time, directed only a couple of music videos. The Warners video executive was less than enthusiastic about the somewhat arty premise of his ideas for *Seven Seas* and didn't believe that the photographer had enough of a track record to approve funding the video. By this point, however, the video was literally ready to shoot, and according to Hollingsworth, Drummond took out a loan against his house to fund it himself. Of course, the results were visually stunning, and had the producers of shows like *The Tube* salivating and wanting to give the single a big visual push when it was released. "So, can I get my money back?" Hollingsworth recalls Drummond asking Rob Dickens, who was quick to issue a positive response. Aided by the video, *Ocean Rain* went top ten and Drummond recouped his outlay.

That Drummond actually borrowed the money himself to fund the shooting of a video demonstrates how different he was from other A&R men. He was gutsy enough to financially back his own decisions, even in a corporate environment, very much in keeping with the way he'd operated when running Zoo Records, where he financed the first sessions for The Teardrop Explodes debut LP. He was a maverick who got things done, but who also saw things that other people didn't see.

"Bill was a natural talent spotter," recalls John Hollingsworth, "but the one thing I never got was those two Scottish guys he signed the publishing on – The Proclaimers. He saw them before anyone. I went to see them do a gig with him and he said, 'John, I'm going to sign their publishing. I'm going to ask them for the rights.' I went 'Really?' They had some catchy songs and that, but it was never going to happen. But he was completely right about that." Another artist he backed early was Rolo McGinty, formerly of the Wild Swans.

"For a few years, Bill had a little bit of Rolo radar going on," McGinty recalls today, "I think he thought that I had something, and he always had a little bit of time for me." This led to Drummond signing him to Zoo Publishing for an advance of £10,000, which got The Woodentops off the ground. "But I still had a bit of time in my job to finish off," laughs McGinty, "I was the cocktail barman in the Inebriated Newt in Fulham and he came in. He came in with all of these guys and they were doing some kind of business meeting. He walked in, turned around and went, 'Hang on a minute? What are *you* doing here? You are not supposed to be in here.' I was like, 'I'm just finishing off some time before I get on with it.' He said, 'I have given you £10,000, *what are you doing here?*' I said, 'Don't worry about it, but I will be making your cocktails, so order away.' They were *well* looked after that night!"

One thing Drummond was not always right about was train times or the possibilities of delays during his daily commute. "Bill used to run in from Paddington station because he used to live with his wife out in Aylesbury," laughs Hollingsworth, "He sometimes used to be late and he would call up and go, 'John! There is someone delivering some kilts.' There were always weird packages being delivered and one was a pile of kilts. I would have to sign for it or there was money left in his drawer or a cheque. There was also a fancy oil painting he'd spotted at Christies or somewhere once and bought."

According to Hollingsworth, Dickens considered Drummond something of a fancy painting himself, and had a huge regard for his talents. "I always thought he was the alter ego for Rob Dickens in a way, as Bill was doing the stuff that maybe Rob wished he could." Whether Dickens would have licensed The Residents' album *George & James* to Korova in 1984 is unknown, but their cover of James Brown's *It's A Man's Man's Man's World* was the nearest the iconoclastic San Francisco collective ever got to the bottom rungs of the charts.

Of course, Dickens had to run Warner Brothers as a business and keep an eye on the bottom line. He was, at times, quite hands on, and would always take calls from sales reps out on the front line to get an insight into which records issued by his labels were selling and needed an additional promotional push. The job of the A&R department, in which Drummond worked, was to sign artists and make records to put in the hands of these sales reps which would sell and make money for the company. "Bill, like anybody else, needed hit records in those days," recalls Hollingsworth, "to keep going, as there wasn't an endless resource of money. Dickens was not endlessly going to fund him." So, like any other A&R man, Bill Drummond needed to sign artists who, like the Bunnymen, would not just be fondled by the music press in endless features and reviews but get into the charts. By 1985 he needed something. Something Brilliant.

"We've got you a deal with Warners," Youth recalls David Balfe telling him as his negotiations to get them a major label deal bore fruit. "'Go and do the album. We've got you two weeks in the studio.' This was when we were a seven or eight piece band." Balfe had sold Drummond on the idea that Brilliant had potential, and the money was found to send them into Vineyard studio in Borough to record the tracks they'd honed live. A line-up of Youth (bass), Stephanie Holweck (bass), Jimmy Cauty (guitar), Jake Le Mesurier (drums), June Montana (vocals), Marcus Myers (vocals), Ben Watkins (keyboards) and John Chester (percussion) recorded tracks including *Escape From New York*, *Kiss The Lips Of Life*, *Somebody*, *Ruby Fruit Jungle*, *Elephants*, *The Growler*, *Subtle Manoeuvers* and *Push*. The session was produced by Barry Andrews, who managed to capture the genie of the Brilliant sound, and along with Youth and Holweck, who played off each other and Le Mesurier to perfection, Jimmy Cauty was also in his element, serving up guitar parts ranging from Jimi Hendrix pyrotechnics to funky licks that were right out the *Theme From Shaft*.

"We laid it down and thought – 'Yeah we've nailed it,'" Youth recalls, "We had the songs and we had the Kiss FM electro dance thing. It was all there. But Bill and Balfe were, 'No. It's no good.' We played it to Warners and they rejected it."

As you might imagine, the band were gutted, but Drummond and Balfe revealed a silver lining. "They said, 'You have a choice. You can split the band up into a three piece – that was their idea – and do the album again with these pop dance producers Stock, Aitken and Waterman, who have just started. They've just done *You Spin Me Round Like A Record*.'" One imagines that the other option was no further interest from Warner Brothers at all.

It was Bill Drummond, wearing his A&R hat, who'd driven through a possible union between Brilliant and Warner Brothers via Pete Waterman. Waterman had started off as a DJ, worked at MCA and Rocket Records in the early '80s and had produced a number of hit records, from the Belle Stars to Musical Youth's *Pass The Dutchie*. In 1984 he set up a production team with Mike Stock and Matt Aitken, and the first record they recorded together was a track called *The Upstroke,* issued as Agent's

Aren't Aeroplanes, which not only got John Peel raving but became a big gay club anthem. The team then cut their chart teeth with a massive hit in 1985, *You Spin Me Round* by Dead Or Alive, who were fronted by Pete Burns, a man Drummond had first encountered working behind the counter at Probe Records in Liverpool, and later on stage at Eric's, back in the late '70s.

At this time, Waterman was in the process of establishing what would become The Roman Empire of '80s pop production - Stock, Aitken and Waterman. Initially, Waterman's working process was to book studio time for recording sessions and then bring in all of his modern equipment - synthesisers, drum machines etc - as well as his boys, to make the record. He even toyed with the idea of buying his own up-to-date SSL (Solid State Logic) mixing desk for £210,000 and having it put in a flight case so he could bring it into whatever studio he booked. Waterman made business decisions on intuition and worked out how to pay for them afterwards, which saw him taking over Vineyard studio and installing his SSL desk with plans to turn it into a modern studio fit for his needs. After sessions for EMI trying to turn a band called Spelt Like This into a new Pet Shops Boys were aborted, he was looking for business, so when Pete Burns mentioned that he knew Bill Drummond from the early days of the Liverpool independent scene and that he was now an A&R man at Warner Brothers looking for acts, Waterman made a point of going to see him.

In his book, *17,* Drummond recalls how Waterman literally turned up at his office, sat down and began a conversation that peaked and creviced like a mountain range, "He starts telling me how he used to manage The Specials, that he had spent Christmas with Michael Jackson and he is about to be the biggest thing in pop music in the 1980s, and then he started going on about steam trains and why The Beatles were still the greatest pop band ever ('until they went weird') and Tamla Motown was the greatest label ever and he was the new Berry Gordy."

It appears that Waterman did everything but play Drummond's piano, and Drummond invited him down to the Wag club to see Brilliant. He turned up halfway through their set, "and before he had heard one complete song said that they were shit, but if I would sack the band but keep the singer and give him £3000 next week he knew just the song she could sing and we would have a Top Ten hit in a matter of weeks. Then he left." Talk about making an entrance! When Drummond and David Balfe later asked what the song was, Waterman replied that he wouldn't tell them until Drummond had paid £1500 - half of the advance he was asking for.

Drummond later went down to Waterman's new studio and recalled that he even had his bank manager there when he arrived. Little did Drummond know that the bank manager had allowed Waterman to borrow so much money to rent and equip the studio that his own future was probably tied to the success of the fledgling Stock, Aitken and Waterman empire. In fact, it was this same bank manager who arranged a further loan of £30,000 to Waterman a few months later to set up his Supreme record label and press copies of its first single *Say I'm Your Number One* by Princess after hearing the track. One imagines that if Rob Dickens had found out about that he would've offered the bank manager a job in A&R.

At this time, the singer Waterman wanted to work with - June Montana - was spreading her time between working with Brilliant and The Dream Academy. She'd initially shared a flat with Kate St John, singer with that trio, and when The Dream Academy started to rehearse at the flat she began to sing backing vocals for them. She would go on to sing backing vocals on their 1985 hit *Life In A Northern Town,* and do some live and TV work with the band when they promoted the single and subsequent eponymous LP. So it's easy to see the appeal that the good-looking Montana held to Peter Waterman, but Drummond had to break the news that to market Montana alone or as Brilliant was not really possible as it was Youth's band, and guitarist Jimmy Cauty also "did really good artwork". Instead, Waterman agreed that they slim the band down to a three piece, so Drummond went to see if this was possible.

Montana was later quite frank when speaking to *Record Mirror*, "I was in both bands at the same time, and then it came to the crunch. Brilliant was more of a commitment when the deals came up so I went with them. It's more me. And who wants to be a backing singer when you can be a lead singer?" As for the boys, "It was a tough decision," recalls Youth today, "but we had to give it our best shot. Me, Jimmy and June were like, 'Let's do it.'"

Although it was via Food, Brilliant now had a major label deal, and with Drummond calling the shots at Warner Brothers and Balfe serving as their manager the plan was to turn the band into a massive chart-topping act like Dead Or Alive. Pete Waterman was given his £1500. "Then he told us another thing," recalls Drummond, "He wouldn't be wanting Youth or the guitarist who wanted to be Jimmy Page playing on the record."

Waterman and his boys finished the backing track in a week and he was soon calling Drummond to say, "we need that girl singer of yours in here tonight to get the song finished." Waterman also wanted his second £1500 as fast as possible and didn't really care that Youth and Cauty were upset that they weren't playing on a track that was going to be released under their name, and didn't even know the title of the track! In fact, the song was a cover version of James Brown's *It's A Man's Man's Man's World*, but recorded with a more laid back and modern vibe. Although Montana was initially unhappy about the song being somewhat chauvinist, she relented and added an excellent vocal, and Youth and Cauty were 'captured' playing bass and guitar by a Greengate sampler and added to the record. "This went some way to placate Youth's and Jimi's desire as musicians to have played on their own record without having to go through the messy business of actually having musicians playing real instruments," Drummond deliciously wrote later in *17*.

When they *were* allowed into the studio for the first time, Youth was probably pleased to see Phil Harding, who'd engineered the first Killing Joke album. By this time, Harding was a vital cog in the Pete Waterman machine, and had worked with him on tracks by Tracy Ullman, Nick Kershaw and Musical Youth. He'd also mixed *The Upstroke,* as well as *You Spin Me Round*. "We got on very well with Jimmy and Youth," Harding recalls today, "We also got on well with Bill Drummond, he seemed to understand what Stock, Aitken and Waterman and myself were capable of at that time."

Although it was early days, what they were capable of was making hit records, and they wanted to continue that success with Brilliant. Of course, this meant working *their* way, and Harding confirms this included, "wanting to keep the band out of the studio as much as possible due to space restrictions and too many opinions flying around from Jimmy and Youth." Waterman's team would record most of the music that appeared on the tracks, and Cauty later related that he turned up at one session with his guitar only to be told, "Well, we did the guitar last night."

When it came to promoting *It's A Man's Man's Man's World,* Warner Brothers went the whole hog roast, including producing an eye-catching video that could be touted around the TV stations. "It was Bill and Balfe's idea to get in a Hot Gossip dancer in to choreograph our videos," laughs Youth today, "We were like – 'It's going to be too pop!' But Bill said, 'No, it is going to be totally Supremes' and Balfe was like, 'It's going to be cool.' Then me and Jimmy said, 'Fuck it. Let's just have a laugh.' Which is not the best thing..."

In fact, looking at the video today, Youth and Cauty were taking matters *very* seriously indeed, from dressing in fashionable clothes to performing choreographed dance moves behind and beside Montana with their guitars. Speaking to the music press at the time, Cauty was very keen to put a lot of water between the earlier incarnation of Brilliant and this three-person, dancing confection, "It just wasn't going to get anywhere, that early stuff. I still really like it all, but it really wasn't going anywhere. Not enough people like it. I mean, *Soul Murder* was one of the best ones from that time, but most of the others are just a load of shit."

Sadly, people thought the same about the new Brilliant single. Warner Brothers worked hard to promote *It's A Man's Man's Man's World,* but a sticker attached to a copy sent to John Peel says it all really - "CHART POSITION 102 Going up slowly but surely." Sadly it went up too slowly, and the single failed to become a hit, only reaching number fifty-six in the charts, although Warner Brothers' legwork apparently did get it into the top thirty in Belgium and Holland.

"That track in particular stands out as one that we all thought would be a big hit," recalls Harding, "the version was quite unique, and we all liked the way June sounded on the track - it was different from the James Brown version and so unexpected for a woman to cover it at that time." As for Montana, she played the misfire ice-cool when speaking to the music press, "Everybody expected *Man's World* to do really well and everyone was surprised it didn't, everyone apart from me of course. I'm so *cynical* about everything. I'm constantly coming into the record company and being told, "Yes it's going to be a hit."" Nevertheless, Brilliant and their production team soldiered on in the studio with the intention of turning another track into a chart song.

Around this time, one of David Balfe's more *interesting* ideas had bubbled to the surface – that Cauty and Youth help out a graphic designer for *Flexipop* and *Metal Fury* magazines. "I was editing *Flexipop,*" recalls Kris Needs, "and my art guy was Mark Manning, who was this lunatic genius artist from Leeds who looked like a biker and had created Zodiac Mindwarp as a gross, alter-ego biker rockstar. It was actually the forerunner of all the people who did that kind of thing - and still do - and take it seriously." Manning had given Balfe a demo of a track he'd recorded on a porta-studio called *Prime Mover,* and Balfe was impressed enough by this back to basics growl of a song to decide that Manning needed a band behind him and get out onto the live circuit to build a buzz around this new Zodiac sign.

"He dragged in Jimmy, Youth and, I can't remember his name – it was a guy who died. (Jake Le Measurer - drums) It was basically Brilliant," recalls Manning today. Youth probably didn't protest too much as Manning had done the cover art for the early Brilliant single *Colours,* so they knew each other socially through Kris Needs already. A gig was arranged and the band prepared for the Mindwarp debut. "Youth and Jimmy don't really rehearse," laughs Manning, "they just jammed it as it is pretty simple music - the music The Love Reaction plays is just basic rock and roll. They're professionals, they don't really rehearse, they just jam it out live on stage, which can be fantastic but it can also be a fucking disaster.

I think it was a mixture of the two really."

One imagines that proper rehearsals did take place and some thought and effort went into how they presented themselves. Kris Needs was standing front row for the Zodiac debut, "They all came on in cut up denim, biker style, all sprayed up and covered in muck and paint and it was an unholy racket. By the time I saw Zodiac play New York two years later he'd almost turned into Guns 'N' Roses, but that first gig definitely had the air of a mischievous hobby band. They caused a bit of a ruckus at a time when every other band was getting a bit squeaky and clean." As for Axl Manning, he loved performing live - "I remember thinking, I can do this, I like this, I want to do more." This line-up, however, was for one night only. "I thought, this lot are already in a band, I want my own band, so that was it. We did the gig and I just decided to get my own band as they were already in Brilliant and had a singer."

So Manning went off to recruit a new Love Reaction, and by the time they played their second gig at Dingwalls in London a positive review stated that they were "top of the so bad they're brilliant stakes." Zodiac issued his debut *Wild Child* EP on Food in 1985, and was soon writing directly to John Peel in the third person - "for many years we of the planet freakout have observed the decline of your decadent music makers. To arrest this unfortunate development we have sent you an interstellar ambassador of the force: Zodiac Mindwarp. Assist the warped one in his mission and many rewards of a physical nature will be yours".

Zodiac was soon garnering acres of press coverage, and later enjoyed a hit single with *Prime Mover*, circumnavigating the globe like a rock and roll satellite in the process. He also gave David Balfe, who produced a lot of the Zodiac Mindwarp material, his biggest dose of front man ego trouble since he worked with Julian Cope, but more on that later...

Meanwhile, back on Earth, work in the studio continued as Stock, Aitken and Walkman tried to craft a Brilliant hit single. "We had to twist their arms to let us hang out," recalls Youth, "They'd never worked with a band, they just worked with singers. We said 'we're a band and we want to be involved in the creative process,' I almost got kicked out of the band as I was giving Mike Stock a hard time about sugary lyrics. They did not like bands interfering."

By this time Stock, Aitken and Walkman had scored a top ten hit with Princess and knew their formula worked. They even drafted her in to provide backing vocals on some Brilliant tracks when she wasn't working on her own material. At a time when recording a single or

BILL IN JAPAN Courtesy of David Palmer

Open Eye Gallery Courtesy of Michael Knowler   **MVCU Studio** Courtesy of Michael Knowler

The Whippets From Nowhere Courtesy of Simon Patterson

Cressida fronts Big Hair Courtesy of Martin Cottis

A Mythical Tets Gig 1978 Courtesy of Simon Patterson

Jimmy Cauty (far left) in Evil Baby Courtesy of Simon Patterson

Alex Paterson and Killing Joke Courtesy of Frank Jenkingson

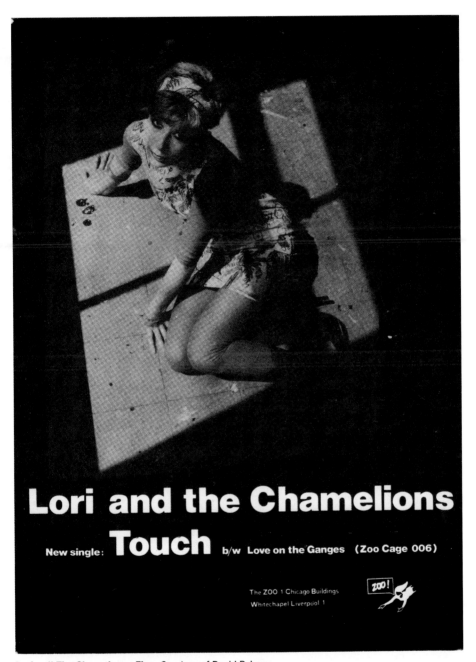

Lori and The Chameleons Flyer Courtesy of David Palmer

The Zoo Compliments Slip Courtesy of David Palmer

Brilliant as a three piece Courtesy of Ian Shirley

Bill Drummond, Jimmy Cauty and Ford Timelord in Sweden Courtesy of Lawrence Watson

Building a fire out of 1987 LPs Courtesy of Lawrence Watson

album could take weeks or months, the SAW team worked fast, and sometimes completed a whole track in a day. "They would start by traditionally looking at the song arrangement and structure, then program the keyboards and guide drums," recalls Phil Harding, "then prepare to record the vocals as early as possible. Once the vocals and backing vocals were recorded, the rest of the instrumentation would then be added to compliment them." Despite writing most of the songs but being relegated to the back burner, Youth, Cauty and Montana did manage to assert themselves enough to be able to get some time in the studio alone. Youth: "I would interfere more, saying 'do what you want on the A-side, just let me do the dub. Give me a night in the studio and I will go in with Jimmy and do the dub.' Pete Waterman let us do that and it was great fun." Brilliant-produced tracks like *The Red Red Groovy* or *The Burning Necklace* would appear as B-sides on 7" and 12" singles.

The second Brilliant single, *Love Is War*, was excellent. Whereas *It's A Man's Man's Man's World* had been too fast to be a ballad and too slow to work on the floor - "I wouldn't quite know how to dance to that" stated one review - *Love Is War* was more in tune with the electro funk pop of the time, and, with its catchy chorus, seemed like a hit. Once again there was a lavish video shoot, and, although he had flu, Youth soldiered on especially as he and Cauty had spent part of the week in a dance studio perfecting their moves with the guitar and bass.

"He never dances when he goes out," bemoaned Cressida, who was now Cauty's wife, at the video shoot attended by one music paper, "but look at him now!" Along with Youth, Cauty had spent a long time in make-up and hairdressing, and, dressed in a leather jacket, again went through a number of dances moves around a car in a desolate studio landscape. Meanwhile, Montana, in a black evening dress, make-up and jewels, looks like she is in a different video to these attractive ruffians, until the end when she also dons a leather jacket, picks up a guitar and fights for love, with her bandmates, through the medium of dance moves with guitars. At the end of the video she turns her back to the camera to reveal the words 'Melt Down' on the back of her leather jacket. This jacket, and those worn by the boys, was designed by Cauty, who was soon gushing to *Smash Hits* about how he crafted them, "It took me weeks at first to do one because you've got to wait for the paint to dry, but I use these new paints now. It's much quicker. I can do one in three nights. People are pretty startled by them. It's like an ad for Brilliant. Art school? ...nah... I'm self-taught."

With Warner Brothers investing so much money in videos, photoshoots and marketing, Brilliant were soon on (UK kids' TV show) *Blue Peter* discussing their leather jackets and plugging *Love Is War*. Cauty even discussed his artistic background with the *New Musical*

Express, stating, "I did some Tolkien stuff for Athena, and some Stonehenge and Glastonbury posters, all based on John Michell's books. He was into ley lines, all that kind of stuff. I got into that and did these posters, which were incredibly successful. But I keep really quiet about it." Unless he was talking to the music press of course! Saying that, his interest in Michell is interesting, as the author and writer was one of the first to popularise interest in ley lines and link them to mythical power and UFOs in the '60s and early '70s. His book, *The View Over Atlantis,* became a counter culture hit after it was first published in 1969, and in 1971 Michell even designed the pyramid for the first Glastonbury music Fayre, making sure it was located at the juncture of two powerful ley lines.

As for Youth, he had the throttle fully open when discussing what he wanted for Brilliant, "We *want* to appeal to Radio One DJs. We *want* to be popular, we want to be on the front line of media attack in people's homes everywhere. We're *pop!* I'm really into pop music at the moment - Simple Minds, the new Grace Jones single, Kate Bush." Kate Bush? This might have something to do with the fact that Bush apparently rang Youth around this time asking him to play bass on the *Hounds Of Love* LP. Sadly this didn't come to pass, but Youth, June and Jimmy were more than happy to give their thoughts to a proper teen magazine on a subject of national importance: "What is Brilliant about the 80s?" As well as praising Prince and Tears For Fears – "they're a great pop band, it's just that they look so bad." – Youth was keen to state that, "I love hi-tech architecture like the Nat West Tower and designer furniture and designer hi-tech pens." Cauty was straight behind him, "Wristwatch TVs are groovy and biological micro-processors are gonna revolutionise everything!" He was also quick to state that, "Our forthcoming album's really groovy, and I think guitar solos are becoming fashionable…" But, when June stated, "I like breakfast television," Youth could only groan, "Ooooh no!"

To help hoist Brilliant into the charts, along with an appearance on *The Tube* strings were even pulled by the Warner Brothers press office to get the band on *Wogan,* which was prime time TV exposure on the BBC. Augmented by two female keyboard players and a drummer flanking Montana, Cauty and Youth toned down their moves as they had to pretend that they were playing their instruments rather than dancing with them. But once again, *Love is War* failed to detonate, only reaching number sixty-four in the UK on release in March 1986, leading to more head scratching.

"*Love is War* was another big track from the album that we at PWL all expected to do better in the charts than it did," recalls Phil Harding. John Hollingsworth, meanwhile, recalls that Brilliant did at least top one chart, "They used to use the West One taxi company a lot, and they had an account with Warners. Jimmy and Youth were the only two people that the cab company were told, if they misbehaved or they were too drunk, the taxi drivers had one hundred per cent permission to throw them out of the cab anywhere in London."

The next Brilliant single was called *Somebody,* and, crucially, after lavishing money on two expensive videos – and perhaps too many taxi journeys – Warner Brothers did not finance a third. Of course, what frustrated Montana, Youth and Cauty was that all of the Warner Brothers investment through Food had gone into studio production and photo and videos shoots rather than tour support for a band that had cut its teeth as a live act. "I'm dying to do it again," continued Montana, "I felt really inhibited last time we played, but I've developed a lot since then so, for my own sake, I want to see how I could cope with an audience now."

Youth and Montana expressed similar sentiments to *Melody Maker* later in the year, although Youth was particularly frustrated due to legal wrangling, "over a disagreement that we can't discuss. We've done no promotional work for the new LP and single." The entire feature was given over to discussing the LP, which was in the process of being issued in a number of Warner Brothers territories, although Youth was, in many respects, true to his word about not selling the album. "I think the LP works well on a general level, but we fell out with the producers at the end, because they're a bit of a hit factory. Their attitude is something is only valid if it's going to be successful. If we were trying to express ourselves it wasn't important to them, unless it had that contemporary sound. That's why every track sounds like a single. They've got no morals, but I suppose that's why they're successful."

Ironically the final Brilliant single was another cover version - *The End Of The World* – and a fine metaphor for what was happening to their career. As for the legal issue, this was contractual - Warner Brothers had forgotten to renew. "Warners had spent a lot of money, not had a hit return and forgot to pick up our option for two weeks," Youth recalls today, "So Balfe went shopping for a new deal, and was getting a good deal for us, then Warners injuncted us and won the injunction, even though it was in black and white. The company had spent so much money that the judge thought it was only fair that they should have a second chance on the option on a clerical error."

That was the end of the world. It has been stated that Warner Brothers spent some £300,000 on recording the album and promoting the singles with very little return, and although they now had a legal right to take up an option on the band there was bad blood between both sides, especially between themselves and David Balfe. On a corporate level, the Warners-Brilliant battle probably put Bill Drummond in an awkward position - not only had he signed the band and worked hard to make them a success, but he had a close working relationship with Balfe, who had been in an out of the Warner Brothers offices ever since Drummond had taken up his appointment with the label.

Although Drummond wasn't party to the legal dispute over the Brilliant contract, the dispute went the full ten yards legally, and his immediate boss Rob Dickens had to deal with a matter that may have created some uncomfortable moments before a court ruling decided in Warner Brothers' favour. The only people who did well out of it all were the lawyers employed by both sides, and whilst the deep pockets of Warner Brothers could afford the outlay it was a big financial hit for Youth, Cauty, Montana and Balfe. As a result, Brilliant decided to call it a day and split up, and Montana later went solo, issuing *I Need Your Love* on FFRR in July 1989. Despite being accompanied by a glossy video, the single was not a hit.

By this time, Bill Drummond may also have been growing uncomfortable working in a corporate environment, where A&R men were measured in the weekly Thursday 10am meetings by sales, chart placing and the latest profit and loss figures from the accounts department. At one of these meetings, probably early in 1985, John Hollingsworth brought a 7" single to play those assembled around the table. It was by the hottest new band on the independent scene, The Jesus and Mary Chain, who were playing short, twenty minute sets that were provoking a reaction amongst audiences and the music press. Hollingsworth had bought their debut single on Creation Records, *Upside Down*, after seeing the band live, and, doing his job, suggested that this was the sort of band Warner Brothers should sign, playing it at full volume in the A&R meeting. Rob Dickens, who was working in an office nearby, came in and told him to turn it down in no uncertain terms.

Some time later, Hollingsworth recalls Alan McGee from Creation Records and Geoff Travis coming into the office. Whilst Travis was running Rough Trade, Dickens had cleverly seduced him by allowing him to set up Blanco Y Negro under the Warner Brothers umbrella and sign bands that were either not suitable for Rough Trade or needed a bigger push than the label could give them. The fact that The Smiths were detonating hard at this time suggested that Rough Trade Records and Distribution could push a band as far up the single and albums chart as Warner Brothers, and by backing Travis, Dickens was being very astute in siphoning off his A&R skills for the Warner Brothers empire.

Blanco had already signed Everything But The Girl, and initially Mike Alway had been part of the label with Travis. But when he went to set up his El label with Cherry Red, Travis brought Alan McGee on board. At this time, Creation was releasing critically acclaimed singles but wasn't making any money - The Jesus And Mary Chain might have music critics fawning over them, but even during these drug-addled days McGee knew that for them to break on through to the other side they needed major label muscle behind them.

Thus, McGee, Travis, Drummond, Hollingsworth and Dickens had a meeting during which Geoff Travis played Dickens the same 7" that Hollingsworth had played at the Warner Brothers A&R meeting some weeks earlier. "This is the most important band of the decade. I have got to sign them to Blanco," Hollingsworth recalls Geoff Travis gushing to Dickens. At that meeting it was agreed that Blanco Y Negro would sign The Jesus And Mary Chain and Hollingsworth – who was not known for keeping his opinions to himself – considered reminding Dickens about his earlier thoughts on the single. He was stopped, however, by a look from Bill Drummond, who knew this was not really the time. Even he knew that there were times when you played the corporate game rather than rocked the boat.

Indeed, timing was everything in the music business, and whereas the signing of The Jesus And Mary Chain was evidence of good timing there were other bands for whom the timing just went wrong. "I went into Warner Brothers to play demos of my new band, Shook Up," Neil McCormick recalls today, "I used to insist - because I had learned - that when they asked us to send demos we refused, and the only way we would do it was by going into the office an playing them ourselves. I was shuffled into this office where this pimply kid no older than myself stuck our lovingly crafted cassette tape into this shitty stereo, which proceeded to play our tracks in a muffled way, and he didn't pay any attention to them. He skipped through them, and he didn't hand it back, but I took it back off him. I was so angry with him that I wouldn't let him keep the tape. I walked out of the office, and as I walked through Warners I saw Bill Drummond, who I already knew, in his office, or maybe I met him in a corridor. He said, 'Neil, what are you doing here?' Then when I told him he said, 'Come and play me these tracks.' So we went in and he listened to them really intensely on a good stereo, paid attention and commented interestingly on what we were doing and seemed fascinated by the whole thing. He said he would come and see us play. That felt like a victory. It was a small office, and he was kind of playing the record executive at that point, when he probably should have being paying much more attention managing the careers of the great artists that he had in this thrall. But Warners had given him some money and he was trying to sign bands."

Shook Up put a lot of effort and energy into the planning and presentation of their next gig as a showcase for a number of labels who'd promised to come and see them perform. They pulled out all the stops, but when the dust had settled they discovered that only two of the long list of record company people on the guest list had turned up. "It was devastating," recalls McCormick, "We'd put all that effort into it and the fuckers didn't even come. We went home and got drunk, drowned our sorrows and woke up in the morning to a phone call from Bill Drummond saying he wanted to sign us! Which is the most amazing phone call a wannabe rocker can ever receive." Of course, Drummond was one of the two…

From this point things moved fast, with the band being wined and dined and Drummond assigning David Balfe – who else! - to produce some demos whilst the contract was prepared for signature. On the 22nd June 1985, McCormack went to the Milton Keynes Bowl with his brother, who was also in Shook Up, not only to see Spear Of Destiny, The Ramones and REM but to hang out with the headliners - and their old friends from Dublin - U2. "We were swanning around backstage and I bumped into the old guitarist in our first band, Frankie Cork and The Undertakers. Everybody was celebrating the fact that my band had a deal. The lawyer who was negotiating the deal was there and he said, 'Haven't you heard?' He looked rather pale and in shock. He said that Warner Brothers had pulled out. 'Has nobody told you?' It rather ruined my day. Possibly ruined my life."

At the first opportunity, McCormick rang Bill Drummond to confirm that this was indeed the case. Rob Dickens had just returned from a meeting with his boss in America, the meeting hadn't gone well and Dickens had been told that the UK operation was spending too much money on acts without a significant return. Drummond actually told McCormick this, and that Dickens had, "come back and gone through the A&R, all the new signings and the business going on, and just chucked it all out. Bill said he took a look at our photographs - he wouldn't listen to our demos - he just took a look at our photographs and said, 'I don't like this guy, he has short hair. I don't like the look of the singer.' Just noxious behavior and our deal was dumped."

McCormick was devastated, but Dickens had to justify his own position as acts were signed as investments to generate a financial return. The investment in Brilliant, for example, had been significant and not paid off, whereas a band like Simply Red were scoring hit singles and albums and generating cashflow. It was, ultimately, the accountants who ran the business, and John Hollingsworth recalls an amusing story when, at one point, there was talk of dropping The Jesus and Mary Chain or not renewing their option, until somebody senior in the accounts department stated that they were, at that time, the *only* band – through licensing and sales – on the roster who had recouped, were actually making money and should stay on the label. To paraphrase the JAMC song it seems that accountants are also happy when it rains – money.

As for Neil McCormick, he returned to journalism and recalls, some years later, being at an awards ceremony when, "somebody approached me, a guy with glasses, and he said, 'Hi Neil, it's Dave Balfe. I just wanted to apologise to you. We really let you down.' He then walked off. That's all he said to me." This comment is intriguing, and one wonders today if the *Brilliant v Warners* legal issue may have had something to do with the band not being signed. Whatever, McCormick not only established a successful career as a writer but penned a book called *Killing Bono*, which ended up becoming a very enjoyable feature film in 2003, although a character based on Bill Drummond did not appear. So, he made it another way.

Someone else who made it another way was Youth, who went on to enjoy a very successful career as a remixer, producer and recording artist. He believes that the experience of working under the SAW yoke gave him a positive insight into how to craft and produce hit records which he later employed himself, and can now fondly look back upon the experience of his time as possible pop candy with Brilliant, "Me and Jimmy were just laughing all the way through generally, but making notes. Ultimately, the band did stall at number fifty-eight in the charts and didn't have commercial success. Bill worked with majors like Warners and he knew that the hit ratio was unlikely anyway, but we had a good innings and I thought it was bold and noble of him to sign us as a multi-racial pop group, not doing straight pop but interested in different things. It was bit risky at the time, but good. Later on M People got successful with a similar formula, didn't they?"

Indeed they did, and nobody would have imagined that, by the time Heather Smalls' group started hitting the charts in 1991, former Warner Brothers A&R man Bill Drummond and failed Brilliant member Jimmy Cauty would already have enjoyed a number of massive hit singles under their own steam.

ALL YOU NEED IS LOVE...
AND A SAMPLER

"If a magazine wanted me to pose naked with just my socks on, I might not be completely comfortable with the idea, but I'd do it if the deal was right. £100,000?"
- Bill Drummond to Melody Maker, April 1987

"And a week later, after my piece, I think the NME did a tiny little piece about it but no one else took any notice. I honestly think that if I had not done that we wouldn't be having this conversation."
- James Brown to the author, 2016

Just when is a mid-life crisis supposed to occur? Has anyone written a PHD thesis on the subject or a clickbait article for *Daily Mail* Online? The common perception is that that most men hit the crisis button in their late forties and early fifties, when sexual prowess begins to decline, the hairline recedes and drinking and eating catch up with the liver, kidneys and stomach. We could be here all day on this particular subject - my own mid-life crisis just saw me cycling more and more, which shows how boring I am, although I do now have chunky thighs that would put a free-range chicken to shame. But, thighs aside, the strangest thing about all of this is *the math*s. If you have a mid-life crisis when you're, say, forty four or fifty five, then that suggests you're going to live until eighty eight or peg out a decade or so after receiving a telegram from the current monarch. In fact, the life expectancy of a man in the UK is seventy nine.

Bill Drummond, being Bill Drummond, chose the exact date of his midlife crisis. He scheduled it in his diary for the day he turned thirty-three and a third years old, on the 11th September 1986. We've seen that, by this point in his life, Drummond had enjoyed something of a roller coaster career in the music business. He'd cut his teeth musically in Big In Japan, then founded Zoo Records, where he nurtured The Teardrop Explodes and Echo And The Bunnymen to critical and commercial success and world tours. But, as we've also seen, his most recent professional low was not being able to turn Brilliant into a hit machine, despite throwing in excess of £300,000 into the oven and baking a cake that refused to rise.

Although he was apparently disgusted with the music business and wanted to have nothing more to do with it, Drummond was so embedded in the mechanics of the industry that he trumpeted his departure through the medium of a press release on Korova headed notepaper, dated 31st July 1986. Here we go:

> I will be 33 1/3rd years old in September, a time for a revolution in my life. There is a mountain to climb the hard way, and I want to see the world from the top. These foothills have been green and pleasant but I want to smell the rock, touch the ice and have the wind tear the shirt from my back.
>
> I entered this party on May 5th 1977, forming a band that had no right to be, and I leave by leaving two gifts, the first, Zodiac Mindwarp and the Love Reaction, the only band that can save us from the future. The second is yet to come, and in between was the greatest album ever made.
>
> In the last nine years, I gave everything I could, and at times some drops too much; and to those who wanted more, I'm sorry it wasn't for the giving.
>
> The reconnaissance party arrive to pick me up on September 11th, on which date my office will be empty. Gold discs will gather dust and telephones will be left to ring.
>
> Comrades and rivals, thanks.
>
> Bill Drummond

Drummond was not giving notice of an assault on Ben Nevis or Mount Everest but a determination to swim to the other side of the lake and carry on in the music business as an artist, rather than a label boss, producer, cajoler-in-chief, manager and A&R man. He later wrote that he'd intended to hire a sledgehammer and destroy the piano in his office on his last day, but didn't get around to it. In fact, he left on good terms. "People were very upset, Rob (Dickens) the most," recalls John Hollingsworth, "Bill was unique. Most people in the building thought he was a bit of an oddball, and that's fine because you want an oddball because most people there were kind of straight, it was old school record industry. But the people who knew and valued his work, people like myself and those in creative areas of the department, really missed him."

Working at Warner Brothers had allowed Drummond to meet fellow Scot Alan McGee, who'd begun working closely with Rob Dickens funding his Elevation label, which saw him yoking bands like Primal Scream and the Weather Prophets to a major label's extensive promotional and distributional organisation. In an interview with Richard King in 2012 for his excellent *How Soon Is Now?* Drummond stated that, "One of the major differences between us was Alan would think everything he was working on was brilliant – 'This is the future of rock 'n' roll' - whereas I spent all my time thinking, 'Oh my God, this is just the worst record ever made. How can we put this out? I'm letting the band down so much...'"

Ironically, then, it was McGee's enthusiasm and gung-ho approach to A&R that allowed Bill to make a record of his own. According to his biography, *Creation Stories*, signing Drummond for a solo LP was an intriguing and no-risk option to McGee, who later wrote "when he quit, still in his early thirties, he decided to record his own solo album and asked me if I would put it out on Creation. He was disgusted with the industry. He wanted to say goodbye to it with an album he'd write in five days and record in five days, and thought I'd be the only one mad enough to put it out. Even so, I think he was surprised when I agreed without having listened to a note. I just thought that the guy was probably a genius and he was offering to cover the cost of recording himself."

So Drummond signed to Creation records to record a solo LP. "Originally I thought the record was going to be a thrash record with really loud and noisy guitars, then I started writing the songs and it came out like this," he told the *Melody Maker* in November 1986 whilst doing promotion for *The Man*. According to John Hollingsworth, the LP was supposed to be called *The Manager*, "Apparently on the release schedule they couldn't fit on *The Manager,* so they just typed it as Bill Drummond *The Man,* and he went, 'That's a much better title.' Typical Creation-like bumbling."

As for *The Man* being recorded in a week, that was true. "Just to see if it could be done," stated Drummond, "Also, because I'd spent so much time telling other people to re-record and re-mix, going behind their backs sometimes to add things onto their tracks so'd they'd be played on Radio One." *The Man* was recorded at The Village in Dagenham, with a range of musicians that included Nick Coler. Drummond had first met Coler whilst wearing his A&R hat at Warner Brothers and overseeing album sessions for a soft rock group called Ya Ya - although Coler was not a full member of the band, he played keyboards with them live and was asked to play on recording sessions Drummond had scheduled in Los Angeles with Mike Chapman, who, as a writer and producer, had a long string of hits to his name, from Suzi Quatro to Blondie.

Ya Ya flew out to America and, as he'd toured there before, Coler was more than happy to man the wheel. "We got a massive Lincoln Town car and I was driving down to LA, down the freeway, and every time we got to a set of lights there was this massive 'Boof' noise. I saw a Nissan 280X (behind me) and saw this guy (at the wheel). What was he doing? Every time we stopped at a traffic light he was ramming me! When we got to the other end I said, 'Are you having a bit of trouble with it?' He said 'I've never driven an automatic before,' and at that time – I'm sure he's a lot better now – he was a dreadful driver. It was Bill running into the back of me all the way."

Although the sessions for the Ya Ya album were aborted due to a problem with the lead singer, Drummond obviously liked what he heard Coler play and asked him to work on his solo LP. "He did it with his brother in law, who was a guitar player," Coler recalls, "We came in and a guy who was in Ya Ya played drums and bass on some of the tracks. The Voice Of The Beehive also sang backups, and The Triffids were also on it. I played all the organ parts and stuff - in fact there is one of my favourite organ solos on that LP. We would just go in and do it, as it was all done quickly in a few days."

There was not much chance of *The Man* getting played on the Radio One breakfast show. It wasn't a bad record, it was just not *that* sort of record. Instead, it blended instrumentals and folk with echoes of '60s pop, over which Drummond sang in a thick Scottish accent that made Rod Stewart, Jim Kerr and Edwin Collins sound like public schoolboys. He even brought his father, the Reverend Jack Drummond, in to narrate on one track, *Such A Parcel Of Rogues In A Nation,* a folk song based on a poem by Robert Burns. "*The King Of Joy* was the last track I did for *The Man*," Drummond later told journalist Roy Wilkinson when discussing the LP, "The night before the last day that we were supposed to be recording I got these two tunes – *The King Of Joy* and *I Want That Girl. The King Of Joy* was celebrating having finished the record – it's just how I felt that morning. One doesn't feel like that all the time. Just enough of the time."

The LP received some excellent, as well as baffled, reviews - "ripe with Celtic sentimentality and telling personal revelations, this is surely one of the oddest records of the year," as one stated. For many, one of the most intriguing songs on the LP was *Julian Cope Is Dead.* This was Drummond's recorded retort to the song *Bill Drummond Said,* which appeared on Julian Cope's second official solo LP, *Fried,* in 1984. Whether Drummond ever did say, as Cope sang, "If I sit and pray my Christmas tree will die" is something only he and The Drude will know, but the song fell into the memorable Cope category, with the lyric "Bill Drummond Said" serving as part of the chorus. On *Julian Cope Is Dead*, Drummond put into folk song a fantasy master plan about killing Cope by shooting him in the head, thus making him immortal, increasing sales and turning gold selling records into platinum.

In addition to the LP, Creation issued *The King Of Joy* as a 12" single. As well as an instrumental version of the title track, the B-side was a spoken word piece called *The Manager*. This was the soundtrack to a ten minute video funded by Creation records to the tune of £1,000 and directed by Bill Butt, wherein Drummond pushed along a rubbish cart containing an electric guitar and a broom, ruminated upon the music business and offered to become The Manager for every band, record label, music newspaper and TV programme in the UK. He had some conditions, including musicians not being allowed to spend more than ten days recording an LP - "and *no* remixes" – and there also had to be one standard contract for all musicians and record companies, and no more advances. Drummond offered anyone his sage advice in return for £100, which he would send by letter, "once the cheque has cleared." The video ended with the address of a PO box in Aylesbury, where Drummond lived. It's believed that this short promotional film was not shown at the time, although Drummond later told a journalist that he did receive two cheques, "before the record had even been released," although he would not say who they were from or what advice – if any – he passed on.

As well as speaking to the music press, promotion for *The Man* also took another form. According to Nick Coler, there was a Bill Drummond solo gig at the Knitting Factory in New York sometime in 1986 or 1987. By this time The Proclaimers had signed to Zoo Publishing, and it appears Drummond may gone to New York on Proclaimers-related business. Coler also had to visit the Big Apple as he was working with a singer based there. "Bill was like, 'I've got this gig.' So we rehearsed in a hotel room with all of this shit (musical equipment) that we got from somewhere and then just went on stage. He just went 'Shut up!' to all of these super trendy people." At that point, the band began to play. As for the reception, Coler states today that, "They loved it. They didn't have any choice, otherwise they would have been beaten up. The place was full. You know what he's like - he can take *command* when he wants to."

Although Drummond had started writing a book before recording *The Man,* he took command of his life on New Year's Day 1987, when he began brainstorming a rap whilst out walking and he decided there and then that he wanted to make a hip-hop record. Clearly, making a hip-hop record would be nothing like recording an LP like *The Man* - it needed to be fabricated rather than played, and Drummond needed somebody who not only had a sampler but also knew how to use it. Fortunately, all of that money invested in Brilliant hadn't been wasted – Drummond knew that Jimmy Cauty owned a sampler and, as they got on personally, decided to call him and ask him to collaborate on the proposed track.

Drummond later related that the phone call took place on Cauty's 30th birthday, and he didn't take kindly to a "happy birthday" wish at a time when his own musical and artistic career was at something of an impasse. Cauty was also setting up a studio in the basement of his shared squat BENIO, and although he had some instruments and the Greengate sampler acquired during his time with Brilliant, some of the funding for the additional gear was to come from an unusual source - Lambeth Council. Many years later, Cauty shed some light on this when talking to Bo Franklin about this period of his life. "They basically made all the squatters join housing co-ops," he recalled, "otherwise you'd get kicked out. So we joined North Lambeth housing co-op." This meant Cauty could apply to the Council for funds to improve his house. "The council actually gave me about £3,000 to put into my private account to do the house up, which seems bizarre. Especially as we were a band and needed to buy equipment... I put a studio in the basement. I don't know how I got away with it. The poor neighbours. I mean now I really feel sorry for them, but at the time it didn't bother me." This studio later became known as Trancentral.

Drummond and Cauty first got together to record one track. Drummond knew what he wanted to do and it was just a case of he and Cauty getting on with it. The fact that it was a hip-hop track and new territory for both of them was not an issue - both were musicians with a lot of experience under their belt, and when it came to sampling some of the music to build up the track Cauty had the means. The Greengate sampler, better known as the DS:3, had been developed in 1984 by a team of UK computer programmers and made commercially available for £350, although it only ran on an early Apple computer, which also had to be purchased in order to use it.

"The DS:3 is, in effect, an instant four channel digital tape recorder with the added capability for unlimited sequence creation and storage," ran the first press release for the product, "The unit will accept ANY audio signal, real sound or otherwise, up to 15kHz and will store this sound first in the computer memory for instant replay, or it can archive the sound to computer floppy disc for future recall." It was this facility to 'sample' brief chunks of other songs and mix them with other music that allowed Drummond and Cauty to craft a track that was groundbreaking not because of how it sounded, but what it sounded like.

With the track recorded and mixed, a small batch of one-sided 12"s were pressed, and in March 1987 Drummond started sending out packages containing letters like these:

DEAR MIKE,

THIS IS OUR FIRST 45. WE ONLY HAD THE MONEY TO PRESS UP 500 WHITE LABEL COPIES BUT AS SOON AS WE GET OUR HANDS ON MORE CASH WE WILL HAVE IT OUT PROPER AND FINISH OUR LP.

YOURS,
KING BOY D

DEAR JOHN,

THIS IS OUR FIRST 45. WHEN WE GET SOME MORE CASH WE WILL RECORD A B-SIDE AND GET IT OUT WITH A PROPER SLEEVE & LABEL.

HOPE IT ISN'T TOO OFFENSIVE TO PLAY.

WE CALL OUR MUSIC "HIGH COURT" CAUSE THAT'S WHERE WE'RE GOING

YOURS,
KING BOY D

Mike was Mike Reid, a DJ at Radio One, and John was John Peel, who was, well, John Peel! As well as radio DJs, the record was also mailed out to journalists at all of the major UK music papers, where one of them found its way to James Brown, at this time an up and coming freelance writer at *Sounds*. "I was on a little bit of a roll in discovering new acts that were actually getting into the charts or getting deals," he recalls. One morning he was on his way to the office and "there was a huge forty eight sheet billboard opposite Capital FM, a huge photo of James Anderton the cop. It was for (the) *Today* (newspaper) and the advert said, 'People With ideas Above Their Station'. It was when he was pretending to be in touch with God. So they were quite striking looking, newsy sort of ads. They were statement ads. Anyway on this one had been pasted – which is quite common now, people paste up their graffiti – it was bubble writing that said, 'Shag Shag Shag.' I just noticed it and wondered what it was."

Once he got to the *Sounds* office there was a pile of 7" and 12" brown and white mailers for him, records he'd been sent to either listen to or review. One of them was from what he assumed was a new band, who called themselves The Justified Ancients Of Mu Mu. It was a white label 12" with a pasted on logo depicting a beat box on a pyramid as part of the band name, and beneath that a title, *All You Need Is Love*.

Brown: "There was a letter scrawled in massive handwriting, purporting to be from somebody called King Boy D. The address was in Glasgow or somewhere in Scotland. It said, 'We like the Beastie Boys, we really like your writing, we hope you like our debut record.' So they were passing themselves off as being young Scottish rappers. I took it home with the other records and played it. It was great! It was really good. It was really noisy, it had (the) "Kick Out The Jams Motherfuckers" (sample). It was full of samples, and then this sort of rapping over the top of it. One of the reasons I liked it was that I knew it would have a story behind it. Because I was freelance and inquisitive and wanted to find new things, I rang the number. I went 'Hello, Is King Boy D there?' and somebody, some English voice, went, 'Oh hello, hang on.' Then King Boy D came on the phone and we had a bit of a chat and I think I arranged to meet up for an interview or something."

As luck would have it for King Boy D, Brown was reviewing the singles for *Sounds* that week and was in a position to make *All You Need Is Love* Single Of The Week. He didn't just review the record, he raved about it: "The Justified Ancients of Mu Mu (The JAMs) have produced the first single to capture realistically the music and social climate of Britain in 1987." He was quick to point out the list of bands sampled on the record – The Beatles, MC5, Hall & Oates, Samantha Fox and the Government Aids advert. "The Jams overlay sweetly sung rhymes, inject funk action drum beats, splice in dirty metal guitar riffs, heavy breathing and some Clydebank rap, and then scratch it all to a seething terror ridden pulp."

At this time, for a debut single to get a positive review in any of the music press was important. To get Single Of The Week meant readers would take note and be curious enough to go out and buy the record. Distributors would also take note, contact the label and offer a deal to get the record into the shops all over the country for these very readers to buy. Even A&R men and women at record companies would take note and wonder if this was an act they could sign and develop into the next big thing. Back in 1979, this had happened with the Zoo label when reviewers had slavered over The Teardrop Explodes and Echo And The Bunnymen singles, leading, in turn, to both bands establishing internationally successful careers. It all started with a review.

Ironically, in the case of The Justified Ancients of Mu Mu, the fact that the record featured a number of purloined samples from other records meant that distributors like Pinnacle and The Cartel were, when they read about this, a little nervous about taking copies. The only shop that had no qualms was the independent Rough Trade in Talbot Road, Notting Hill, who took a hundred copies from Drummond and Cauty – or, to use the names under which they were now operating – from King Boy D and Rockman Rock. Faced with the dilemma of a record that had piqued interest and had a market but could not be distributed, Drummond and Cauty soon retooled the track so that Samantha Fox's *Touch Me*, The Beatles' *All You Need Is Love* and The MC5's *Kick Out The Jams* were, "sufficiently trimmed from the new version to allow the single to slip through the lawyer's fingers," as the *Melody Maker* reported on 9th May.

There was also a bizarre report that Alan McGee had taken out an injunction against the original version, "claiming he had given Bill Drummond an advance to record a follow up to his *The Man* LP, not a Justified Ancients Of Mu Mu single." As Drummond had financed the recording of *The Man* himself, this may have been just another spin of the publicity wheel to get more attention for the JAMs single when it was being reissued and made more widely available. In later years, Drummond stated that he actually spoke to McGee about releasing the debut single by The Justified Ancients Of Mu Mu on Creation records.

Was the first JAMs single intended to be a Bill Drummond solo record? Or were The Justified Ancients of Mu Mu from the outset a two-man collaboration? It was, after all, Cauty who designed the arresting label artwork - actually cut out by hand and stuck onto one side of the first 500 white label copies - as well as the headed notepaper upon which Drummond wrote his letters to DJs and music journalists. Cauty was also behind the "Shag Shag Shag" artwork that was pasted on the *Today* newspaper billboard, although getting it in place was a two-man job.

Shortly after making *All You Need Is Love*, Cauty pondered moving to America. With the failure of Brilliant, and legal action against Warner Brothers souring matters further, he was at a loose end and possibly contemplating - along with his wife Cressida - a fresh start. James Brown, who recalls speaking to Cauty in recent years on his radio show, remembers, "I talked to him on or off the air about that period and he said it was over. 'We made the single and thought, no-one is going to get into this' and he said as far as he was concerned it was a dead project - it was finished – and he had moved to New York. He said Bill called him and said, 'You have to come back, there's this kid and he's really championing us.' That's when Jimmy came back and we did the interview that went on the *Sounds* cover."

As a freelance writer, Brown pushed his editor and was given a green light to write a feature on The JAMs, which duly appeared on 16th May 1987. Brown had gone the whole hog, speaking to the band on three occasions at their "south London studio," which was basically Cauty's squat, the *Sounds* conference room and, "on top of the twenty storey block of flats where they were painting the name of their LP, *1987 (What the F*** Is Going On)*, on the lift for use as record sleeve artwork."

Although The JAMs didn't know it, Brown had encountered some resistance because Drummond was a known quantity in the music business. Also, "Jimmy had been in that sort of glam pop band who made a record with Peter Waterman - Brilliant – but then again they were one of many record company bands who didn't get anywhere. And Bill had been an A&R man and obviously knew more people in the music business than I did, but I was kind of fresh and up for it and didn't give a fuck where they came from." For Drummond, *All You Need Is Love* was his new beginning, and he *gushed* rather than spoke to Brown;

"I had this idea as I was walking around with this pretty crap hip hop tune, *MC Story*, in my head, and I just started rapping this thing that became *All You Need Is Love*. All the samples on the single came into my head on that first day. They don't fit beat wise, but I knew I had to find out how to put it together. I had no idea how to go about it, but I was down in London at the beginning of the year and I met Rockman and we got talking and he was into it."

As well as the genesis and recording of the single, the interview was wide ranging and covered the recording of their upcoming debut LP. Cauty was prescient in his sparse comments, "I used to play electric guitar, but now I'd rather sample someone else's guitar and just play it on a keyboard. I get more out of it than playing a guitar. Because if you're playing a guitar you're always trying to be a good guitarist. You've got to practise playing it and I just can't be bothered anymore. Sampling now is like the electric guitar thirty years ago." Whilst Drummond made reference to Cauty's possible flight to America - "Rockman is going to be sorting out our first gigs in New York next week" - Cauty was defiant about accusations of theft through sampling other people's material: "It doesn't bother us. Their records are still there. It's not as if we're taking anything away, just borrowing and making things bigger. If you're creative you're not going to stop working just because there is a law against what you're doing." Drummond was quick to back him up, "It's like saying Andy Warhol just stole other people's graphics, which he didn't. He took other people's images and re-cycled them and reused them. That doesn't mean he's robbed them and left them with nothing. We're just doing musically what he did with Campbell's soup cans and a picture of Marilyn Monroe."

By the time the interview ran, *All You Need Is Love* was in the shops, and the *Sounds* feature was followed up by a short piece in the *New Musical Express,* which described The JAMS as a five-piece (Rockman Roc, KingBoy D, Nigerian born Chike and "Lovers rock duo Burning Illusion"). An unattributed quote, one assumes from the lips of

Drummond, also bent history into new shapes, "No, we've not been in bands before, and, yes, I suppose we were originally influenced by The Beastie Boys to actually get up and do something. I mean, if you were fifteen and living in America you'd be getting up and doing something after hearing The Beastie Boys."

Drummond even pretended to be a young, eighteen year old kid called King Boy D, "who says he's never heard of Bill Drummond," on the phone to another interviewer. Unfettered, Drummond then waxed lyrical, "Forget all these drongos discovering Led Zeppelin and the equally misguided Edwyn Collins and Buzzcocks clones. The JAMS are coming to town, stealing everything in sight and giving back more – this means real change." It did, although Drummond soon dropped the pretense and had to step forward as King Boy D after a photo shoot for the *Sounds* cover.

John Higgs referred to *All You Need Is Love* as being "shit" in his 2013 book on The KLF, which suggests that, whilst he is widely read, his adventures in sound are less extensive. *All You Need Is Love* was, and remains, a wonderful musical sophon. It's an incredibly detailed and imaginative price of music that, when unfolded, contains all of the elements that make up the rest of Cauty and Drummond's musical adventures. There is the crude but imaginative purloining of sampled music, the deadly beats and smears of lyrics, the melodic hooks, ranging from an insistent synth line that sounds like a singing cat to sing-song female backing vocals from Cressida, and more sexual panting than a porn film. It also has, like many game changing records, an unmistakable energy and panache that is hard to contain, especially in Drummond's vibrant rap about sex and AIDS. It has something magical about it, even if today it's seen as something of a musical curio.

Crucially, Brown's championing of the band, and the energy of the record itself, gave The Justified Ancients Of Mu Mu a small shop window, and they were quick to produce more goods for sale. The most important thing, though, about *All You Need Is Love* is that Drummond and Cauty discovered that they could work together. There were common interests, and although Drummond played down his Bunnymen period interest in ley lines when talking to the *Melody Maker* in April 1987 – "I don't know anything about ley lines, never read any books about them or anything… it started out as a myth, then everybody would ask me about it, then people like Killing Joke's Jaz started going on about them…" – this may have been something he could discuss with Cauty, who'd been interested in them in the 1970s after reading the works of John Michell. The fact that Drummond had been the record company executive who'd signed Brilliant wasn't an issue as Cauty had witnessed first-hand how hard Drummond had worked to try to break the band, even if that had involved musically frustrating time spent on the sidelines as Pete Waterman and his team crafted the records.

The crude sampling of other people's material to create the debut JAMs release inspired them to begin work on songs for an album with the subtle title, 1987 *What The Fuck Is Going On?*, and to promote the LP Drummond and Cauty decided to create an enormous advert. So, on the night of 11th June 1987, whilst the nation was celebrating or bemoaning the re-election of Margaret Thatcher for a third term of office as Conservative Prime Minister, Drummond and Cauty climbed up onto the roof of the National Theatre on the South Bank of the river Thames and painted the album's title onto this iconic concrete building. It was Big Hair all over again, but on a somewhat larger scale. "It took us two hours and we could be seen from the road," Cauty later told *Face* journalist Ian McCann, "But we got away with it."

The LP – released on the 12th of June – comprised of six tracks, kicking off with *Hey Hey, We're Not The Monkees*, whose opening rhythm was comprised of 'shag' noises similar to those heard on *All You Need Is Love*, before Drummond began rapping in his distinctive Scottish burr. The track developed into a clever wrestle between Monkees samples and Drummond hilariously screaming about his dislike for the band, and eventually everything drops out, to be replaced by a female chorus singing what would become a familiar "Justified and Ancient" refrain. This was, in fact, the core of the song, rather than the Monkees concoction, and the first aural manifestation of what would become one of Drummond and Cauty's most memorable musical calling cards.

Next, *Don't Take Five (Take What You Want)* sampled the JB's *Same Beat*. At this time, everybody was sampling the output of James Brown, from Public Enemy to Jazzy Jeff, and early in 1988 Housemartin Norman Cook, who would soon begin to craft his way towards a famous career as an international DJ and remixer, compiled a list of artists who'd done so, as well as the purloined sources, for the *New Musical Express*. "This list is by no means complete. By this time I was sick of listening to grunts, screams and that snare sound. You could write a weekly column of updates," he joked, after listing twenty five tracks, which included *Don't Take Five*... The track also featured a purloined sample of Paul Desmond's famous alto saxophone line from The Dave Brubeck Quartet's jazz standard *Take Five,* recorded in 1959, and was, all told, an excellent slice of funk, underpinned by a beatbox and a number of sampled effects.

The album's third track, *Rockman Rock Parts 2 and 3*, meanwhile, was a fantasia of stolen riffs and samples, ranging from Led Zeppelin to Jimi Hendrix, and saw Drummond, like many rap MCs, take time to pay fulsome credit to the man behind the music - Rockman Rock.

Again, female backing vocals played a strong part, and amongst many things included a reference to the famed Roland TR-808 drum machine, as well as stroking Cauty's ego by informing us that Rockman 'showed them the way'.

1987's second side, however, kicked off a million miles away from Side One's sample-fest, with a short, fetching ballad sung in Vietnamese by Duy Khiem and titled *Me Ru*. Khiem was actually a session musician, who Drummond had first encountered when working with the Bunnymen and later drafted in to add some parts to this new LP. As Drummond later wrote on the *Edits* sleeve, "We never planned to have this on the LP, he just sang it while the tapes were running when he was down in the studio doing the bits of tenor sax and clarinet that are on the other tracks. It blew our minds." The piece was later issued on a 7" titled *All You Need Is Love (Me Ru Con Mix),* although it had nothing to do with *All You Need Is Love* and featured no samples whatsoever.

The track that followed Khiem's was *The Queen And I*, which revolved around the sun of an ABBA sample. Next, *Top Of The Pops*, was composed of a number of sampled song introductions and chart rundowns from various editions of the popular BBC show of the same name, including the Beastie Boys. Next came a version of *All You Need Is Love,* upon which Drummond and Cauty cut their musical teeth, before *Next* provided another Drummond rap and sampled inspiration, ranging from Stevie Wonder's *Superstition* to The Fall's *Totally Wired*. Sampling *The Lonely Goatherd* from the *Sound Of Music* soundtrack and underpinning it with a beat was inspired, and the track again showed that Drummond and Cauty could create driving music, albeit of a rough and ready nature.

Unlike their debut 12", *1987* not only had a sleeve but also labels which, in keeping with their position as musical outlaws, stated around the rim that, "All sounds on this recording have been captured by the KLF in the name of Mu. We hereby liberate these sounds from all copyright restrictions without prejudice." Publishing and Copyright were not credited to Zoo but attributed to the Sound of Mu(sic), and review copies were quickly sent out to journalists and DJs, including John Peel:

DEAR JOHN,

I DON'T THINK YOU PLAYED OUR SINGLE, BUT THIS IS OUR LP.

OUT NEXT WEEK.
K.B.D.

There was rabid approval from James Brown, and *Melody Maker* also got onboard with an analysis headlined *Licensed To Thrill,* a pun on the Beastie Boys' *Licensed To Ill* album from the previous year. "This is a roller coaster ride through rock history, the tapestry wrapping itself around your head as Samantha Fox strokes *Totally Wired* and *Top Of The Pops* gets a particularly glamorous skin disease… The Justified Ancients Of Mu Mu have made a scabrous celebration of 1987's dizzily wide eyed appeal, while still managing to kick the people that count in the kidneys with more grace than the rickety spliff Red Wedge could ever muster. Inspirational."

Reviewer Paul Mathur was soon in front of Drummond and Cauty with a microphone for a *Melody Maker* feature article. "The thing about The JAMs that annoys a lot of journalists is that there's no theories, no manifesto," waxed Drummond, "Manifestos are usually for people to hide behind when they don't know what to do. So many people come along to us and try to get us to be something that we're not." He also conveniently let it slip that they'd received a letter from an American warning them not to try to contact Robert Anton Wilson, who had co-penned the *Illuminatus!* trilogy of books which The JAMs had "sampled" their name from, as if they did they would end up in "deep shit." Drummond loved it, "Deep Shit. That's brilliant. It's going to be the working title of our next album." Another wide ranging interview included mention that the entire project was only supposed to generate one single before it evolved into an album. "It's like when you have a crap and you squeeze it out and think I'm never going to need another one. Then half hour later you're thinking maybe you will."

Moving away from the bowels of The JAMs, Drummond was incisive when discussing the possibilities of the sampler for creating new and exciting music, "I haven't a clue about technology, but Rockman has and, between us, we spend lots of time touching things and seeing if it hurts. Whereas we have people like the engineer who got all stroppy about us putting a Phil Collins bass drum on the record like it was sacred or something." This Engineer was Ian Richardson, Nick Coler's musical partner at the time. He was no fan of what Drummond and Cauty were doing in the studio and let them know about it. As for the interview, there was even talk of The JAMs playing live gigs, with Drummond musing about starting at Hammersmith Odeon, "but not telling anyone, so there'd be no one there but a few roadies and a pile of unsold T-shirts. We just want to see what it feels like."

There never were any live performances in 1987, but there were Cauty designed t-shirts that were sold mail order, although the "JAMS axes, skateboards, pneumatic drills, cars and rocket launchers," and even a helicopter, that were advertised in the *1987* insert never did roll off the assembly line. The mail order side of the equation would carry on, with Cressida taking charge, and many visitors to Cauty at BENIO would later recall records being put into mailers as three rings blazed on the hob in the kitchen to keep everybody warm. Even Rolo McGinty pitched in, "I enjoyed that. It was really interesting watching that work as I had record company management and all I'd done was make music and worry about that. I never had anything to do with the background stuff." Of course, the background stuff was part of parcel of the JAMs/KLF operation and would carry on throughout their existence.

Drummond and Cauty were also interviewed by the *Record Mirror*, who had seen positive merit in the album - "at times their adventures are a little too freestyle, too busy, yet there's never anything mundane here. An extraordinary heist indeed." Once again Drummond rolled out the story of how he'd been inspired to record the original single, as well as giving his thoughts on the legal aspects. "We were aware of copyright, but it was only once we'd done *All You Need Is Love*, finished our album and been told that we couldn't do this sort of thing that we came out with The KLF - the Kopyright Liberation Front. It's like 1955, and you've got yourself an electric guitar, and then somebody from the Acoustic Guitar Society comes around and says, "I'm sorry you can't do that, it's against the law to use electricity in instruments". And that's what it feels like - we've got these samplers, how are we meant to use them?"

It was also here that Drummond tied up, for the first time, the link between the *Illuminatus!* trilogy by Robert Shea and Robert Anton Wilson, The Justified Ancients of Mu Mu and the messages about the AIDS situation on *All You Need Is Love*. "In the book I was re-reading, it was saying there was this disease that was going to be manufactured and was going to get everybody. The swinging sixties was a front to get everybody into freer sex, and then they were going to throw in this disease." That Drummond was re-reading the *Illuminatus!* trilogy – or trying to – was prescient, although it was Cauty who'd taken more inspiration from its pages, including the formation of his earlier band, The Tets. The trilogy had also informed his design of The JAMs' pyramid blaster logo, and lyrical references to Mu were also purloined from its pages to serve as JAMs choruses. The book was a handy reference point to Drummond and Cauty for visual and lyrical ideas, rather than a deep well of philosophy that informed and guided their every action. It was 'sampled', just like music, for their needs. Indeed, they even spelt the name of The Justified Ancients of Mummu incorrectly. *Illuminatus!* was tangential rather than central to their story, and whilst they played around with the number twenty three they never contemplated, to my knowledge, issuing a record as The American Medical Society, a fictional band referenced in the books.

On 17th August 1987, either Bill Drummond alone or he and Cauty had a meeting with the Mechanical Copyright Protection Society, probably in their offices in Streatham, at which they presented the MCPS with copies of the *All You Need Is Love* 12" and the *1987* LP. At that point, the MCPS referred the matters to their solicitors and wrote to Drummond and Cauty on the 28th August with some bad news. Not only had they not complied with Section 8 of the Copyright Act 1957, but, "even if you had abided by the above, the very nature of making a record of a work which comprises a part of a work takes this outside of Section 8 and would, therefore, require the prior permission of the copyright owners. Certain works which you have used have also been clearly arranged, which may not be done without the consent of the owners of these works."

In effect, in lifting samples of other artists' materials and working them into their own songs without prior permission, The JAMs had breached copyright. There was further grief in that, "One of our members, whose work is used substantially on the *1987* album, is not prepared to grant a license in respect of their work. We must therefore insist that in respect of this record you:

(i)   cease all manufacture and distribution
(ii) take all possible steps to recover copies of the album, which are to be delivered to MCPS or destroyed under the supervision of MCPS
(iii) deliver up the master tape, mothers, stampers and any other parts commensurate with the manufacture of the record.

The question of damages or the infringement will still need to be assessed, but these may be minimised by your co-operation in the above."

The one member concerned was ABBA, whose hit *Dancing Queen* was the fundamental backbone of The JAMs' track *The Queen And I*, which appeared on the second side of *1987*. To say Drummond and Cauty had been creative with *Dancing Queen* was an understatement - alongside Drummond's Clydebank Beastie Boy rap about meeting the Queen, the ABBA track was, at times, played unadorned, whilst at other times it sounded as if it was being sung by a very tuneful South London tomcat. The track was, and remains, unbelievable fun, and even features a snip of the Sex Pistols' *God Save The Queen*. We assume they, along with other members, did not object at this juncture.

Being told to cease and desist production and destroy all copies of the album was, in some respects, Mu(sic) to the ears of Drummond and Cauty. Whilst the threat of possible legal action and having to pay unknown damages hung over their heads - and must have created some worry - it did give them a platform upon which to generate more publicity. What they chose to do was a case of wish fulfillment - on *The Queen And I* Drummond asked, "Have you ever met ABBA? I'd *love* to meet ABBA" and so a plan was made to go and meet the band in Sweden. "I want to see the band personally," Drummond told the *Melody Maker* in early September, at a time when they were also getting ready to release their next 12", *Whitney Joins The JAMs*.

Drummond and Cauty's adventure in Sweden is one of the cornerstones of the JAMs/KLF mythology. Whilst it's not without question that ABBA or their management objected to the sampling of their material, and that the MCPS were in a position to issue their cease and desist letter, lest we forget Drummond had worked in the music business since 1978 as a label boss, A&R man and producer, and still owned Zoo Publishing, so he knew exactly how the music business worked. He'd read *Music Week* and sat in numerous executive meetings - if he'd wanted to contact ABBA or their management he would have been able to find a phone number in quick order. This was, after all, a man who, a few years later, recalled being able to speak to Tammy Wynette around twenty minutes after he and Jimmy Cauty first thought it would be a great idea to work with her.

Of course, what Drummond also knew was that a few letters back and forth between himself and ABBA's management, and maybe more meetings with the MCPS to agree a royalty percentage to be paid to ABBA, was not going to generate any media traction to add to The JAMs' reputation as South London sampling pirates. So he came to the decision - along with Cauty - that it would be more fun and, importantly, more newsworthy to go to Sweden to try to confront ABBA. The duo's main champion in the music press, James Brown, was now on the staff of the *New Musical Express* and didn't take much convincing. He cleared it with his editor and, along with photographer Lawrence Watson, jumped into Cauty's battered old American police car and rode shotgun to Sweden.

The subsequent feature appeared in the *New Musical Express* in October 1987. Written in the best Hunter Thompson style, it told the tale of a breathtaking journey that saw the car run down and kill a moose before Drummond and Cauty indulged in a ceremonial burning of copies of the *1987* LP that was only halted by an irate farmer, who blasted at them with a shotgun for trespassing and burning the records on his land without permission. In Stockholm, unable to find ABBA or anyone connected with the band at 3am in the morning, they gave a gold record to a local prostitute, carrying the dedication "Presented to Benny, Bjorn and Stig, to celebrate sales in excess of zero copies of The Justified Ancients Of Mu Mu's LP *1987*." This was cracking copy, and was accompanied by suitable photographs of the burning and the prostitute holding the record, as well as Drummond (with binoculars) and Cauty (in cowboy hat) standing on the stern of the ferry.

As for the real story of what happened, here's James Brown today, "Basically, we just went to Stockholm and it was the middle of the night and we came home. That is what happened. That was the reality of that. Basically, we went to Stockholm and back in a police car that broke down. Jimmy and I hung out in this little town. Bill went to bed early in the motel we checked into. I don't know what Lawrence was doing, maybe he was with us...."

It may have been the *following* night, after the car broke down, that Lawrence Watson recalls, "we ended up crashing in someone's house and being chased out by his drunken father, who thought we were hitting on his wife and daughter. His son had been locked up the week before for scaring horses on the estate with his motorbike. It was very surreal, all the things that happened. The father woke up pissed out of his head and came out in his little Y-fronts and chased us. We grabbed everything and ran for the door, afraid that he was going to beat us up." Sadly for Brown's diary of purple prose, the angry Swede did not give chase riding a moose with a shotgun cradled in his arms.

Brown had to justify to his editor - and probably the accounts department - spending four days travelling to Sweden with a photographer with not much to show for it, and thus added lashings of purple prose to the feature. "I had to turn it into something as I'd told the editor that I was going to Sweden to meet ABBA (laughs)." Also, it became evident once in Sweden that Drummond and Cauty, "didn't know what to do when they got there – didn't even have ABBA's address." In fact all they had was a PO Box!

"It was all flannel on their part," recalls Watson, "they were going to present this disc for no sales, but all we did was buzz the intercom of Polar Music and were told to bugger off in no uncertain terms around three or four in the morning." That said, for Watson the photographer, from a visual perspective everything was perfect. "When we met them they turned up in the old American police car, and that began the fun from the start. It was a gift having that as a backdrop all the time, that car, as it looked so photogenic, although we got loads of looks as we drove through Sweden in it. Jimmy would occasionally shout at people through the loudhailer."

On the way out, Watson also snapped photos of Drummond and Cauty throwing copies of the 1987 LP off the back of the ferry, although sadly he kept his camera in his bag when Drummond entered a karaoke contest on the ship and won a large Toblerone for his efforts. On a mad early morning dash to catch the ferry back, just before Cauty's car broke down, "Jimmy pulled over into a field and in the corner of that field they proceeded to set light to all of those *1987* albums," Watson remembers, "I think James slept through all of that in the back of the car!" Watson photographed the burning, although even this set piece was nearly ruined when Cauty ran over his camera bag when reversing in the car. Luckily, Watson's cameras were around his neck at the time.

When the car broke down shortly afterwards, they missed the ferry back and had to wait a couple of days for the next one. Watson recalls that Cauty or Drummond had wisely joined the AA the day before the trip, which not only allowed them access to roadside assistance in Sweden but also gave them a book of AA vouchers, "that you could use in certain restaurants, so we were living off AA vouchers. I'd just got my first credit card but I didn't let that be known until the last night, when I bought some beers and stuff. I was not going to let that lot – James Brown and The KLF – loose on my credit card. So I kept it quiet until the last night."

One of the most interesting things James Brown recalls about the Stockholm trip was a telephone call that Drummond made or received from - I assume - David Balfe. "Bill said to Jimmy, 'I might have to go home. There's a problem with the Zodiac album.' That was the only chink, a glimpse that Bill was kind of playing at it. Despite saying 'we're confronting the record industry', he was in the pay of Warner Brothers." Indeed, in an earlier JAMs interview with *Melody Maker*, Drummond had described recording *1987,* as "five days in the studio like one long, mad party," and then continued, "I have to admit, it does get difficult when I do things like what I'm doing at the moment (producing one of the King Grebos). Fortunately, he's a good bloke so I can get back to that more."

Whilst Drummond was no longer working at Warner Brothers, he still had a working relationship with David Balfe. Not only did they co-run Zoo Publishing, but the pair were still a coalition on other fronts. Whilst Balfe was taking his early steps towards becoming a record company mogul by taking his Food label under the umbrella of a major, he was also undertaking production work and managing the career of a number of artists, including Mark Manning, aka Zodiac Mindwarp.

As we saw earlier, Balfe had initially put Manning, Youth and Jimmy Cauty together for the first Zodiac Mindwarp live gig, but when that hadn't worked out Manning and Balfe recruited other musicians, including guitarist Cobalt Stargazer, to form a new incarnation. It wasn't long before Zodiac Mindwarp And The Love Reaction exploded with the *Wild Child* EP, a mini album, a top twenty hit in *Prime Mover* in May 1987 and the kind of bad behavior that garnered plenty of press coverage - both positive and negative - and put swaggering rock back on the map. It appears the call Drummond handled in Sweden was related to the *somewhat* difficult sessions for the first full-length LP, which the record company and their sales staff were gagging for. Manning was living the rock and roll life to the full and, according to one source, amongst other things drinking a bottle of vodka a day. This may account for some issues in the recording studio, and according to my source, "Zodiac was terrible at remembering melodies, so we had him hypnotised into thinking he was Bon Jovi, it did improve things." To be fair, if you or I had drunk a bottle of vodka we'd probably encounter similar difficulties walking in a straight line, let alone recalling melodies to songs.

Crucially, Drummond and Balfe were helming the sessions for the Mindwarp album and, speaking today, Manning gives an interesting insight into their production dynamic. "It was always unique. I don't know if you know about Bill and his recording techniques, but he does very strange things. He wears costumes and stuff. He was wearing Ghandi outfits when we were doing that album. Big nappies and stuff. That's one of his things, as other people will tell you - he has a fondness for wearing costumes, really bizarre costumes. A lot of the time he was doing it bollock naked. Cobalt (Stargazer) really didn't like it. I just said, 'Look, that's the way he works Cobalt, don't take it personally.' 'But he's sitting there completely naked!'. 'Just ignore him, pretend you're in India and you're not looking at people shitting on the street and that kind of thing.'"

According to Manning, Drummond's off-the-wall behavior created a good working environment. "They were a good team because Bill is completely wild, he's like wandering around in the studio, peeing in the car park, not wearing any clothes, and Balfe is sat there with a calculator actually counting the beats, timing the beats so he can say that is thirty-three or something or other. He does it with a calculator, and Bill is the complete opposite."

As David Balfe declined to be interviewed for this book, I was unable to confirm whether Drummond did wear his birthday suit at this recording session, but in a wide ranging interview about Food Records in the *New Musical Express* in April 1989 he not only reflected on how Zodiac Mindwarp laid down the template for bands like Guns 'N'' Roses to follow him to the bank, but also stated that, "He's also largely responsible for the fact that it's now totally OK to like heavy metal." Whilst not mentioning his calculator, Balfe added, "He is so megalomaniacal, he got a bit deranged for a while and we cocked it up." A reference, perhaps, to these fraught LP sessions, some of which were attended by Nick Coler, who has a great tale to tell, "Him and (friend and roadie) Gimpo had been drinking all day. Zodiac was drinking a bottle of Jack Daniels and Balfe was being Balfe and saying, 'Can you do it with a bit more…' All I heard (from Zodiac) was 'I'm going to go round to your house and fuck your wife!' Then he (Balfe) went, 'No, lads could you do a little more…' Then we heard him go right over and fall down behind the desk - this was Zodiac - and I thought, where's he gone? He came up, and he used to wear these little round glasses, and the glass from one had gone right through his skin here (indicates right cheekbone) and there was just blood pouring everywhere. He was still going, 'Gonna fuck your wife!' Gimpo just got a bit of gaffa tape and stuck it over the cut, then he stuck Z on his motorbike and off they went into the night."

When the *Tattooed Beat Messiah* LP was released, Manning told the *New Musical Express*, in March 1988, that "I'm one of the Morrisseys, the Bill Drummonds, the Mark E Smiths, I'm one of the crazy gang. But the real beauty is, nobody really knows what the fuck I am." He turned up to the interview wearing John Lennon glasses and told the interviewer "If you find them disconcerting I'll take them off. I can't see a thing without them though."

This digression illustrates that Drummond would have received cash flow from his production duties, which was probably channeled into his work with Cauty and the JAMs, which itself might have been generating ideas, great music and coverage in the music press but no significant cash flow. It must have also helped pay for studio time, printing costs and the pressing of records. It was also Manning who later brought Gimpo (Alan Goodrick) into the orbit of The KLF after he'd served time as Manning's roadie and, later, his manager.

So, when he returned to London from his adventures in Sweden one imagines that Drummond had to go back into the studio and help Balfe wrestle Zodiac Mindwarp And The Love Reaction into musical submission. But in the meantime there had actually been another Justified Ancients of Mu Mu 12" released to the public. Whilst *All You Need Is Love* was a vicious piece of spiteful sampling, almost polemical in nature, the one-sided 12" *Whitney Joins The JAMs* was the complete opposite. The title sums up the song perfectly – after opening with the sampled theme to *Mission Impossible* and a driving beat, Drummond dives straight into the fray - "Mission impossible we were told, she'll *never* join The JAMs" - before a blast of the *Theme From Shaft* blows in. Drummond sounds like he is just having the greatest time of his life, and when Whitney Houston joins the song - and thus The JAMs - through a sample of *I Wanna Dance (With Somebody)* he is so excited – *"Whitney!"* - he sounds as if he's about to have kittens. Running for seven minutes, the purloined samples are used to craft an excellent dance track. Apparently, the original plan was to record a song based on Isaac Hayes *Shaft,* but when Drummond went to a record shop to buy the album he ended up purchasing the Whitney Houston LP instead, and the rest is, as they say, is history.

Whitney Joins The JAMs received positive reviews, and would not only be repressed but was also the first song the duo filmed a video for, when one was requested by *The Chart Show* after it reached number three in their independent chart. "They keep pestering us for a video and we were saying, 'Oh no, we haven't got one and we don't want to do one. Just get it out of your charts fast'", Drummond stated at the time, "Eventually our ego won and, with the loose change we had in our pockets, we hired a video and got one of our mates to film us driving in the JAMMmobile to the place where they made *The Chart Show.* When we got there, we took out the cassette, handed it in at the gate and said, that's your video! The next day it was on national TV. It cost us £19.96. Most record companies spend up to a hundred grand on their videos and almost as much on lunches trying to get people to screen them. We did it for under twenty quid."

One imagines that their reluctance to provide a video stemmed from their troubles with the continuing saga over the *1987* LP, although at this time they were not the only ones swimming in increasingly hot waters. *Pump Up The Volume* by M/A/R/R/S was near the top of the singles charts in early September 1987 when Pete Waterman arranged for his lawyers to take out an injunction against their parent label 4AD because the song used - among many other samples - part of the Stock, Aitken and Waterman track *Road Block.* "Our claim is that they don't have any right to use Road Block without our permission and without paying the artists and the writers," Waterman told the music press at the time, "We both have to go to court for the law to decide what the law is on sampling, because nobody knows. We are the first to say, 'You cannot sample somebody else's talent, put it on a record and get away with it.' We've got nothing against 4AD or the record." Although the matter was settled, it was ironic that part of the tools in the Stock, Aitken and Waterman armory that served up so many hit singles at this time included the sampling of bass and drums!

Whilst the Swedish trip and the subsequent feature helped to maintain The Justified Ancient's Of Mu Mu's profile in the music press and attract curious readers to their music, they didn't have the financial resources to fight legal cases, or the balls of Peter Waterman. But the next step in the *1987* saga was a brilliant piece of vinyl theatre – the genius idea of re-releasing the *1987* album as a 12" single with all of the offending samples removed, but giving details on the rear of the sleeve as to how to re-create the original album with the aid of the 12", a turntable and the original records from which the samples had been taken. Thus, in early November the music press began reporting that the edited version of *1987* was now in the shops, "it's been available for some weeks but only on an exchange basis for people bringing in their original copies of *1987."*

In many respects, the release of this 12" record was something of a watershed in the development of the Drummond and Cauty partnership. Musically, it made no sense - after all, parts of the tracks were missing - but it was another brilliant opportunity to garner publicity for The Justified Ancients Of Mu Mu, not just as musicians but as an artistic project that was challenging the existing order through the medium of sampling and graffiti. Although *The JAMS 45 Edits* was reviewed and there were some more extended pieces written about the band on the back of it, the most interesting consequence of this act was the fact that the reputation of The JAMs broadened sufficiently for them to start appearing on TV. Both Drummond and Cauty were always open to interviews, and Cauty's BENIO squat was fast becoming their acknowledged headquarters and, as such, a location not only for interviews but for visits by television film crews. With Cauty's American police car parked outside it was more in keeping with their image that Drummond's suburban Aylesbury home, where his wife and children were based.

In one TV feature, Drummond was interviewed sitting on the bonnet of the police car holding, for some reason, a set of stag's antlers, and gave a condensed history of the band so far, including how they'd ended up getting into hot water with ABBA and the MCPS. Drummond and Cauty then became actors, driving to a Virgin Record store in Marble Arch, London, to retrieve banned copies of the *1987* LP. "Our case went to court," continued Drummond as the piece cut back to him sitting on the bonnet of the car, "we ended up being fined and were told we could release the same record without the offending parts. So we did this edited version with all these gaps, with instructions on the back on how to put the whole thing back together again in your own at home. But it was really just to send up the situation we found ourselves in."

The next segment showed Cauty playing a JAMs fan going into the Rough Trade shop on Ladbroke Grove to return a copy of *1987,* where he is given a free copy of the *Edits* 12" as a replacement. The man serving him behind the counter was, of course, Bill Drummond. Cauty returned home to BENIO with the 12", started playing it, and then, at one point, declared, "Shit! I can't hear anything. What's the matter with it?" He goes back to Rough Trade, where Drummond gives him copies of albums by Fred Wesley and The Sex Pistols and *Dave Brubeck's Greatest Hits* - three artists sampled on the LP. Returning to BENIO, Cauty attempts to recreate a track from *1987* following the instructions, which include deploying three turntables, a video machine and a TV. When he gets frustrated he not only breaks a record in two - not one by The JAMS - but symbolically throws a record player at a poster of Samantha Fox which is conveniently hanging on his wall. A poster of 2000AD anti-hero Judge Dredd gazes on with approval from another wall.

Meanwhile, whilst this *1987* related drama was being played out, Drummond and Cauty had been busy in the studio, and the third JAMs single, *Downtown*, was issued in December 1987. In an interview given to the *New Musical Express* in December 1987, King Boy D was keen to throw out a vision of musical chaos when it came the recording of the new track. "This is going to sound ludicrous. We didn't even know it was going to be called *Downtown*, we didn't even know what it was going to be like when we started doing it. One day I was in the studio and I just started humming the chorus of *Downtown* over the intro. I thought, 'That's funny, I wonder what key it's in...'"

A snatch of the famous Petula Clark record soon found its way into the mix, along with beats and a gospel choir. What's intriguing about *Downtown* is that Drummond and Cauty were already displaying a skill for collaboration, bringing in DJ Cesare to work on a version of the track that appeared on the flip of the 12". Cesare had gotten involved in music after giving Adrian Sherwood a tape he'd mixed in his bedroom that saw him invited to do a session in the studio with the On U Sound boss. As well as artists like Tackhead, and even M/A/R/R/S, Cesare also now worked with The JAMs. "I mixed Pet Clark's *Downtown* into the JAMs single, but that was a straight session job. I turned up with the idea, "I'm the arms, you're the brains boys - use me". As it happened they left the studio and left the mix totally to me since they weren't really interested in making a statement so much as squeezing the juice out of the JAMs concept." This quote was from March 1988, when Cesare was promoting his first 12", *Drop,* wherein he'd remixed a number of Public Enemy tunes, and by which time he'd also worked on other tracks with the JAMs, like *Burn The Bastards*. "I'd rather work in the underground indie market in a dance field rather than, say, become the new Stock, Aitken or Waterman. I match beats and I like to do it in as adventurous a way as possible. I'll mix Adonis into Front 242 or Skinny Puppy into Wagner."

Although *Downtown* was officially the last JAMs 12" of 1987, there had also been another single issued by the KLF axis that year. This was a 12" by Disco 2000, who were marketed as a couple of raunchy girls The JAMs had discovered whilst on patrol - "Cress used to work in a Sten Gun factory greasing barrels, she met Rockman at an Army and Navy fashion show where The JAMs' sample sergeant was modeling camouflage underwear. It wasn't long before the pair had moved into a South London munitions dump." As you've probably guessed by now, the wonderful, free flowing fictional style was the output of James Brown, writing in the pages on the *New Musical Express*. In fact, one half of Disco 2000 was Cauty's wife, Cressida, who, with her own musical background in The Whippets From Nowhere, The 39 Steppes, Big Hair and Angels One 5, was not going to let her husband have all of the musical fun and limelight. The other member was Mo Brathwaite, who had, at one time, sailed on the good ship Brilliant when they had enough members to man the ferry Drummond and Cauty sailed to Sweden on.

Musically, *I Gotta CD* was pop-house, clubby electro with smears of guitar, scratching and even those JAMs cats. It was a crucial record, in that it showed that Cauty, who, one assumes, did most of the spadework, was starting to draw from the well of Chicago house and early techno from Detroit that was, by now, filtering into clubs around the country. Over this broth, Cressida and Mo rapped in unison like a deranged version of chart duos such as Mel and Kim or Pepsi and Shirley, and King Boy D made a brief contribution. What's particularly interesting about the Disco 2000 release is that Drummond and Cauty used a PR company - 10 Better - to service the record to radio stations and the music press, although the press release was probably still penned by the duo as it was somewhat raunchy, "Mo has her fingers in quite a few pies (not to be mistaken for pants). 'What's that smell Mo?' 'Oh that's the last A&R man I was sampling.'"

When Disco 2000 were interviewed by James Brown for the *New Musical Express*, the resulting feature carried on this theme and read at times like a cross between a *Carry On* film and an episode of Benny Hill. "You've got to come across as sexy feminists. Not having huge bottoms, always wearing dungarees and never a bra. You've got to have feminists who wear mini-skirts." But Cressida did find time to talk about the song, "We didn't want political slogans or anything like that, we just wanted it to be funny. The use of abbreviations is a comment on the planned obsolescence in today's society."

It was a funny and frothy feature, much in keeping with the record itself, and one of James Browns musings on this release, and the earlier *Whitney Joins The JAMs*, was to prove spookily prescient, "Likewise the accessibility of *I Gotta CD* can't go ignored. And though The JAMs only produced it, the surprising dance-awareness that has infiltrated both releases has come as a surprise to both The KLF and myself. If they were prepared to destroy their abstract political ideas, The KLF could quite rapidly become something akin to King Boy, Rockman and Waterman. A wall of sex and a string of hits could be built in no time."

Speaking of walls, in December 1987 Drummond and Cauty rabbited on to *Melody Maker* on a range of subjects, from sampling to Pete Waterman, as well as creating a photographer's dream by backing Cauty's car up onto the pavement and defacing a billboard with the message MERRY XMAS FROM THE JAMS. "We do it all the time," boasted Cauty, "I can't believe that nothing ever happens."

By this time Drummond and Cauty were already recording their second LP, which was "written, recorded, pressed and packed" in two months between late November 1987 and January 1988. Drummond explained why the finished product had no track listing to the growing army of JAMs fans in their second information sheet, sent out in March 1988 to those on their mailing list:

"The reason there was no track list with the record was to enable us to get the record out as fast as possible after we'd finished recording it. We had to deliver the artwork to the printers before Christmas, at which time we didn't know what the tracks were to be called." This was because Drummond and Cauty were still recording them, but the key point here is the urgency with which the duo were operating, which was going against all of the normal record company policies of a considered release schedule that they were both used to working with. Drummond sounded like Miles Davis in his fertile electric period of the late '60s and early '70s when he told one journalist that, "as soon as we've finished doing something we're itching to get onto something else, so by the time the people who have bought the record have got into it, we've moved on."

Unlike *1987*, the cover art for *Who Killed The Jams* LP was full colour, featuring a photo taken by Lawrence Watson during their ill-fated trip to Sweden. It showed Drummond and Cauty standing by the door of Cauty's Ford Galaxie police car amidst a pall of white smoke generated by the burning of copies of the *1987* LP - conveniently shown on the back of the sleeve. Their status in the music press saw album reviews that were mostly positive, although in his analysis Edwin Pouncey did muse in the *New Musical Express* that, "Twisting the existing ideas of others into the shape they want and hammering them home is a cute trick, but for how long can the boys keep pulling the same rabbit out of the hat?"

Released in February 1988, *Who Killed The JAMs?* was, in fact, a musical step forward from *1987,* and showed, in some respects, the duo's future direction of travel, and that their rabbit ears were tuned into wider listening habits. *Candystore* opened with a sample of The Shirelles' *Leader Of The Pack, with* Drummond adapting the song's lyrics before it quickly moved into a driving dance track, complete with piano parts played by Nick Coler and a house-themed chorus from Cressida and Mo. This was Chicago house, South London style, and the track would be retooled and issued under the name *One Love Nation* as the second Disco 2000 single in April 1988. There was even a video shoot, and a journalist from the *New Musical Express* was on hand to document the event. Cressida was quick to pass on the plot, "Yeah, tons of people crowding around... Then we jump up as if to start rehearsing the song in our bedroom. Then Mo starts to... she sort of..." Mo: "I start to masturbate!" It was *Carry On* again, and all that was missing was a cackle from Sid James.

Disaster Fund Collection, with its pulsating synth line, female chorus lines and brass, again dropped anchor into the realms of house music and was again much more musically - and in sampled terms - sophisticated. Whilst Drummond railed - "I've paced the cage of freedom for all it's worth!" - it was sonically more Pet Shop that Beastie Boys. Next, *King Boy's Dream* started as a pure rap and saw the inspired use of a sampled Cauty cough as part of the rhythm before shifting into the *Porpoise Song,* electronically prowling terrain that, at times, sounded like an updated version *Riders Of The Storm* by the Doors. Here, Drummond narrated about his days as a nineteen year old working on a fishing trawler, as well as trying to get a porpoise to join The JAMs. It was an excellent track.

The lyrical content of Drummond's rap on *Prestwick Prophet's Grin* told of his epiphany to create the music that became *All You Need Is Love,* as well as the story of The JAMs so far, but the charm was in the wonderful music, underpinned by a funky, almost jazzy, guitar riff, organ and a winning beat that sounds like it was constructed from the barking of a musical dog. Female backing vocals took the track into the realms of gospel, despite a short Indian music interlude.

The album's final track, *Burn The Bastards*, drove the record home with a JAMs version of Sly and The Family Stone's *Dance To The Music*, with Drummond singing lyrics tweaked from the original as the song pounded away, driven by house piano (again provide by Nick Coler) and an insistent chorus of "Dance Everybody." There was also the first deployment of the famous "Mu Mu!" chant, sandwiched between Drummond's demands to throw the bastards on the fire. The record wound down with the chimes of Big Ben, from Westminster, counting in the New Year, before Drummond declared the party 'crap' and asked Rockman if he knew of any others.

The album ended with the sound of a collaborator who would be central to Cauty and Drummond's next major musical step forward - the engine of Cautys's Ford Galaxie police car, soon to be rebranded as Ford Timelord.

DOCTORIN' THE TARDIS

"Between engagements these two hooligans came along and bought me. They turned out to be none other than those two chaps. They're good lads, but when they started playing me the new stuff they were doing on my car cassette I thought it was time I showed them how it should be done. They haven't got much of a clue on the music front."
- ***Ford Timelord to the Melody Maker, 11th June 1988***

"Anyway, as it happened Ford told us that we had to start a band called The Timelords. We thought OK, fair enough, there aren't many people who've got a car that's telling them to form a band."
- ***Bill Drummond to New Musical Express***

After the ups and downs of 1987, early in 1988 Drummond and Cauty abandoned The JAMs - "King Boy D and Rockman Rock have ceased to exist" – shortly after the release of their second LP. At this time they were probably at a low financial ebb – although they could still afford to place an advert in *The Face* offering the last five copies of 1987 for £1,000 each - but by the summer Bill Drummond and Jimmy Cauty were winners. They'd jumped onto the hit train and made a fortune by scoring a chart topping, hit record, *Doctorin' The Tardis,* under the name The Timelords, and their wives, families and friends - and maybe even members of ABBA - got to see them prance around on that great British institution, *Top Of The Pops.*

In a move no doubt instigated by master strategist Bill Drummond, The Timelords even published a book that appeared early in 1989, titled *The Manual (How To Have A Number One The Easy Way).* In this slim but juicy tome, issued in the names of both Drummond and Cauty but mostly penned by Drummond, they detailed exactly how they'd recorded, produced, marketed and promoted their hit single and how, if you followed their justified, ancient and sage advice, you could have a hit record as well.

The book even came with full money back guarantee. As for the contents of *The Manual,* as Joe Strummer of The Clash sang on *London Calling,* "And you know what they said? Well, some of it was true."

"It was all done down in Dagenham, that one," recalls keyboard player and programmer Nick Coler (described as a 'genius' in *The Manual*). "They had the idea and we reconstructed all of the parts." Coler was familiar with Tony Atkins' Village Studios in Dagenham as he'd previously recorded there with both Ya Ya and Drummond, and as a hard working session musician. *The Manual* stated that, "Studios are in the most unlikeliest of buildings, and the most unlikeliest of settings." Set between a printers and a carpenters shop, The Village occupied the perfect example of the incongruous location, and, despite not being listed in *Music Week's* annual round up of London studios, was not only an excellent studio with modern facilities but was also reasonably cheap.

Whilst *The Manual* suggested that the artist went into the studio with a blank canvas, Cauty and Drummond went into The Village with a good idea of exactly what they wanted to achieve. As Drummond later told *Snub TV,* "We wanted to be Number One so we made a Number One record... we were going to make a dance record, a house record, using the *Doctor Who* theme, and Jimmy had been working on some rhythms for it, and he played it to me in the car when we were driving off to the studio and I said, 'It can't be, we can't have a Glitter Beat on a house record. That won't work at all.'"

In fact, this was the only way it would work. Musically, the bones of *Doctorin' The Tardis* fused together elements of The Sweet's *Blockbuster,* from 1973, and a sequenced retooling of the *Doctor Who* theme, over which infectious lyrics were shouted to the vocal line that graced Gary Glitter's 1972, mostly instrumental, hit single *Rock and Roll Part 1.* They even threw in the word 'Loadsamoney,' referencing the popular Harry Enfield comedy character of the time, who also had a chart hit in 1988 with a song of the same name. As Drummond stated, Cauty first struggled to give the song a rhythmic engine, and however hard they tried they couldn't give the song a house beat. So, a song that found so much inspiration from glam rock just had to be underpinned by the Glitter Beat. "We had to go with it in the end," Cauty also told *Snub TV,* "We were trying to make it into quite a hip kind of record, but it just wasn't happening, so if it is going to be poppy let's go for it."

The Glitter Beat underpinned most of Gary Glitter's hit records from the early '70s, as well as a number of other glam-inflected chart singles, and Drummond and Cauty got exactly what they wanted through Nick Coler, whose musical partner at the time, Ian Richardson, was brother of former Rubettes drummer John Richardson, a man who knew how to create the Glitter Band drum sound as he was the session drummer on a lot of those tracks. "So he came into the studio and we basically just put tea towels on everything," recalls Coler, "So the drums weren't sampled, they were played. As far as I remember it was Jimmy playing one floor tom-tom with dishcloths gaffa taped to it, overdubbed loads of times to get it nice and big. Then the kick and the snare were triggered from an Akai S900 (sampler), controlled from an Atari computer."

One thing that was not mentioned in *The Manual* was exactly how they got the *Doctor Who* effects on *Doctorin' The Tardis* to sound like those from the BBC TV series. Was this proto-sampling in action or hard work in the studio? No - this was a stroke of divine fortune. "The weird thing was that at that time I was working with a guy who was doing the theme music for *Doctor Who*," recalls Coler. Enter Dominic Glynn.

Glynn's own involvement with *Doctor Who* was also down to another stroke of fortune. "I'd been in a band for so many years, and it was a familiar story of the '80s - lots of bands struggling to get record deals, then getting a deal and then it didn't really come to anything. By that time I'd really got the bug for working in the studio and making music, electronic music and all that kind of stuff, and there was no getting away from the fact that I wanted to make a living from it." At this time, *Doctor Who* was one of the few TV programmes broadcast in the UK that used electronic music, and Glynn had written to the producers of the show in the vain hope of securing some work. Amazingly, he was asked to send in some demos, and this led to him being asked to work on the show.

Originally, Glynn was commissioned to provide incidental music for one of the episodes, then he was handed the golden ticket. "The first thing that I actually did was a rearrangement of the theme tune," he recalls, as the show's producer "suddenly had the idea that they ought to change the theme tune every now and then. So he thought he would ask me to give it a go. At very short notice I did a rearrangement of the classic tune, the first thing I finished for them. It was done in about a week, it was very short notice between getting a call saying, 'Would you like to have a go at doing the theme tune?' and, 'Oh and I'll need it next Tuesday,' or words to that effect." The reason for the hurry was that, "They needed it fairly instantly because they were going to dub it onto the episode that they were putting together, so it was a last minute thing, but the music went on the first episode of the season, which started in the autumn of 1986."

Whatever the quality of the writing, acting or storylines, the *Doctor Who* theme was something of an institution, and like any musician doing a version of a classic song, Glynn was guaranteed a reaction, "That was quite funny," he laughs, "in those days there was no email response, it was letters to the *Radio Times* and letters on (TV's) *Points Of View*. I think there was a bit of an outcry as there always was when you tried to change a British institution, and there was no doubt that *Doctor Who* was a real institution. I thought it was quite daunting, so when they asked me if I wanted to do it, of course I said 'Yes,' but at the same time I went into ultra-panic mode and thought, how do you mess around with something that is universally loved? Naturally there were lots of people who didn't like it, but fortunately a lot of people did like it. So it became a sort of you either loved it or hated it version, which I would much rather that than a bland version that everybody thinks is kind of alright. It did create a bit of a thing, with people having letters (read out) on *Points of View* and comments in the *Radio Times* like, 'Come on BBC!' or 'What are you thinking?'"

So how did Nick Coler get involved? Well, the music that Glynn recorded for the *Doctor Who* theme was only for the opening and closing credits, and each lasted for around twenty-five to thirty seconds, but at this point the BBC decided they wanted Glynn to record a full-length version that they could issue as a single. "So the minutes were adding up,' recalls Glynn. "At this point Nick was a friend of mine and an accomplished producer, and I was quite green and starting out, so the difference between making music for TV and making a record meant I wanted to get somebody else involved."

Coler was the obvious choice as he'd produced tracks by Glynn's band Strange Persuasion when they'd secured a deal with Dakota records a few years previously, although nothing had been released. He'd helmed the sessions with skill, expertise and good humour, and they became friends, "So I got Nick involved. Also Nick had some nice synthesisers that I didn't have, so getting his expertise and these synths meant that we could make improved 7" and 12" versions of the theme I'd done. Basically, we went to a studio in Kent and took my original eight-track recording of the theme, he and I chopped it up, added a few extra sounds and basically spliced that together to make a long version. That would have been in 1986, possibly even at the beginning of 1987. Before *Doctorin The Tardis* he worked on that with me."

So, when Coler later worked with Drummond and Cauty on a track that drew inspiration from *Doctor Who* and needed some sound effects, he knew where to go. "I knew about the *Doctorin' The Tardis* single through Nick," Glynn says, "and I somewhat illicitly provided some samples of the sound effects from the show." According to Nick Coler, "I had all the samples from the real *Doctor Who* as he had them, and he told me how they were made." As you might imagine, whilst making a record that took its lyrical and musical impetus from *Doctor Who*, this was *something* of a benefit. "I took them over and we stuck them on the record and that's why the sounds are real - I got them from this guy who was doing *Doctor Who!*"

Later on, it has been suggested - but not confirmed - the BBC came sniffing around The Timelords, questioning how they'd got the sounds. But Drummond and Cauty could have countered any threat of action by describing exactly how they had recreated the sounds as Glynn had been told exactly how the sound of the Tardis materialising and other effects had been originally created, thus clearing that particular hurdle. "To be honest, I would think it's a myth," states Glynn, "because in 1988 there wouldn't have been a problem. If someone wanted to go and pinch a sample you would go and buy a *Doctor Who* video and you could have sampled it of off there if you wanted to. It was just the fact that I knew Nick well and he only lived a few miles away and he said, 'Have you got any sounds?' And I said, 'Yes.' I doubt very much if the BBC would even think, 'How on Earth did they get those sounds?' They could have got them from anywhere, and even taped them off the telly. It may well have been questionable whether or not they should have used them, but I doubt if there would have been any question of where they got them from."

As for the Dalek-type voices that pepper the record, these were recorded in the studio, and again Coler's experience came in useful, "I knew that they'd used ring modulators to make a Dalek sound, and I had a fuzzbox, so all the 'You What?' and 'So What's' and other (vocal) stuff was Jimmy. We put all that together."

The title of the track was a clever play on words - not only had they messed around with the *Doctor Who* theme, but it was also a tip of the hat to Coldcut, who'd scored a top ten hit earlier in the year with a track called *Doctorin' The House*, although there was no musical similarity.

"We all knew it was going to be a hit," recalls Coler when the song was finished, "at the time novelty records were popular, and we just had a feeling." The first mention of the track appeared in a JAMs 1988 Information Sheet dated 10th March. Whilst the main body of Drummond's hand-written note detailed what the band were planning - "In 1988 Rockman and myself want to have a low profile year" - there was also the cryptic heading, "Watch out for new KLF signing - The Timelords. Bosh Bosh Bosh," which suggested that the track had been completed. Drummond, more than anybody, knew *Doctorin' The Tardis* was a potential hit, but also knew that it was important to use the machinery of the music business to get there. In *The Manual* he wrote, "Between you sipping this cup of tea and getting to Number One you are going to be involved with a lot of people along the way, and from all of these people you can learn a lot." His own expertise and knowledge as a label boss, producer and A&R man meant he knew exactly what needed to be done to give the record every chance of success - recording a potential hit record was one thing, but selling it was *much* more important.

Drummond had known and worked with publicist Mick Houghton since the early days of Zoo as he'd done the publicity for The Teardrop Explodes and Echo And The Bunnymen. Houghton knew everyone in the business and everyone knew him, so he was the perfect man to write press releases, pick up the phone and set up interviews and photo shoots. According to *The Manual*, he was paid £1,000 for his work, and recalls today that things went well from the beginning, "I can't remember how Bill and Jimmy saw it, but I always thought the Timelords single could have completely backfired on them until I took it into the *New Musical Express* offices and played it to (then editor) Danny Kelly. He just loved it - I hesitate to use the phrase 'went mad for it' because I've never said that in my life - but he did, and he just played it on a loop in the office, grabbing anybody he could to find to come and listen to it and saying, 'This is genius.' The following week they ran a two page story about it, and a few weeks later The Timelords were on the cover."

As for radio and TV, Scott Piering was recommended by distributor Rough Trade, and was also employed. Piering had worked for Rough Trade before going it on his own, and his Appearing company (whose offices were in the Rough Trade building) was the best in the business at promoting independent releases and getting them played on the radio, promoted on TV and into the charts. Drummond admitted in *The Manual* that, "without him this book would have to be retitled *How To Get To Number 47 – With A Certain Amount Of Difficulty.*" At this time, plugging a record was a not so dark art deployed by major labels to ensure that acts were given every opportunity to sell lots of records by having them played on the main nationwide station, Radio One, Capital Radio in London (which reached 43% of listeners in the capital) and other regional outlets.

One well-known team was Nick Fleming and Ollie Stallman - "By appointment to the record industry. Purveyors of rather large hits for quite a long time" - who once arranged for decorators working on the exterior of the BBC's Egton House to hoist them up to the fourth floor window where the Radio One playlist committee was meeting so they could deliver a record. "Ollie Stallman is always great fun," Radio One mainstream DJ Steve Wright stated at the time, "He has the right mix of healthy cynicism and sincerity. He's subtle, he doesn't ring you every day like some people, he rings you every other day!" Fleming and Stallman were to plug one of the biggest selling singles of 1988 - *The Only Way Is Up* by Yazz – which spent five weeks at the top of the charts.

Scott Piering also delivered a similar personal service, especially to John Peel, who never needed any coaxing to play any record that he liked, although Piering's role here was to get acetates and test pressings to Peel for him to play before anybody else, which was another dark art of the record plugger. Although we don't know how much Piering charged The Timelords, some well-known pluggers charged up to £2,500 per record, which - if it led to a hit - was good value for money. "If, as an MD of a major record company, you've signed a new band for, say, £100,000, then, with studio, video and marketing costs all adding up to an average of another £100,000, you're talking a serious investment," wrote Guy Holmes of pluggers Gut Reaction in a letter to *Music Week*, "Would you suggest that that investment is put into cardboard mailers and posted to Radio One, or would you employ people who you recognised as having experience in promoting bands to radio and TV for a fraction of your initial investment?"

At this time, although *Music Week* actually listed airplay charts, giving an indication of strong chart performance as well as evidence of hard plugging, the explosion of the dance underground was beginning to serve up major chart hits that had received little or no airplay on major stations before crashing into the charts. But with an average of seventy five new singles being released each week and only seven getting any major national radio airplay, selling your record through a plugger was still a vital business, and if it was an independent record Scott Piering was your man. "He became famous as the most brilliant independent radio plugger the world has ever known," recalls Adam Morris, who, like many other people, employed his services, "Most of the indie bands like The Smiths, The Undertones - all those kind of bands - he plugged them to radio and television." And now he was going to plug The Timelords.

As well as airplay, equally important were the salesmen whose job it was to sell the records to the shops, and in *The Manual* Drummond lifted the lid on how the entire process worked, including paying an independent sales team like Impulse, Bullet or Platinum a fee to work the record as a priority release, as well as paying them a bonus for the record's success. "These are the men that make the hits. Without them there would be nothing. Even if everybody stopped buying singles for a month there would still be numbers going into GALLUP computers. Still midweeks on Thursday and predictions on Friday and charts on Sunday. Nothing would change." It was the combination of press, publicity, radio play, distribution and these records selling and stock being swiftly replenished that was the litmus of chart success.

Drummond and Cauty came up with a brilliant price of marketing for the record - it wouldn't be released as The JAMs, or as the nascent KLF, but issued under the name The Timelords. This played the *Doctor Who* card for all it was worth and, in the spirit of aiming for the commercial jugular, they also decided that the record would be fronted by somebody more photogenic than Lord Rock or Time Boy (as they were credited on the record) – Cauty's old American police car. The car already had form, and for his assault on the charts he'd not only be allowed to operate on a full tank of petrol but would also be named Ford Timelord.

The marketing plan was a publicist's dream - Ford Timelord would do all of the press for the record. He would conduct all of the interviews and do all of the photo shoots. He would also appear in the video to promote the single, and, when the time came, appear on *Top Of the Pops*. Even the front cover of the single featured a picture of Ford with a speech bubble stating, "Hi! I'm Ford Timelord. I'm a car, and I've made a record." This was very clever indeed - editors and journalists love nothing more that something fresh and unusual to break their standard diet of record reviews, constant badgering by press officers, conducting artist interviews, writing features and producing gig reviews.

Of course, Ford Timelord also wrote the press release that went out with promotional copies of the record, a highly amusing piece that ended with the compulsive, "So I told these two plonkers to change their names to TIME BOY and LORD ROCK and stay well in the background, pressing the buttons, twiddling the knobs and counting the money while I do all the photo sessions and interviews and generally be star-like." It was a four-wheeled answer to Morrissey.

To say that the record took off would be an understatement. Reviews - "this time they manage to create a glam-rock house record by mixing together Sweet, Gary Glitter and the *Doctor Who* Theme! It's so crass it could work, too." – didn't matter as the song was so infectious. *Doctorin' The Tardis* crashed into the independent charts and, due to the legwork of Scott Piering, became a Radio One staple, which also saw it crash into the national charts at number twenty-two on the 4th June 1988. All aided by the smooth running of Rough Trade's Cartel distribution system, and a sales team that assaulted shops across the country making sure not only that the record was ordered but the correct numbers were entered into the computers of those shops who compiled chart returns.

Ford was also on full throttle and happy to do anything and everything to promote the record, from appearing in a cheap and cheerful video with an even cheaper and more cheerful mock Dalek to fulfilling any promotional duties required of him. "Everything about The Timelords was wonderfully tacky," recalls Mick Houghton, "the video was the antithesis of big budget videos, with their old Ford Galaxie driving round mythical Wiltshire chasing crudely constructed Daleks. And the idea that the car was the star and that only the car would do interviews was even more preposterous."

In the past, reviews and articles about The JAMs and offshoots like Disco 2000 had been confined to the *NME, Melody Maker, Sounds* and *Record Mirror*, but as *Doctorin' The Tardis* took off into the charts the reach widened to include more pop-orientated publications like *Smash Hits*, who even printed the full lyrics to the song. Ford Timelord even got into the pages of the BBC's *Doctor Who* magazine, where he not only admitted some attraction to former Doctor Jon Pertwee and his old "Edwardian roadster, Bessie," but also that, "I'm attracted to K9 (the Doctor's robotic dog) for some reason, but I hope it's just because he's mechanical." The magazine gave away twelve copies of the single that Ford had personally signed as a competition prize – "he's run his tyres over the covers!" The only trick Ford missed in the publicity stakes was doing a photoshoot with Harry Enfield's Loadsamoney character's wheels of choice, a Ford XR3…

In some instances Drummond and Cauty would provide the music press – probably via Houghton - with written answers to questions: "It's my ambition to be a mega pop celebrity. I see myself as moving on from that to be a general all round celebrity once the record has been a big hit," stated Ford on one occasion. "I'm basically a child of the '70s and I thought that if I mixed two essential elements of that great decade - *Doctor Who* and Gary - I would very definitely have a hit on my hands." On location, journalists and photographers would be brought to the car or the car would be brought to them and then speak to them through the medium of its loud hailer.

"When they used to do interviews they would fill it up with stage weights so it would drop right down and someone would be under a load of carpets in the back and that would be the interview," chuckles Nick Coler. An associate of the band would be inside primed to answer questions. "He was under the carpet. It was all cheap and cheerful. It was, 'Where do you come from?' 'I come from another planet,' and all that stuff. The papers were really trying to kill it. They hated it. They did not want to play along. Who is it? Who is in the car? Who made the record? We are not printing that shite!"

Cauty later related similar concerns to *Snub TV* - "saying that the car is fronting the record (was) because Bill and I didn't want to front the record as we were too embarrassed. It sort of backfired on us a bit as the media hated the idea that we were saying a car could make a record. They just didn't believe us."

Although *Smash Hits* played along, even they joked about someone being hidden in the car talking to them and pointedly asked, "Why have you got those bits of cardboard stuck on your windscreen?", but the question was part of a feature that covered a whole page and was great publicity for the single. Houghton believes it was all part of the fun, "Such was the credibility that Bill and Jimmy had - and I hesitate to say this, but that I had as well - that the press went along with it. I don't recall them being sniffy about standing around in a car park to speak to a car. If Bill and Jimmy were taking the piss then the press were happy to conspire in something they saw as undermining the music industry and, to some extent, undermining their own part in the process. The JAMs were renowned for bucking the system after all."

But was there enough air in Ford Timelord's tyres to go to number one? Comedian Freddie Starr didn't think so. He was a regular at The Village in Dagenham, laying down tracks of his own, and was around when *Doctorin' The Tardis* was being finished. He was so convinced that the song wouldn't be a hit that he bet Nick Coler and Ian Richardson £10,000, or a brand new Jaguar XJS, that it would *not* make it to number one. When he was told that they couldn't afford to match his bet he told them not to worry, it was a one-way bet that he thought he wouldn't have to pay out on!

But Starr was wrong. *Doctorin The Tardis* was an infectious cocktail that everyone adored and it climbed to the summit on 18th June 1988. Even today, it's surreal to read in that week's music press, "In a seesaw battle for chart honours which saw Wet Wet Wet, Bros and The Timelords each achieving their highest sale on individual days last week, it was the latter that came through to claim the Number One spot with their single *Doctorin The Tardis*." It should be stated that both Bros and Wet Wet Wet were not only huge acts at the time but also had the massed ranks of two major record companies behind them, including an army of press officers, pluggers, salesmen and distributors. But they were beaten at their own game by the sales and distribution team of an independent army.

As they were playing the game to the hilt, Drummond and Cauty jumped at the chance to appear on *Top Of the Pops.* Ironically, the BBC producers wouldn't allow Ford Timelord into the studio to promote his own record, mainly, one assumes, due to the logistical issues of getting him on and off the stage. So, with two drummers and a fake Dalek, Drummond took to the stage in a white suit, cape and top hat whilst Cauty wore a similar, all black outfit. Both played flying V guitars (white for Drummond, black for Cauty) as they mimed along to the song, and, amusingly, when not punching the air or kicking out a leg, indulged in syncronised dance moves with their instruments similar to those deployed by Youth and Cauty a couple of years earlier in those failed Brilliant videos.

That *Doctorin' The Tardis* was a glam rock stomper that deployed the Glitter Beat and vocal melody from *Rock And Roll Part 1* was not lost on the music press. In July 1988 the *New Musical Express* ran a full discography of Gary Glitter, stating "Hello, hello, he's back again – the man who brought you blubber rock, the very fellow who took on the Osmonds and The Rollers and left them both for dead. Now he's inspired The JAMs." Glitter not only made money from the record – along with co-writer Mike Leander he had a publishing credit – but also featured in a full page advert printed in many publications that showed him dipping his right hand into a huge jar of skin rejuvenating cream under the heading, "The things people do to keep hold of their Young Persons Railcard."

In June, as the record was topping the charts, Glitter also went into the studio with Drummond and Cauty to record a new version of the song that was reported in the music press to be called *Gary And The Tardis* or *Gary Joins the JAMs*. White labels were quickly sent out to radio stations to keep the song on the top spot, "so he could front a performance on *Top Of The Pops* (being) as ludicrously camp and over the top as back in his glory days," recalls Houghton. As the record was only Number One for a week, this wasn't possible as the programme never featured acts that were falling down the charts, but it did lead to a somewhat surreal *New Musical Express* cover when Drummond, Cauty and Glitter did a photoshoot and interview at Stonehenge. This was Glitter's first and only *New Musical Express* front cover and he did most of the talking:
"Did Bill Drummond and Rockman rip off my patent Glitterbeat without asking me? No way. They asked me for permission on behalf of the car, Ford Timelord, who had this idea for what turned out to be *Doctorin The Tardis*. I, of course, agreed immediately. You see, me and Ford Timelord go back a long way. In a previous in-CAR-nation, before he grew wheels, Ford was the twin drum kit in the Glitter Band." Obviously Glitter had been well-briefed by Houghton, Drummond and Cauty. The feature revealed that at one point the BBC thought that Glitter was behind The Timelords, and in keeping with the surreal location Glitter also aired his thoughts on near death and out of body experiences.
With regards to appearing on *Top Of The Pops*, Glitter eventually got his wish when The Timelords were booked to appear on the Christmas edition of the programme, which showcased all of the hits from 1988, including one of the biggest chart topping singles, *The Only Way Is Up* by Yazz. Ironically, not only had the song been given a special fillip, mix and arrangement by Youth, who was beginning to deliver some serious hits of his own, but Yazz had also appeared on the Coldcut hit *Doctorin' The House*, which had also been a top ten hit in February 1988.
As well as adding Gary Glitter to the line-up for the show, Drummond and Cauty decided to make a visual statement that saw the band decked out in long black robes with pointed black hoods. Nick Coler, who had just returned from a tour in Russia with Ya Ya, was drafted into the line-up and recalls that, as they were rehearsing the song, "The door

opened and Yazz – *The Only Way Is Up* – came in, and she saw it all and she called the producer and said, "This is racist! It's the Ku Klux Klan!" The BBC guy came in and he said, "Amazing. This is *so* visual." In other words, all he could see was that The Timelords were going to look fantastic on the TV screen!"

In truth, there was nothing vaguely racist in what The Timelords were wearing - they were the sort of robes that monks and members of a religious order might wear. So, despite Yazz's misgivings, they performed in the outfits, whose headgear, according to Coler, was simply "rolled up bits of cardboard for the hoods with gaffa tape to hold it onto your face." Gary Glitter, who wore a red outfit as befitting his status as a '70s glam star, gave everything he had in front of the cameras, although Coler recalls, "He was right in front of me with the whole of his shirt ripped open, and you could see all the fake tan dripping down as he'd only done around here (indicates face and neck)."

Whilst *Doctorin' The Tardis* helped breathe air into Gary Glitter's career, Ford Timelord also enjoyed several brushes with celebrity as the car was easy to recognise when parked outside BENIO, or whilst being driven about by Cauty. Alex Paterson, who was a friend and starting to work in partnership with Cauty as The Orb around this time, recalls that one particular admirer who stopped Ford Timelord was a policeman. "There were about eight of us in there. Pretty titted (drunk). And he said. 'Is this the Timelords' car? Are you a Timelord, sir?' This was to Jimmy. 'Well, yes, this was at Number One, this car had a number one.' 'Wonderful Sir, Perchance is there a Killing Joke member in the car?' 'Well, yes.' And he stuck his head in the car and went, 'Hello Youth!' then walked off. That was a really, really bizarre moment."

Drummond's decision to write *The Manual* after the success of The Timelords was inspired, and in keeping with the skill with which he and Cauty were now using the tools of the music industry for their own ends. Crucially, upon publication, as they had recently enjoyed a Number One hit the book received a lot of publicity in the media, and as the main author Drummond not only spoke to the press but also made a number of TV appearances to promote it. The most surreal saw him being interviewed by Tony Wilson (on *The Other Side Of Midnight),* who held up the book and stated that it was, "the new thing from the cranial recesses of Bill Drummond."

He not only challenged Drummond's assertion that many performers were puppets – "is there not something puppet-like about constructing a number one single?" – but also the fact that he was sporting a fake moustache. Drummond, who was dressed in a tweed suit and plus fours and looked like a modern incarnation of John Cleese in the classic BBC comedy *Fawlty Towers,* fired back with the quip, "It's what I am going to wear for television. I understand that moustaches are very important in television." Eventually, Wilson moved away from the upper lip to concede that it was probably the best book written about the inner workings of the music business as it was so truthful. Considering that Wilson also co-ran Factory Records, he should've known.

Drummond also appeared in the same outfit on a show called *Reportage*, where Cauty could also be seen sporting a fake moustache in his white Parka. The show not only interviewed Drummond and detailed how the book could work for any artist or band, but even roped in an old bandmate from Big In Japan for a quote. "I don't think it should be taken too seriously, you know," said Holly Johnson, "it's written in a light-hearted way, and it's very expensive - if you read the book, it's quite an expensive episode." Speaking of Drummond's former Liverpool colleagues, Julian Cope was also asked what he thought of The Timelords in an interview with the *New Musical Express* in October 1988. "If it wasn't Bill Drummond, if it was The Tweets or the follow-up to *Star Trekkin'*, I would have thought it was shit. But because it was Bill, I started thinking, what does he mean? And it wasn't helped by the fact that, two weeks before he put the record out, he came to see me to ask me to play bass on some other project, and he also went to see Pete De Freitas. Now, I've always had the theory that Pete and me are the two father confessors to Bill Drummond, because we're the only two people who totally suss him. And that's why he came to see us, because he was trying to cleanse his soul before he completely sold his arse! But it was cack…"

The Manual sold out and came with a full money back guarantee – "You get the price of the book back if you do not get a Number One," Drummond told Wilson, "We will refund the price of the book."

No one ever asked for one, although Freddie Starr did buy Coler and Richardson a Jaguar XJS.

I WANT TO LEAVE THIS BODY BEHIND

"KIDS! WANNA BE King Boy D's Best Boy? 'Thrills' can offer you the chance to have your name in the credits of THE JAMs' apocalyptic new movie! Impress your friends as the credits roll and YOUR NAME is there as "GAFFER" or "BEST BOY/GIRL" or "KEY GRIP"!
- New Musical Express, 25th February 1989

"Bill Butt asked the question, "Would your regular punter give a fuck or not whether The JAMS made it to THE WHITE ROOM? No. They would rather see Cauty get pumped full of lead while his pompous partner was blown into Hell as their car hit a land mine."
- Information Sheet Eight, 1990

"The 'Kylie' single was unusual because that was a public failure. Usually they'd reach that conclusion themselves, ditch recordings and projects and would just move on no matter what they'd spent on them."
- Mick Houghton to the author

Having a Number One single in the UK was a game changer for Drummond and Cauty. When the dust settled and the accounts began to be tallied, they suddenly had an abundance of something they'd never had before - money. *Doctorin' The Tardis* was released on their own label, so all of the profits - after pressing, distribution and other costs - came to them rather than being filtered down through a record company, where they would have only received a percentage as a royalty, offset against any advances that had been paid out. It had also sold well in other territories where it had been licensed, so there was additional income from those sources. Drummond and Cauty also controlled their part of the publishing income, which would have been lucrative once airplay had been factored in. All told, it's believed that *Doctorin' The Tardis* probably generated a figure anywhere between £300,000 and £500,000.

So, whereas in the past everything in their world up until this point had been hand to mouth, there was now a massive cash injection. Chart success and money also gave them another type of boost according to publicist Mick Houghton, "I think it proved to Bill and Jimmy not only that they could get away with absolutely anything but that they could push their ideas even further to the limit."

At one point there was discussion about staging a joint exhibition at a London gallery, but one day, according to their Information Sheet Eight, "Driving down the Marylebone Road on a wet September afternoon in 1988 in their infamous US Cop car, Cauty suggested, instead of doing the art exhibition they should make a film."

Drummond agreed, and plans were soon drawn up to make a road movie. Budgets, storyboards and a vague script were pulled together, and by November 1988 they were shooting in the Sierra Nevada desert in Spain. The action was directed by Bill Butt, working with a small film crew, many of whom had just worked on the third film in the Indiana Jones series, *The Last Crusade*. As old friends and collaborators, Butt and Drummond had been here before with The Bunnymen's *Shine So Hard* film project.

For all its faults, *Shine So Hard* had a traditional logic about it, depicting The Bunnymen preparing for, and then performing, a concert before their fans. The Justified Ancients Of Mu Mu, The Timelords and even Disco 2000, however, were not going to perform live, and Drummond and Cauty were not going to be filmed in the recording studio laying down tracks and giving a visual demonstration of how to put *The Manual* into practice. This meant that the 'road movie' concept had to have a plot 'driving' it forward. At first, the weather in Spain was so bad there were worries that the film wasn't going to feature anything at all, and even when things got better on the weather front there were other problems, as Drummond related to *The Catalogue* magazine in 1989, "We were stuck on the top of a mountain in Spain, with this whole full-scale 35mm film crew, the camera people, sound crew, PAs and everything, and suddenly I thought, what are we doing? And when I asked our people what it would cost us to stop the whole thing right now, and they said, 'Oh, at least £65,000', we just had to go with it."

Going with it meant filming pick up scenes of Drummond and Cauty driving around the desert in Ford Timelord, sitting beside a burning fire, consulting a map on the bonnet of Ford Timelord, painting Ford Timelord white and then driving up a mountain road laden with snow. Drummond even walked down a railway track carrying a large dead eagle that he'd found by the roadside. "The significance of this at the time could not be argued," Drummond later wrote in Information Sheet Eight, "Meaningless but dramatic."

As they intended to record a soundtrack to the film upon their return, there was, at this stage, no dialogue. But when the cameras stopped rolling in December 1988 they returned to England and "viewed all the uncut rushes that had been shot. They knew then that they'd just thrown away the best part of £250,000."

At this stage there were discussions amongst themselves, with Bill Butt and with their accountant, about cutting their losses and abandoning the project. The movie was far from complete and would require more money to film additional scenes and to edit the existing footage together into a coherent narrative. It was, however, decided to continue, and a revised plan and plot was drawn up to complete "a film within a film," which included hiring actors to play parts and adding dialogue. Drummond later talked about approaching Paul McGann, who had numerous TV roles under his belt and whose debut movie as a co-star was the iconic *Withnail And I* (1987), but nothing came of it.

With some residual money flowing in, one assumes, from *Doctorin' The Tardis* and sales of a low-priced, 2LP JAMs compilation titled *Shag Times* and released in January 1989, additional scenes were filmed at BENIO in Stockwell. "Youth was there as well," recalls Nick Coler, "and they had all of the windows taped up as they had lights inside." This was intended to be the opening sequence of the film, depicting a rave and featuring all of their friends, who Cauty and Drummond leave behind to go off on their quest in Ford Timelord, armed only with a map and vague instructions.

Exactly how this quest was to end was still, at this stage, up in the air, and by the time *The Manual* was reviewed in the *New Musical Express* in February 1989 there was even a competition to, "suggest how best The JAMS can end their movie, preferably with style, panache, and loads of BLOOD!" One imagines that a number of readers submitted their ideas in order to win a free copy of *The Manual,* but the eventual ending was more prosaic, with Drummond and Cauty finding two fake moustaches in The White Room and affixing them to their upper lips, after which Drummond inspects a contract before they walk off and vanish into a thick cloud of white smoke.

According to a later treatment, the title of the film came from a fan or organisation called Eternity, who had earlier written to Drummond and Cauty asking them to enter into a contract and – conveniently – "make an artistic representation of themselves on a journey to a place called THE WHITE ROOM." It's interesting that Cauty was to first appear as The Orb with Alex Paterson on an LP called *Eternity Project One* in 1989, which also featured tracks by an artist listed as Eternity. Was this a coincidence or just the work of the Illuminati?

Thus, the title of the film became *The White Room*, and a vague plot was added in which their road journey was to unravel elements - and the meaning of - the contract, as well as how to extricate themselves from it. In addition to the rave at BENIO, a number of other scenes were filmed featuring Drummond and Cauty's real-life solicitor David Franks playing himself. One, for example, showed him eating a meal in a White Room, waiting for them, and he's also there at the end, when Drummond inspects the contract. As 1989 rolled on, Bill Butt and editor Rob Wright knocked the film into shape, ending up with something that was fifty-two minutes long, but still not long enough for a theatrical release. According to Information Sheet Eight, "Some of the scenes that had been planned and shot had to be dumped. Others that had been shot on the hop had now become vital to the shape of the film." More vital to the shape and completion of the film was the soundtrack that Drummond and Cauty stated that they'd begun to record in February 1989.

Whilst all of this was going on there had been a third and final throw of the dice for Disco 2000, namely a retooled, upbeat version of the Stevie Wonder song *Uptight*. According to Nick Coler, part of the impetus for this came from David Balfe, "He wanted to do that. We always said that on his gravestone it would say, 'I wish I'd thought of that before Bill!' (laughs). He thought that would be a good idea to do." *Uptight* was recorded at Village Recorders in Dagenham in 1988. "I think that Jimmy started it and we ended up dubbing over it," recalls Coler. The plan was for *Uptight* to chart, and the single was issued as a 7", 12" and CD single.

The loyal James Brown stated in his review, "few bands have been both stupid and clever enough to use Bananarama as role models, but Disco 2000 have gone for it in a big way and will probably benefit by way of a hit." Cressida and Mo were even interviewed by *The Face* although the list of questions were dictated by *The Manual* ranging from the importance of Steve Wright's show on Radio One to the Stock, Aitken and Waterman formula for success. Mo was keen to state that Disco 2000 were totally flexible in their approach to the pop business, "We can laugh and joke, or we can be serious and politically-minded. It depends who we're dealing with. We're not icons, for sure, we're not perfect. We're just entertainers, performers, but there's tongue in cheek attitude because we hope people will pick up on us."

There was even a cheap promotional video produced, where Cressida and Mo danced, sang and had fun in front of the camera, starting in knitted jumpers with the words "DISCO" (Mo) and "2000" (Cressida) on the front and "KLF" on the back, and ending up as black and red sex kittens. But *Uptight* failed to detonate, and lived up the *The Face's* opinion that, "Disco 2000, unfortunately, are too clever to get to number one." It didn't help that the song was rather pedestrian, although the flip side, *Mr. Hotty Loves You*, was an excellent, mostly instrumental, house track. As for their lack of chart action, Cressida told *The Face* that that "We're not sweet enough," and would have to wait until The KLF hit pay dirt before she got to appear on *Top Of The Pops* promoting a hit single.

Having scored a hit single in 1988 and talked up *The Manual* and *The White Room* project, Drummond and Cauty were now go-to artists for the established music press. This included interviews, photo shoots and frequent updates in news sections about their real and planned activities. There was not only talk of a comic resurrecting King Boy D and Rockman Rock (which Cauty started but never finished) but even an article that suggested that The JAMs logo had been "sampled" for the cover of a comic book drawn by the American artist Bernie Mireault and called *The Jam*. "*The NME* got in touch with me by phone for an interview," recalls Mireault today, "I thought it was because they liked my comic art and was happy and proud to have a bit of notice from the other side of the Atlantic. Then, months later, I actually saw the article and was shocked to find that I was deeply embroiled in a copyright battle over the cover of my first colour comic book, *The Jam - Super Cool, Color-Injected Turbo Adventure From Hell No. 1*. I'd designed a diamond shaped crest instead of a more traditional logo, and I learned that the design had obviously been lifted whole-hog from an album cover by The Justified Ancients Of Mu Mu, of whom I'd never heard. I remember the friendly tone of the interviewer, and how he gave me zero indication as to what the interview was actually about. If only he'd been straightforward, we could've cleared it up right there."

It was, in fact, a coincidence and nothing more, but it showed that the music press was so keen to feature Drummond and Cauty that they gladly made something up. James Brown had done the same in April 1988, devoting a whole hilarious page in the *New Musical Express* to the demise of The Justified Ancients Of Mu Mu: "Even in this early *Shag Shag Shag* promo shot, Rockman Rock (left) can be seen holding an opened umbrella... even though it isn't raining. A well-known sign to the Gods, often used by Scottish tribes to signal the imminent death of a clansman."

Drummond, who was always willing to give good copy, even appeared in a feature concerning the first single he bought. In the company of David Gedge (The Wedding Present), Thurston Moore (Sonic Youth), Paddy McAloon (Prefab Sprout), Vince Clarke (Erasure), Shaun Ryder (Happy Mondays) and even Robert Englund, who played Freddie Krueger in the *Nightmare On Elm Street* films, Drummond, who normally hated looking in the rear view mirror, opened up like a tin of sardines, stating that it was The Beatles' *Strawberry Fields Forever*: "I never play it. It's just too much. The sheer inexplicability of it. Musically and emotionally I still think it's the greatest record ever made. Best sleeve too. You'd have all those boring record sleeves that were just brown bags with the record company name on, and they had that brilliant picture in a gold frame. Basically, it brings all those early adolescent feelings welling up inside me. I loathe nostalgia with a vengeance, but its survived nostalgia."

In June 1989 Drummond had to reflect upon his past again, but for more unfortunate reasons, when Echo And The Bunnymen drummer Pete De Freitas was killed in a motorcycle accident near Rugerley in Staffordshire. De Freitas was en route from London to Liverpool to meet up with The Bunnymen to work on material for a new LP. In 1987 he'd been demoted to hired hand rather than a full member of the band after he'd gone AWOL in 1985 and used Bunnymen money to start a band called The Sex Gods and pay for recording sessions in New Orleans. The Bunnymen he was en-route to work with on his motorbike was a line-up without McCulloch, who'd left the band to go solo in 1988.

"I don't want to say much until I've spoken to Pete's wife," McCullough told the *New Musical Express* when asked to comment on the tragic early death of his former drummer. "It's a very difficult and upsetting time for everyone." As their former manager, who had invested so much energy and emotion in the Bunnymen, Drummond was also hit hard by De Freitas' passing. As well as relating how he and David Balfe had found and drafted De Freitas into the band, he reflected warmly on his strengths and motivations, "He was the one member of the Bunnymen who understood reason, he was the one who would always unblock situations between other band members or the band and ourselves, the management…. He lived for his motorbike and that whole Jack Kerouac lifestyle, he lived it for real, and at times the band got in the way." This may have been a reference to De Freitas' Sex Gods period - it was actually Drummond who had gone out to America and brought him back to the UK.

Musically, although they worked on a number of tracks aimed at the underground dance market after The Timelords, as 1989 progressed Drummond and Cauty probably felt that they should record another hit single to refloat them financially, having spent much of their profits on *The White Room* film. To that end, they, in some respects, followed their own manual and went into the studio to craft another hit.

The Pet Shop boys had, by this time, developed a niche wherein their electronic pop meditations, cutting edge dance beats and melodic, hook driven sheen was winning them an international fan-base. After the single *West End Girls* went to Number One early in 1986, they began to turn out a regular series of charting singles and chart topping albums, such as *Please, Actually* and *Introspective*. At the same time, Jason Donovan and Kylie Minogue had broken out from the successful Australian soap opera *Neighbours* into massive chart success, produced by Pete Waterman and his boys.

As actors, Jason and Kylie were perfect for the PWL production team in that that they were used to receiving direction and doing what they were told. The only difference between TV and the recording studio was that, whereas on set they uttered the words written for them in front of a camera, with the PWL team they sang what they were told to sing into a microphone. When it came to making promotional videos, taking part in magazine photo shoots or appearing on shows like *Top Of the Pops* and other teen-related fare, their youthful good looks made them perfect pop fodder. *Neighbours* was so popular in the UK that Waterman was effectively tapping the ball into an open financial goal from two yards out.

Drummond and Cauty's cunning plan was to blend together elements of the Pet Shop Boys' winning electronic sheen with lyrics that referenced the two characters from *Neighbours* who were now hot property in the charts - they began to craft a new track, which was to be called *Kylie Said To Jason*.

Nick Coler is pretty open about this follow-up to The Timelords' single. "After that, they thought it would be easy to do it all and wanted to copy the Pet Shop Boys, basically, so we made that." This was one of the last tracks worked on at Dagenham, and Coler also recalls that, "Jimmy wanted me to make everything sound like it was from Southfork, Dallas (the ranch in the TV series), so I was playing all those string lines (on the keyboard)."

With the track recorded and vocals added, everything was put in place to prepare the way for the record to climb up the charts. This included the production of a glossy video which utilised segments of footage filmed for *The White Room,* ranging from Drummond and Cauty leaving the rave at BENIO and driving Ford Timelord around London to Drummond carrying the dead eagle along the Spanish railway track. Cut into this was close-up footage of Drummond's face as he sang *Kylie Said To Jason*, like a Scottish version of Neil Tennant. "I remember Bill practicing the lip-synching for this for ages," chuckles Nick Coler. The only thing missing from the video was a moody looking Cauty standing behind a keyboard wearing the "BOY" baseball cap that was something of a Pet Shop Boys trademark.

Kylie Said To Jason was released on 31st July 1989 under the name The KLF, and Scott Piering's accompanying press release sent out to broadcast media came with a 'top ten' fact list about the band, which ranged from stating that Bill Drummond "formed a group called Big In

Japan" to telling us that "Jimmy collects old American cars. He has never paid more than £500 for any of them." This was the sort of information intended to appeal to a broad range of media outlets, from radio disc jockeys to the editor of *Smash Hits*.

When it came to the music press, Drummond came out swinging. "I know this sounds cynical," he cynically told the *Record Mirror,* "but I think we know what is going to make a top selling record. We can almost program ourselves to write hits, and we always knew that *Doctorin' The Tardis* was going to be a Number One, no doubt about it." The machine-honed *Kylie Said To Jason* was also intended to hit the playlist and chart bullseye, although Drummond was keen to stress that, "We're not really *Neighbours* fans, and we couldn't tell you what colour knickers Mrs Mangel wears. But when we're in the studio the television is on for rather a lot of time, and if you're watching *Neighbours* twice a day you easily get hooked."

With Cauty playing the strong silent type, Drummond continued, "I wouldn't mind meeting Kylie, and if we went on a date I'd take her to Paris for a trip up the Eiffel Tower, followed by dinner. But Felicity Kendal, who's also mentioned in the song, is really my ideal woman. I seem to recall she even won best bum of the year in a newspaper survey once. But I doubt if Felicity could sing as well as Kylie. *I Should Be So Lucky* was a classic song, and I'm sure Kylie has a long career ahead of her. I can't remember anything I've heard by Jason though. But never mind, he has nice teeth."

Jason's teeth aside, whilst the music was fantastic things might have been different if Neil Tennant had been drafted in. As it was, Drummond's lyrics ranged from the inane to the surreal. Putting aside the elements of astral projection described in the chorus - "I'm gonna leave this body now" – and besides references to Jason and Kylie, Drummond took the listener through a tour of old TV sitcoms, from the '70s self-sufficiency themed BBC comedy *The Good Life,* in which Felicity Kendall – and her bum - appeared, to the American *Archie Bunker Show.* He even referenced Skippy The Bush Kangaroo! Sensing a bandwagon forming, some of the music press were quick to pen positive reviews. "I can tell you now that this record is going to do horrendously well," gushed Helen Mead in the *New Musical Express,* "In fact it'll probably top the success of last year's *Doctorin' The Tardis.*"

However, despite the video, press releases and a charm offensive in the music press where Drummond even appeared wearing a Kylie Minogue T-shirt (whether Cauty wore one featuring Jason Donovan cannot be confirmed), *Kylie Said To Jason* was' 'exterminated' across the country. Even the lure of a free poster in the 12" version didn't send Timelords or *Neighbours* fans rushing to the shops, and it failed to chart

- Scott Piering couldn't even get it onto radio playlists. According to Mick Houghton, despite expectations it was the opposite of *Doctorin' the Tardis*, "Where The Timelords' single was a shameless exercise in making a pop hit, it worked within the context and the concept of The JAMs, even if it eventually sold mostly to people who'd never heard of The JAMs," he states today. "*Kylie Said to Jason* didn't have that cache. I remember that there was a real record company/media buzz about that single being the massive follow up hit to The Timelords, not from Bill and Jimmy - they didn't think that way - but Rough Trade were excited and the pluggers saw it as going straight on the Radio One playlist. (But), whereas the press loved the idea of The Timelords and bought into it, I think they were pretty indifferent to *Kylie Said to Jason*."

In short, after such a spectacular failure Drummond and Cauty could have written to themselves to ask for a refund of the cost of their own copy of *The Manual*. To add insult to injury, on 5th August Kylie Minogue's new single, *Wouldn't Change A Thing,* went straight into the singles chart at number four, and her debut LP, *Kylie*, which had originally been released in 1988, re-entered at number thirty-nine. Jason Donovan's LP, *Ten Good Reasons* was still in the top ten. I have been unable to find out what he thought of Bill Drummond's teeth.

The failure of *Kylie Said To Jason* was particularly keenly felt as it was intended to provide another influx of cash to fund the completion of *The White Room*. Indeed, the single had even been billed as being part of the soundtrack, which Drummond and Cauty announced was complete and would be released in September, although this date came and went without the album seeing the light of day. According to Houghton, this original version of the album was scrapped after *Kylie Said To Jason* flopped, "Its failure did have a really positive effect though, because Bill and Jimmy abandoned the original *White Room* tracks and mixes that they'd recorded and disappeared to get on with making *The White Room* film."

Plans to show the film, however, were also put on hold, although Drummond was keen to stress that after a little more retooling it was just a matter of time before it saw the light of day, "I can't see the film being a huge box office success, but in years to come I think it's going to be regarded as a classic, much sought after cult film. I think we'll be adding a lot of sex and violence to the film later on and we want to use well-known actors, especially for the sexy bits. No names at the moment though, it might ruin the contracts."

When it came to contracts and the business side of the equation, Drummond was usually the spokesman, representative and advocate. He had, after all, run his own record label, managed two huge bands and been an A&R Manager at a major label. Whatever Drummond's view of the music business – especially after his run-in with the MCPS over ABBA - he knew how it worked, and made sure it was oiled sufficiently to allow the gears of KLF Communications to turn. One person interviewed for this book recalls people coming to BENIO for meetings with Drummond, who interacted on a regular basis not only with Mick Houghton and Scott Piering, but also with their distributor Rough Trade.

Through initial nervousness about the *All You Need Is Love* 12" and issues over the *1987* LP, Drummond had established a solid relationship with Rough Trade Distribution, who took care of farming out the growing number of KLF Communications records to shops around the country, and whose sales force helped get The Timelords into the charts. When it came to distribution, Rough Trade had a number of label managers whose job was to each look after a small roster of independent labels, from Mute to Sleeping Bag. It was the label manager's job to be the physical interface between these labels and Rough Trade, to ensure that records were put onto the release schedule in time to allow pre-marketing and pre-sales to retailers, and also to make sure that the records – and the newer CD format - were pressed up and ready for distribution to those who had ordered them. The role of label manager was crucial if both Rough Trade and the independent labels themselves wanted to keep the blood flowing, and it appears that, by this time, the label manager looking after KLF Communications for Rough Trade Distribution was Sallie Fellowes.

By all accounts, Fellowes' approach to any task at hand was no-nonsense, and she got things done. "She was just forceful," recalls one former Rough Trade employee who worked with her at this time. Drummond would likely go to see her on a regular basis to discuss upcoming releases, as well as dropping in on the Rough Trade accounts department to chase up any payments due – or overdue knowing how accounts departments work - to KLF Communications. "Bill used to come in and sit in reception and be really chatty," recalls Andrew Lee, who also worked at Rough Trade at the time, "and gave me a couple of T shirts and things." Drummond would also, on occasion, use a Rough Trade photocopier to run off KLF Information Sheets and other paperwork.

Lee had come to work at Rough Trade in 1989 as he'd been a Smiths fan, but he was also partial to The KLF, "Do you remember all of those fictitious releases that never got released, like *Turn Up The Strobe* and stuff like that? There were spaces for them. There were racks of shelving with 12" singles on them, and I used to go around and flick through them - there was no security or anything, you could wander around and people used to steal loads, it was terrible. I remember seeing all these plastic dividers all racked up against each other, and there were loads of (KLF) releases with no vinyl. I think the reason that stuff didn't get released was because they didn't have any money. I don't think it was intentional. I don't think it was anything majorly artistic. One, I don't think they ever had their shit together, and two, they never had any money at certain times. So there was nothing mysterious. They'd just run out of lines of credit."

Drummond liked strong-minded women, and at some point became romantically involved with Sallie Fellowes. That he was married at this time would lead to consequences outside of the remit of this book, but Fellowes later became his new partner. Their close working relationship at this time meant, on a professional level, that Fellowes not only worked hard on the KLF account at Rough Trade Distribution but began to take a hand in the growing business surrounding KLF Communications outside of her core role. She also began to be weaved into the growing JAMS/KLF mythology as "Distribution Girl", featuring on a number of press releases, one assumes, penned by Drummond as something of an 'in joke' between them.

By 1990, as KLF Communications began to pick up a head of steam, more and more of Fellowes' time and attention would be spent working with The KLF as they began to ascend to a level that would eventually put them in the same league as the Pet Shops Boys, Kylie Minogue and Jason Donovan.

The gateway to this transformation in their fortunes had its genesis in a 'sleeper' that Drummond and Cauty had originally recorded and released in 1988. In her review of *Kylie Said To Jason* in the *New Musical Express* Helen Mead had stroked the first reissue of this track stating that they were, "aiming to teach Kevin Saunderson (of Inner City) a new definition of the good life."

From 1990 onwards there would be no more sadness and only gladness for the duo as they asked the world one simple question...

What Time Is Love?

WHAT TIME IS LOVE?

"'Ride On Time' by Black Box might have been the ultimate record of the '80s, but as soon as its creators were expected to build an act around their almost perfect creation and we could watch them on 'Top Of The Pops' and read what they had to say in 'Smash Hits' it all sank to the level of 'Opportunity Knocks.'"
- Bill Drummond writing in Select, September 1990

"What is clear, is that there is some sort of musical convergence going on. From Chicago to Chippenham, people are discovering the joys of abusing technology, electrical distortion and the ripping of circuits. Necessarily, given the different cultural backgrounds involved, there are already various approaches to acid house evolving."
- Jack Barron, New Musical Express, July 1988

What Time Is Love? is one of the cornerstones upon which the reputation of The KLF rests and, in its reworked, *Live At Trancentral* guise, the song that saw them break into the mainstream in 1990. Whilst everything that Drummond and Cauty had recorded and released before this had merit and bore flashes of downright genius, it was this track that seared their music into the minds of a generation and, like The Timelords before them, sent The KLF towards the top of the singles charts.

The first KLF Communications Information Sheet of 1988 had stated that, "we might put out a couple of 12" records under the name The KLF. These will be rap free, just pure dance music, so don't expect to see them reviewed in the music papers," and, in an interview with *Sounds* in February 1988, Cauty could not resist dropping a hint -"Not something for music papers to write about — a pure sex groove is the idea" - and stating that they would be "coming out on KLF."

At this time, the acronym KLF was best known as the name of their record label, KLF Communications, and it remained flexible as to what the initials stood for, with the Kopyright Liberation Front being best known, especially given the connection to their widespread sampling activities as The Justified Ancients Of Mu Mu. But that was another band and another musical universe a long, long time ago, and Drummond and Cauty had admitted when pronouncing The JAMs dead early in 1988 that, "We're getting into a bit of acid house." Cauty also told the *Sounds* journalist, "so next week we're going to do a song on acid."

Acid house sprang up under the noses of the established British music press. Reading through back issues of the *New Musical Express, Sounds, Melody Maker* and even *Record Mirror,* it's amazing to see how little coverage this exciting and vibrant underground movement was initially given. At the time, bands like Simple Minds, New Order, U2, The Mission and Morrissey had page after page devoted to their every utterance, from set piece interviews and fulsome reviews to on-tour extravaganzas, and this was, in many respects, the job of music journalists – after all, these were successful rock bands backed by major labels who paid a lot of money to advertise their records in the pages of those publications. But, looking back today, the years 1986 and 1987 were almost a return to the positions of 1976 and 1977, when punk and the new wave had to work hard to muscle out pages devoted to established bands like Genesis, The Who and Status Quo. "Punk taught kids that they didn't need to be a virtuoso to make great music," Douglas Hart of The Jesus And Mary Chain, who also began operating as the Acid Angels, told the *New Musical Express,* "A couple of chords was enough. Now you don't even need that skill, just the ability to push a few buttons on cheap samplers, synths and drum machines."

Acid house was a movement that grew organically out of Chicago house and Detroit techno, and which operated mostly under the radar of the music press, but these strands of dance music soon generated an entire DIY industry of record labels, clubs and promoters, and a slow infusion of crossover hits. In many respects, acid house *was* a throwback to punk, but in a danceable form. Not only did clubs up and down the country begin playing the music, but larger DIY raves began to be held in unlikely locations - a field, an abandoned warehouse or anywhere else you could get the electricity to power the decks and some lights. At a time when mobile phones, texting, and social media didn't exist, individual promoters pulled together to throw pre-planned or ad-hoc parties and raves where, once the music got pumping, participants would dance the night away. Many began taking the drug ecstasy, and many didn't, but everybody had a great time.

Washing Machine, recorded by Larry Heard as Mr. Fingers in

1986, and Phuture's *Acid Tracks,* produced by Marshall Jefferson in 1987, were crucial signposts towards this new land, as was the house-tooled *Promised Land* by Joe Smooth, a track issued Stateside in 1987 and released in the UK in 1988. There was even *Jack The Tab*, an LP recorded in a weekend by Genesis P. Orridge and friends and attributed to a number of pseudonyms that imagined what acid house might sound like. "It was done before we'd gone to any of the clubs or heard any of the music," recalls participant Richard Norris, who later went on to form The Grid, "It was better that we didn't hear the music as we just made up what we thought it might sound like." Recorded in 1987, the album was issued in 1988.

A growing number of 'proper' acid house 12" singles began to emerge that were more representative. Baby Ford's *Oochy Koocky* was seminal as it took inspiration from Chicago house but gave the music a particularly elastic UK flavor. Beats Workin's *Sure Beats Workin'* – which took liberties with the *Old Grey Whistle* test theme - was also crucial as mastermind Nicky Holloway had links to Special Branch DJs and the Balaeric beat scene in Ibiza, which played a vital part in the emerging UK dance scene. "It started for me as, "Let's make a club record"" Holloway told the *New Musical Express* in July 1988, "and what happened was that it turned out to be such a catchy record that it's turned into something else. We were all saying, let's do it for a laugh, but deep down there was a little glimmer of hope that wouldn't it be great if we could crack it as well."

One of the signatures of acid house was elastic, synthesised bass taken from the Roland TB-303, along with drum patterns taken from the Roland TR-808 drum machine; just like house music and techno, in fact, but with its own particular flavour. Crucially it was mostly instrumental.

There were, of course, plenty of shit raves and shit tracks, but there were also fantastic raves and fantastic records, and by 1988 this was becoming a cultural movement and a way of life for many who just wanted to go out and have a good time, hear music and dance. At one point, even *The Sun* newspaper jumped on board, supporting this new youth movement and offering their own acid-themed t-shirt to their readers. Had they heard that a segment of those going to raves were football fans and decided to tap into the demographic of their back page readership? Of course, they soon reverted to type with hysterical, heavy handed reporting on the dangers of ecstasy and the disorderly conduct at some illegal raves up and down the country. To be fair, a number of other national papers followed suit - it was *The Filth and The Fury* all over again.

Many of the acts making the early records that became hot tunes on the acid house scene were faceless, as the medium of the movement was a 12" single. A label or an artist might release just one or two records, many of which were simple 12" white labels, which were cheap to press as you didn't have to worry about printing sleeves or labels. You just wrote the name of the track, the artist or the band on the white label - or you didn't even bother. Many of these records would go to DJs or straight into record shops, although, as the movement grew, distributors like Pinnacle and Rough Trade began to shift serious numbers of units as they discovered that fans of house, techno and acid house were like any other music fans - if they heard a track they liked when they were out, and they could remember what it was called and whom it was by, they would go out and buy it. Therefore, companies that serviced DJs with white label promos or finished records and got them played in clubs became an important part of the scene. The phuture was here, and some acts began to chart - D-Mob's rather obvious *We Call It Acieed* anthem went top five in October 1988, but a press backlash around this time hurt other records as the BBC put a playlist ban on anything that was felt to promote drug use. One of the records that suffered from this backlash was The Moody Boys' *Acid Rappin'*.

Like a lot of acts making dance records at this time, the line-up of The Moody Boys was somewhat elastic, and those involved were also putting out records on other labels under different names. It was a good way to get your music out there, and also to get some money from different labels who were all looking for records to release and were happy to pay for them. One of the core members of The Moody Boys was Tony Thorpe, who was also involved in the tail end of the career of industrial pioneers 400 Blows. The band were not only making the transition to dance but putting out records by other artists on their own Warrior Records.

"I was at this flat in Penge and Tony came to live there," recalls Nigel Laybourne, "He was a friend of somebody else who used to live there, and when they moved out he moved in." At this time, Laybourne had taught himself to program early MIDI equipment and drum machines and gotten a job as an engineer in a studio in Bromley. "When he found out that we had similar interests – because he was in 400 Blows at that point – and he saw what I could do he thought he could employ that somehow. He was coming around to my place and we were working out stuff - he was trying to get stuff done, just demos and what have you on the side." Thorpe had eclectic tastes that ranged from bands like The Clash to soul and dance music, and the music that he made reflected the open door policy in his imagination.

By this time, Laybourne had also acquired a piece of equipment that was going to become an essential tool in the armory of anyone serious about making acid house music. "I remember the day my TB-303 turned up in the post. Somebody had been selling it in a classified ad for £65. You know how much they are now? £700 if you want to buy one. It was a piece of technology that was going out of date, and I remember holding it up and going, "Look what I've got!" Then laughing at the cheesiness of it. One year later it was *the* most wanted piece of equipment. It's the thing that gives you those *classic* acid basslines."

One of Laybourne's early collaborations with Thorpe was issued under the name House Addicts, and he also worked as Cultural Thugs. "The reason it's confusing," he laughs, "is that there was a lot of pseudonyms being used." As for the name of the Moody Boys, this was an inside joke, "if you saw the initials you can see it was a bit of a pun," states Laybourne, "Because we were called R and B, that's *Are* Moody and *Be* Moody. It is just a little play on words." Thorpe also deployed his knowledge of the growing scene to compile the *Acid Beats 1* and *Acid House Volume 1* compilation LPs issued on Warrior and BPM Records in 1988.

When it came to *Acid Rappin'*, Laybourne recalls that the original premise was to put a rap over a house beat – hence the title – and the vocals were added by the duo Rhyme and Reason. It was, however, the B-side that became better known on the club circuit, a track called *Acid Heaven*. "Basically, I demoed *Acid Heaven* – the music was my idea and my drum patterns and he (Tony) heard that and said, 'Let's do that in the studio. I want to use that.' So that was something I'd done and it got used." Indeed it did, and what made the driving track so memorable was not just the squelchy TB-303 bassline but the spoken word samples spread over the top. "There was a documentary on the television about Route 66," recalls Laybourne, "which is where loads of those samples come from; all those preachers and the guy juggling the chainsaw at the beginning. It was pretty much all from the same documentary I think."

It was Thorpe who did the deal with Citybeat to release these tracks as The Moody Boys, and there were hopes that the record would chart. "The single features the talents of London rap duo Rhyme & Reason, who have recently enjoyed television exposure on both LWT's *House Party* and *The Bill*," gushed a press release which concluded, "this is a sure track to take a new generation of sound to national recognition… ACIEEEED!!"

But, as we've seen, there was an inconvenient backlash against any record with acid in the title at the time. "We were slightly behind Danny D's record, *(We Call it) Acieed*," recalls Laybourne. "He rose up into the charts and ours rose up to about sixty or something and suddenly the establishment went, 'This terrible thing!' and that was the end of it. It might have charted and all this would have been history, but they put the barricades up and the BBC were not being compliant with that sort of thing any more. We were just that fraction behind Danny D, and he got in the charts and we didn't. And there'd be no chance of anyone getting into the charts mentioning acid after that."

That said, The Moody Boys did issue a follow-up called *First National Rapper*, then moved to XL to issue the seminal *Funky Zulu (You're So Fresh)* in 1990, on which Jimmy Cauty apparently added some guitar feedback. "I think that's the only act that was already signed to Citybeat when I started working as club promo manager there that was transferred to XL when Tim Palmer got it up and running," recalls Nick Halkes who co-founded the label. "My vision for XL was very much about credible underground music and not about chasing pop success, and *Funky Zulu* was essentially that – a cool, rock solid club track that was getting played by all the key guys. Tony Thorpe would pop into the office reasonably regularly – we had a little basement then with no windows and just Tim and I in there."

Thorpe was also regularly popping down to Stockwell to see Cauty at BENIO either alone or with Laybourne, who once recalled seeing that, "the whole front of the house had collapsed – they woke up one morning and they could see out of the bedroom!" It was, however, around this time that Laybourne grew disenchanted with the acid house movement and stopped working with Thorpe, "It seemed like the openness and room to experiment was completely gone within six months. Once it started charting it became a race to get in with big business and things like that, whereas when it was an underground thing it was much more open to experimentation… It was not my idea of fun, doing something because everybody else was doing it at that moment." Laybourne began working with UK hip-hop artists and became famous as No Sleep Nigel. "That name was given to me by Sparki and MC Mell O. They said, 'we have a name for you', and put it on their record *Comin' Correct* (1989). That's where it all began."

As for Tony Thorpe – also involved in *Comin' Correct* - he too had no interest in riding on the same bandwagon as everybody else. "Music is about ideas and songs," he told the *Melody Maker* around this time, "it's a form of relaxation and entertainment. That's all it should be. The problem now is that it's got to the stage where it's all about money and shifting units and that's pretty sad." Even at this stage, he felt that the entire acid house genre was too much of a trend, "As far as I'm concerned the whole thing's just stagnated. It's only going in one direction and not branching out enough. It really fucks me off sometimes, I wish people would use their initiative and do something of their own. I blame technology and drugs – technology for making it easy to make records and E for making people think that crap records are good."

Thorpe continued to make records as The Moody Boys, and under a number of other names, as he moved towards eventually working with Bill Drummond and Jimmy Cauty, both of whom were also interested in the rave and acid house scene - Drummond to a more limited extent as he preferred walks in the county rather that driving to a field to dance. It was Cauty who went down to Shoom to check out that scene, and he also organically began making ambient music as The Orb with Alex Paterson around this time. Despite being in their mid-30s, both Drummond and Cauty also dipped their toes into the chemical waters of rave. It's now part of KLF folklore that, when Drummond once asked Cauty "What Time Is Love?", he was not consciously trying to name the first KLF anthem but asking when the ecstasy they'd both ingested was going to kick in. The question itself gave the answer.

"It was the first thing we did on the new gear we bought with the Timelords money," Drummond told *Making Music* in December 1990 when discussing the first manifestation of *What Time Is Love?* "It was just another riff," added Cauty, "only three notes, you know." This first incarnation was instrumental, and part of a plan to, "do a single a week for five weeks, pressing 2,000 of each," as a chuckling Drummond revealed in another interview, but "Then after *What Time Is Love?* we spent three months trying to write the next one."

What Time Is Love? was first issued as a KLF 12" in October 1988. There was no video and no Timelords-type fanfare. Billed as the first in series of "Pure Trace" records, unlike many acid house tracks it wasn't just a white label but was housed in an arresting sleeve. Later there were 12" KLF records housed in equally arresting black and white 12" die-cut sleeves, of which Drummond had ordered in the region of five thousand, probably to take advantage of a good printing deal. The duo was, consciously or otherwise, actually beginning to transform The KLF into a brand.

Then something happened. Something unexpected. *What Time Is Love?* began to ripple outwards and became an underground favourite, not only in the UK but in Europe. The momentum built up a head of steam at a time when Drummond and Cauty had just enjoyed their success as The Timelords and then blown all of the money funding the early stages of *The White Room* film project. At a difficult time, when they were once again in serious financial difficulties - Drummond's house was apparently under threat of repossession and Cauty was being chased for Poll Tax arrears on BENIO - *What Time Is Love?* began to generate much needed cash flow.

"Then an order for 2,000 copies arrived from an ITALIAN importer," stated a 1990 KLF Information Sheet. "How and why, they had no idea. Every day there were more and more orders coming in from across EUROPE. By June 1989 the track was beginning to be played in 'certain' clubs and on the pirate radio stations in and around LONDON.

The KLF were being feted by all the 'right' DJs." The KLF were on their surfboards at a time when the perfect wave was arriving.

The original, Pure Trance version of *What Time Is Love?* is a classic, based around a hypnotic Oberheim OB-8 synth line and a cool and seductive, slowly building electronic pulse. There were no vocals. As they'd deleted the original version in January 1989, Cauty and Drummond remixed *What Time Is Love?* as *The Primal Mix* and pushed it out again through Rough Trade Distribution, with the original mix on the flip. One thing that helped turn the track into magic may have been Cauty's playback setup at Trancentral. Rolo McGinty recalls that, "what Jimmy was doing was that he was writing his stuff and listening to it not on bass bins but club speakers. Most of us, what we do is have the Gelelec or the Yamaha (studio monitors), but he had a miniature club PA, so he got to hear how it sounded on that."

In many respects *What Time Is Love?* was enjoying a similar trajectory to the track *Flesh* by Belgian Electric Body Music act A Split-Second, with which it shared some similarities in style and arrangement. This cut had originally appeared in 1986 as the last cut on a four-track EP that played at 45rpm, but it was soon noted that the hypnotic, trance-like track sounded better when played at a speed slightly above 33rpm, which started going down well in clubs. It was remixed and retooled and issued as a 12" across Europe between 1988 and 1991 and became a club favourite, although it never had the legs to get into the charts in the UK.

That *What Time Is Love?* was something particularly special became evident when Drummond and Cauty were alerted to the fact that DJs were not only playing it hard in clubs, but people had also recorded cover versions, or taken the instrumental original and put vocals over the top to create a new track. Other artists were doing to The KLF what The Justified Ancients Of Mu Mu had done themselves, but this musical call and response was not played out in the music press or in the legal ledgers of the MCPS, but in clubs across Europe and the UK. Ironically, a duo that had started their career freely sampling others was now being pilfered themselves - Tony Thorpe was right on the money when he told the *Melody Maker* that, "a good tune comes out and for the next three months the market's flooded with rip-offs trying to copy the formula. It's all use it, abuse it and milk it." In fact, at one time The KLF were one of the most bootlegged artists in the UK as a market developed for illegally pressed records on the dance market, records that might sell anywhere between five hundred and two thousand copies as 12" white labels. Not that the British Phonographic Industry was too bothered, "It is a very difficult area to investigate," Derek Varnals of their anti-piracy unit told *Music Week*, "we don't waste our resources by scouring record shops and paying £10 or £20 a time for white labels."

In a brilliant display of musical judo, Drummond and Cauty responded to the pilfering of their material by issuing a mini-LP themselves called *The What Time Is Love Story,* pulling together some of these purloined tracks, like Dr. Felix's *Relax Your Body*, Neon's *No Limit* and Liaisons D's *Heartbeat*. "The next release will be JAMS LP4 - THE WHAT TIME IS LOVE STORY (25th Sept)," wrote Cressida in the KLF Information Sheet of Aug/Sept 1989, "This is a six-track, forty minute mid-price LP. It's a sample of some of the illegal (it's in their karma) cover versions of everybody's favourite arm-waving-in-the-lasers track, that have been popping up all over Europe this year." The original 12" version of *What Time Is Love?* was also included on the LP, as it was, by now, deleted. The KLF also slipped out a new track as the second part of the Pure Trance series called *3AM Eternal...*

Drummond and Cauty also began to assert their rights over *What Time Is Love?* through a small number of 'live' appearances. These were, of course, not concerts in the traditional sense but promotional activity in dance clubs, where an artist might appear briefly to sing a couple of numbers to a backing track. Indeed, the *What Time Is Love* LP contained a version of the song 'performed' by The KLF at the Land Of Oz on 31st July 1989. This 'live appearance' had been a fifteen-minute extended meditation on *What Time Is Love?,* and to make it memorable, polystyrene balls were blown out into the crowd by a wind machine. "At the time they had to do a gig in Heaven me and Alex Paterson from The Orb were basically the sound guys for that gig," recalls Nigel Laybourne. It appears Drummond and Cauty played a pre-recorded DAT rather than live instruments, although they may have mixed in some samples during the performance. "It was pre-recorded tracks," recalls Laybourne, "to be honest they could have walked out to the hall in the soundcheck to know what they asked me to tell them. Still, a soundman's job is like a St John's Ambulance man - there in case of an accident or problem, not to give a medical to everybody that enters."

The duo also did a brief set at The Academy in Brixton, as well as another outing on 30th September when The KLF 'performed' at an open air "dance music spectacular" in Chipping Norton, organised by Helter Skelter. This was a massive affair, complete with car park, medical staff, chillout café and even a craft fair. It was, in many respects, a rock festival approached from a dance perspective, but rather than kicking off during the day it started in the evening and ran all night. There were a number of other acts appearing that night, including Jolly Roger (UK DJ Eddie Richards) whose *Acid Man* was a big underground track at the time, and even ex-Frankie Goes To Hollywood singer Paul Rutherford appeared, trying to kick start a dance career. There were also several sound systems spread around, so the thousands who attended could sample sets from a number of DJs.

As for The KLF, they appeared on top of a narrow thirty-foot tower with a synthesizer slung over the side and played a pre-recorded, extended mix of *What Time Is Love?* and *3AM Eternal* before distributing £1,000 into the crowd. "When we were asked to do the party, we understood it was going to be £15 to get in," Drummond later explained to *I-D* magazine, "They ended up charging £25 which we thought was such a shitty rip-off that we decided to throw the money away as a sort of statement. We wrote 'Children, we love you' on each one, crumpled them up and then threw them down. But even then, as soon as we'd thrown it all away, the people down the front were shouting, 'We want more money, we want more money.'"

One of those – but not shouting - was Mark Darby, who worked at Blast-First records and had driven down specifically to see The KLF. He recalls that, "I was somewhere right down the front and did get a couple of quid." After The KLF had finished, he and his mates went back to their car and drove off to Reigate to sneak into the massive *Phantasy* rave that was going on down there at the same time. Another who saw The KLF at Chipping Norton was Rolo McGinty - as he lived in South London, he often went over to BENIO to see Drummond and Cauty, say hello and see what they were up to. At one time he recalls seeing a massive oil painting laid out on the Trancentral mixing desk, which Cauty told him was part of an *Illuminatus* themed triptych. The other two were screwed to the ceiling above them.

McGinty also vividly recalls The KLF's appearance at Helter Skelter. "I remember *What Time Is Love?* kicking off after some kind of intro. There was smoke, and at one point Bill seemed to be chucking money out to people. It was – I think – comedy money. I believe I picked a note up. There was a crowd around their area - I thought they'd done OK to have that many people, because the choice of places to party was pretty wide. The KLF weren't a big hit yet, so it was funny to watch them in this bizarre country place." As for how the audience reacted to the music, McGinty recalls, "It was more something you watched than got in the middle of the crowd. There was plenty of jumping around, but they'd stop at the ambient bits then start up again when the beat came back. It was more performance art."

Whilst The KLF's performance was intriguing, the real highlight came later when a tour bus rolled into the venue in the small hours of the morning and disgorged some American acts like Two In A Room, The Minutemen and Loleatta Holloway. "Black Box were number one in the charts with their sampled up, cheesy version of *Love Sensation*," recalls McGinty, "Loleatta Holloway said, 'Well, you all know the records

Number One right now, you know the video with… *the girl!* Now it's time to ditch the bitch and do the real thing!' Very funny, but then she let out a "'Waah hoh!' (one of the famous purloined parts from the Black Box single) that felt like it blew you all the way to Banbury. This messy lady, all half-dressed for the stage, had the most powerful foghorn of a voice I'd ever heard. She sang over a backing tape and it was one of the best things I've ever seen to this day. She just killed us all." This was a performance, rather than performance art.

Although *What Time Is Love?* had had already been remixed and retooled, with money coming in from healthy 12" sales a decision was made to upgrade it again in 1990. In some respects it was at this point that Drummond and Cauty began - consciously or otherwise - to deploy the lessons they'd learned during their brief relationship with Pete Waterman and his PWL team and apply them to their own singles, especially after their Pet Shop Boys pastiche *Kylie Said To Jason* had failed to detonate. Whatever was going on in the dance or rock scenes since they'd failed with Brilliant back in 1986, Waterman's team had gone on to deliver a remarkable succession of hit pop singles and albums, spreading them across a broad raft of artists including Kylie Minogue, Rick Astley and Samantha Fox (who had been sampled on the first JAMs 12"). PWL were not only independent producers but also had their own record label to boot. As an operation they were not a million miles from The KLF, just millions of pounds richer.

To do full justice to *What Time Is Love?* - to give it the full PWL treatment and aim it at the charts - it needed the one thing the original did not have….. vocals. Drummond was not going to do it, so who were they going to use?

Over in Fulham, South London, another two-man team were beginning to make a name for themselves in a totally different scene. The Outlaw Posse comprised of Azat Bello and his best friend Karl Gordon. Bello believes that their early career was helped as he was fortunate to have lived in the South Bronx in New York when he was ten or eleven - not only did his older brother bring records home and play them, but hip-hop artists would set up and play in the local park, "so I was hearing all of these dope tracks like The Funky Four Plus One and the Treacherous Three and The Furious Five. I was listening to the guys who started it." Returning to England, it was back to school, where he eventually met up with Karl Gordon. "We were classmates, and then one day he was like, 'Check this tune out,' on his headphones, 'I made beats!' I said, 'I've got raps'. I wouldn't say we were great - we would make demos and they were just for us - but we made music. We weren't like, we can get a deal out of this, but we were making songs in the most basic format, with a 303, an

808 and two turntables from what I can remember. He (Karl) used to mix it on tape."

Gordon had already been broadcasting as a DJ on pirate radio in south London, and his father ran a record shop. He worked behind the counter for a while, so had access to a broad range of black music, from soul to funk and beyond, which he used as source material for the beats and music he created for Bello to rap over. Things took a step forward when Bello plucked up the courage to 'drop a verse' over a beat at a club for the first time. "Little things like that give you confidence later on when you have to perform live," he believes, "the first couple of gigs we did as Outlaw Posse were just to get that experience of working with a crowd and, once we got over that hurdle it was like it was meant to be! I used to feed off performing live." By the time they were both eighteen years old things began to happen for the Outlaw Posse.

Crucially, DJ Ritchie Rich, who was co-owner of Gee Street Records, heard one of their demos and put them in the studio for a day. He then issued their first 12", *Party* backed with *Outlaws In Effect,* at the end of 1988, and their second 12", *Original Dope*, was released in October 1989 and became their breakthrough record on the UK hip-hop scene. "A pulsating dance beat shot through with a haunting melodic flute break that is perfectly balanced by MC BELLOWs (sic) quirky and querying vocals," gushed the Gee Street press release. *Original Dope* was a fantastic record and got Outlaw Posse a lot of attention on the hip-hop underground. With an album in the works they began to tour. "We played all over the country, man. Played to anyone who was into the music at that time. It was wicked."

It was probably *Original Dope* that caught the ears of Drummond, Cauty or Tony Thorpe, who was now beginning to work with The KLF in the studio and helping to provide beats and breaks for their tracks. Whoever heard it, they liked what they heard and thought that Bello would be the ideal person to rap on the new version of *What Time Is Love?* "They went directly through to my management and said, 'Would you be interested in doing this?'" Bello recalls today. "We were working in Gee Street studios, maybe we were doing a remix of *Original Dope*. I think someone brought in a tape – that's how long ago it was, they brought it on a *tape*! - and they played me the instrumental. We all listened to it and I got it straight away, but most of the other people in the room - because we did hip-hop and that's our shit - most of the people in the room were like 'No, man!' There was no reaction to the track! You know what I'm saying? There was *no* reaction! But I was like, 'No - this is *different.'*"

Bello was interested. "You have to remember that I had so many influences, reggae, rare groove and hip-hop, so why not acid house?"

Bello first met Cauty and Drummond at BENIO in Stockwell, and even today can recall how unusual the place was. "I used to go down to the house, the squat. It was raw," he laughs, "When you went in that crib, it was like…. you knew you were in a creative person's house – let's just put it that way! I probably didn't even make it to the toilet. It was raw, that's the only way to describe it."

BENIO always provoked a reaction from those who first visited it. Nick Coler recalls that you could go to the toilet on one floor and look into the kitchen. Most of the internal walls had been removed on the ground floor, with the walls supported by agro props. When a BBC TV crew was setting up lights for an interview with Drummond and Cauty, one of the electricians thought that the living room was a film set and mistook Cauty for one of the film crew, "What time you knocking off, here mate?" Cauty was suitably offended, "This is my house!"

When it came to recording, things were straightforward, "We used to go down there and Jimmy would be working on the music and had all of this equipment - it was quite cool. There would be Jimmy, his wife Cressida, Bill and another guy who used to come in called Tony Thorpe, who used to do all the beats. He used to come in with breaks and stuff." As for the subject matter for Bello's contribution, "they would just fling words at me. This is what we are about - 3AM, Mu Mu, Ancients of Mu Mu and all this stuff. I thought, this is crazy, but as long as you say these words and just do your thing it'll be cool. They gave me the freedom to express myself, and that was it, man. It was a match made in heaven." So Bello got to work, came up with a rap and got to recording. As for the music over which he flowed, Cauty, Drummond and their emerging 'Children Of The Revolution' team had completely rebuilt the song. "*What Time Is Love?* was (re)made from scratch," recalls Nick Coler, who was also involved in the re-recording, "although we used a sample of Jimmy's Oberheim 8 with a delay line as it was just one of those sounds you were not going to see again. So that was the only thing that existed off that." Although Bello's rap was the core vocal, and the "Mu Mu" chants that had originally been recorded at Village Recorders in Dagenham were added the song, *What Time Is Love?* was given a memorable hook when they took a sample from a 12" called *To The Bone* by an American artist named Wanda Dee.

To The Bone was only issued in the US, on Tuff Records, and was only available on import, although ironically her debut single, *Blue Eyes*, *had* been issued in the UK in 1987 as it was a Stock, Aitken and Waterman production! The specific sample taken from *To The Bone* was the powerful vocal refrain "I wanna see you sweat," which was soon to become as memorable as Snap's "I've got the power", Black Box's "Ride On Time" and Nomad's "I wanna give you devotion".

As we've seen, the main vocal hook on *Ride On Time* was a sample taken from Loleatta Holloway's 1980 track *Love Sensation*. Things got very muddy there as Black Box was the creation of Italian DJ Daniele Davoli, who released the original on the Out label in Italy and later licensed it in the UK to Deconstruction, where it became a massive hit, spending five weeks at Number One between 9th September and 14th October 1989. It became a massive hit across Europe too, and a game of musical legal chairs commenced. Holloway gave an interview to the *New Musical Express* wherein she broke down in tears over what had happened, "I told them. 'OK if you want to say Black Box did the song and act as if they did, then let me go on TV and do the song and eventually people will know that I did it. But don't throw me out of the back door and say, 'Bitch, you ain't getting anything.'""

In fact, Holloway was the victim of a new form of accounting torture being deployed by record companies. When discussing the issue, Deconstruction boss Pete Hadfield told the *New Musical Express* that "Deconstruction and its distributing company RCA have been in negotiation with Salsoul Records (who owned the rights to *Love Sensation*) and Loleatta's legal representative to determine royalty compensation for this sample." But paying Salsoul wouldn't help Holloway as, according to Hadfield, "Loleatta is unrecouped at Salsoul," which basically meant that she had not yet earned back advance payments made to her, and Salsoul would keep any money that they received for the Black Box recording and not pass it onto her, despite her voice being the driving force behind a massive hit.

"Sampling as a technique is common to *all* dance records," stated Hadfield, "Unfortunately the copyright law as yet has not addressed the issue of sampling of records, therefore agreement of compensation is a lengthy discussion *every* time an issue like this arises." Eventually a deal was agreed that satisfied all parties, but the issue of legality and payment for samples was now centre stage due to the amount of money being generated by records that sampled other artists. Only Kraftwerk – sampled to death themselves – could take the moral high ground, "We sample our original sounds from twenty years ago," Ralf Hutter told the *Melody Maker* in 1991, "but in a subtle way, not the silly way in which it is done today, with all this montage of old records." But creating these "montages" was already an art form - The S-Express hit *Theme From S-Express,* for example, went to number one as early as May 1988 and was an amazing confection assembled by DJ Mark Moore which remains a classic. The memorable vocal refrain, "I've got the hots for you" was taken from a 1983 single by TZ, horn lines and other parts were taken from Rolls Royce's *Is It Love You're After* (1979) and even "Drop that ghetto blaster" came from an early 1988 house record called

Lick It by Karen Finley. Other samples included Debbie Harry from Blondie but the kernel of the song was Moore's ability to mix and blend music this together to create something new that was, and remains, a compulsive listening experience.

As for *What Time Is Love?,* Wanda Dee's contribution was soon to become another ABBA moment for Drummond and Cauty - although they credited Dee on the record they had not *cleared* the sample.

The opening of *What Time Is Love? (Live At Trancentral)* was also something of a nod to The Justified Ancients Of Mu Mu and the duo's past, sampling the MC5 and their "Kick out the Jams, motherfucker" refrain again, as well as adding crowd noise to give the impression that this house track was being served up live to a massive stadium audience. "This version is everything the original wasn't", stated a KLF Communications press release, "The original was all this could never be. Whether it is a chart bound sound or just another document in the unfolding KLF story is for someone else to decide." The single was released on 16th July 1990, around the same time that the ambient *Space* LP – more of which later - was also released. Both records capture the ambition, scope and groundbreaking nature of the Drummond and Cauty partnership, but of course, whilst the *Space* LP got good reviews and garnered reasonable sales, *What Time Is Love?* exploded like a supernova.

What Time Is Love? was mastered, cut and scheduled for release, and Rough Trade worked hard to pre-sell it to retailers. Scott Piering also pummeled the eyes and ears of radio and TV stations before the single came out, and generated his own press release: "The KLF realised that it was only a matter of time before somebody came up with the ultimate cover, which would at last bring this classic track to the attention of the mainstream. So, in typical KLF style, they decided to cover their own track!"

Piering knew this was going to be a hit, and stated that, "the pre-release demand for this record is huge" and enthused that the band was also available for interview and a video was being shot to promote the record. "With the charts and radio so willing to accommodate the likes of Snap's *The Power*, 808 State and MC Tunes, LFO and Tricky Disco, *What Time Is Love?* should now deservedly find its final resting place in the national top forty." Clearly, as it had already been an underground hit on the club scene, it was just a question of how high the track would climb in the single charts.

Around this time, Sallie Fellowes left her position as a Label Manager at Rough Trade Distribution and went to work for Scott Piering. "Sallie went to work for Scott as his TV booker," recalls Andrew Lee, who was still working at Rough Trade Distribution at the time, "but the deal was that she was going to work half for The KLF and half for Scott, because everyone was looking for jobs when Rough Trade was going tits up." Rough Trade Distribution had, in the past, weathered many a storm and come out intact, but, as we will later see, problems the business began to experience in 1990 would later form the *perfect* storm, with consequences for both The KLF and the entire independent music business.

The fact that Fellowes went to work at Appearing and was to spend part of her time working for The KLF shows that they were beginning to reach critical mass - as well as helping to prepare *What Time Is Love?* for release in the UK there was also the matter of licensing it in Europe and other territories, where there was also significant demand. In some respects, with Piering also becoming a KLF insider his Collier Street office replaced BENIO as the unofficial management HQ of the project.

After contributing his rap, Bello forgot about *What Time Is Love?* and got back to his busy schedule with Outlaw Posse. "I remember one day, maybe three months after we did the tune, I was driving down the A40 - I don't even listen to Radio One but that day I was - I heard the guy say, 'Top thirty KLF!' I almost crashed my car - it was crazy. 'What? That tune I did months ago?' I'd completely forgotten about it, you know what I mean?"

Outlaw Posse planned to issue their delayed debut LP, *My Afro's on Fire,* in September 1990 and, along with around fifty other people, The KLF were thanked on the sleeve as the duo were keen to list their influences as well as their friends. Before the album was released, the band were the only UK hip hop act to play at the New Music Rap Showcase in New York (where they were up against acts like KRS-One) and Gee Street issued a new single called *II Damn Funky,* whose Press Release had to be amended to incorporate the fact that, "MC Bello B is the rapper on the KLF hit *What Time Is Love!*"

What Time Is Love? first entered the charts on 11th August 1990, going in at number thirty-four, and two weeks later it had climbed into the top twenty, making a KLF appearance on *Top Of The Pops* inevitable. The Timelords experience had shown that Cauty and Drummond had no qualms about appearing on this institution, and along with Cressida, who had a strong eye and hand in their look and presentation, they made sure that The KLF had a visual, as well as a musical, impact. Thus, on their first appearance to promote the single, the duo appeared on stage standing behind synthesisers and wearing black weather proof coats with the words 'IT'S GRIM UP NORTH' stenciled in white on the front. Bello stood in front of them, flanked by Tony Thorpe and Cressida, who mimed playing guitar synths with tremendous gusto. The most arresting part of this enthusiastic performance was the fact that Bello wore a massive afro wig and sunglasses.

"Whose idea was that?" he muses today. "I think it was Jimmy's wife Cressida. She came up with some stuff. I think maybe because our album was called *My Afro's On Fire* she may have got it from that - I don't know. I think it was quite cool. It was funny because I wore the afro and everyone still knew who the fuck I was. I thought it would disguise me, being on there with an afro, but as soon as I started dancing everyone was like, 'We know that's you Bello!' But coming from underground hip-hop to go on *Top Of The Pops,* it was great."

Following the *Top Of The Pops* appearance, Radio DJ and fellow publicity seeker Jonathan King stated on air on Radio One that he believed that the man doing the rapping was a white guy, blacked up wearing a wig. "It's all a big hoax," he told the *Record Mirror*, "and everyone's in on it - even the people on *Top Of The Pops.*" By this time King had actually met Bello, who, alerted to the article, ran down to Radio One to confront King, and "to prove my blackness." He stated in an interview at the time that, "It was the first time I'd had to do it and the whole thing was freaking me out. When I got there he just laughed back in my face and started rubbing my hand, asking me if it would wash off!" As you might imagine, Bello found this behavior somewhat bizarre, especially as King still insisted that he was "sticking to his story" and would write about it in his newspaper column. "I told him I didn't really think it was a good idea, but he insisted and told me that if I really was Bello then it would be good publicity."

The success of *What Time Is Love?* propelled The KLF further into the hearts of the music press, and even national newspapers. Whilst Drummond might pen a feature for *Select* on the state of the music industry - *The DJ Backlash Starts Here* - The KLF also gave interviews to magazines like *Smash Hits,* where he was keen to engage on a number of subjects, from his Big In Japan days to the name of the band. "The KLF? We change our minds all the time as to what it means. I should've known you were going to ask me that question and thought of something. I'll phone you if I think of something." The lyrics to *What Time Is Love?* were also reproduced in the magazine.

Of course, this being The KLF there had also been an attention-grabbing stunt shortly before release which was intended to play out across all parts of the media, namely the construction of a KLF themed pyramid blaster corn circle in Wiltshire. "It all started rather innocuously with us trying to find a way to promote our single," Drummond coyly told a *Record Mirror* journalist. "Our idea was to make a huge circle of our pyramid blaster logo and then willingly submit to the subsequent press storm." According to Drummond and Cauty, events didn't go as planned and someone – allegedly a KLF fan – beat them to the punch and made a circle in the same location they were planning to use. "The sickner for us," stated Cauty, "was that someone was thinking quicker than us. I don't like that."

This conversation took place in a car en-route to Wiltshire, where Drummond and Cauty were preparing to be photographed in the corn circle they created. "We don't have any pet theories about the circles, we don't know any more than anybody else. What we do know is the incredible feeling we had when we were making our own circle," stated Drummond, "It took us eleven hours in total to plan it out, make it and film it for the video from the air, and the feeling after we had done it was just incredible. Making it was just a compulsion and now we really do believe that we've been circling for years." John Michell had founded a magazine in 1990 called *The Cerealogist – The Journal For Crop Circle Studies,* and one wonders if the general interest in crop circles at the time might have served as inspiration for the field trip.

The duo became even more sought out by the music press, and were more than happy to oblige if the circumstances were right. So, for example, they helped review the singles in the *New Musical Express* on 1st September 1990. It was interesting that one of them was the *Rollercoaster* EP by The Jesus And Mary Chain - issued by Blanco Y Negro - considering that Drummond had been in the meeting where it was agreed to sign the band to the label. He was particularly taken by the Cocteau Twins *Iceblink Luck,* and sensed kindred spirits, "The Cocteau Twins are another band who've never given a fuck about what is happening around them. They just get on and do what they do and they seem to the (sic) getting better at it. Attitude matters just as much as music in most cases." When slating The Christians' *Green Bank Drive* he outdid Ian McCullogh of the Bunnymen, "The Christians are OK but they do deserve criticism for being the ultimate coffee-table band. As we speak, coffee-tables all over the country are waiting for this record. And the coffee-tables deserve everything they get." As for Cauty he had plenty of time for Primal Scream's *Come Together*, "That's the best dance record we've heard today. Much better than the ones in the charts already."

By the time *What Time Is Love?* peaked at number five in the charts in September, Drummond and Cauty were already getting ready to issue the follow-up and had already completed advance work on the track, which had got as far as a 12" promo that was sent out to journalists. Musically this material was totally different from their JAMs and Pure Trance output, and they cryptically called it "Turbo reality for the bleep generation." The information sheet sent out by Impact, who serviced club DJs and radio stations, invited those who received it to suggest possible titles from a list provided. It became known as *It's Grim Up North* - as we've seen, the title had even been pre-advertised on Drummond and Cauty's jackets during the first *Top Of The Pops* appearance for *What Time Is Love?*

"We went to this rave and the sound system was broken," Cauty told a journalist from *Record Mirror* around this time, and, "all you could hear was this kind of screeching top-end and a really low bass drum and we thought, 'Wow, this is what the kids are into.' *The Black Room* album will all be this kind of electro turbo metal. It's not really industrial like, say, Throbbing Gristle, because it's coming from house and has an uplifting vibe about it. But it is so heavy it will just pin you to the floor." It was revealing that, whilst there'd been talk in interviews and Information Sheets about an upcoming debut LP from The KLF, which would be the soundtrack to *The White Room* film, Cauty was already throwing out information about another LP - *The Black Room*. It was Ying and Yang.

The *It's Grim Up North* promo became one of the most collectable records in The KLF's canon, but there *is* an even more collectable version, due to a pressing error. The way this was created also showed that, when it came to the business side of The KLF, there was now a strong hand at the tiller. Andrew Lee had recently moved from Rough Trade to work with Appearing, "I was an office monkey there. I used to put the stickers on records and prepare releases. There were only four of us in the office and it was basically (to) support Scott." Of course, like any promotional business, Scott Piering offered different levels of service, ranging from sending out records to the right people to Piering going in to radio stations like the BBC or Capital Radio personally and talking directly to DJs and programme directors to get records onto their playlists. At this level, "you were paying for *Scott* time," as Lee puts it.

As you might imagine, a large number of test pressings and white label promos flowed in and out of the Appearing office, and, as Fellowes was partially running KLF Communications, a number of KLF test pressings would be part of that. "You remember when you're working in record companies, when the promos come in it's 'one for me and one for my mate?'" laughs Lee, "I was in Appearing on my own and this (courier) came in - it was the new KLF promo-only thing. It was the grey *It's Grim Up North*. I thought, I've got to listen to this, so I flipped open the box - no one else was in that afternoon - and listened to it. It was amazing. I thought, I love this, and still do to this day. A box of twenty five is usually actually twenty-seven or twenty-eight, so I took one out of each box - one for me, one for my mate...

"Sallie comes in about four o'clock. I said, 'These have turned up - have a listen, it's fucking phenomenal.' She gets one out of the bag, looks at it and goes ape-shit. Not at me, but because they were supposed to have (something) scrawled in the run out (groove). It's an un-labelled record, and there's supposed to be writing and they hadn't done it. She rings them up, and it was like the Alex Ferguson hairdryer. I just sat there cringing as she was going off at whoever had pressed them up. 'You've got one fucking job, this is a specialist release and you've fucked it up!' I sat there thinking, shit, I've got two of these in my bag. 'You get round here and pick them up and destroy them and do them properly - these are supposed to be out in promo tomorrow.' 'We can't get them done.' '*YOU WILL HAVE THEM DONE TOMORROW,*' and they were. They came and picked them up that night and they were all back the next day perfect - they must have worked through the night, and I'm thinking, shit, I'm not saying anything. I hope they don't miss a couple!"

However, although the repressed, one-sided grey *It's Grim Up North* 12" was sent out to journalists and DJs, Drummond and Cauty decided against making it their next release, preferring instead to re-tool the second Pure Trance release, *3AM Eternal*, in their new Stadium House style. Meanwhile, Sally Fellowes, for her part, took on the challenge of helping them widen their net to an international audience by working on licensing, until her work with The KLF began to dominate her working hours. "There was a time when Sallie got really busy, and she was doing much more KLF stuff than her TV plugging, so she left," recalls Lee. KLF Communications proceeded to set up their own small office in Brixton, run by Fellowes and a couple of assistants.

The original version of *3AM Eternal* featured the vocals of a singer called Maxine Harvey, who had become involved with music at an early age. "I've been singing since I was a little girl, when my parents got me up to sing on a coach when we were going to the seaside," she recalls today, "I was singing since school and bounced from one person to another, met Maxi Priest and did his tour and just went from one thing to the next really." The first record she appeared on was *Your Love Is Quality* by Interfaze, issued on the Positive Beat label in 1987. The label even shot a video to promote it, although the song failed to sell strongly.

Harvey can't recall how she showed up on the radar of The KLF, but believes it might have been when she was laying down a vocal track in a recording studio in Catford where Tony Thorpe heard her sing, "and it went from there." Where it went, in 1989, was into the studio with The KLF to work on the original version of *3AM Eternal*. Things were very relaxed when she first worked with Cauty and Drummond, "It was a vibe first, it was a vibe singing and then they asked me to sing something and that all went good. They said they liked my voice, we started on *3AM Eternal* and it went through its various stages... Jimmy would say, 'sing this' and I would sing it, then he would say, 'sing it like this,' and I would sing it. That's how *3AM Eternal* came."

As a young singer, Harvey was bouncing around the scene at the time, "I used to work with all different people, and didn't work with them (The KLF) exclusively. I was working on another album with Papa Levi, *The Lion Ain't Sleeping* (1990). I was just having fun and worked with whoever I wanted to." Indeed, part of this bouncing around actually involved Harvey getting behind the wheel as part of her early KLF session work at Village Recorders, "I remember when we used to have to go to Dagenham, everyone would pile into my old Ford and I had not passed my test." One imagines that, at this time, Ford Timelord was off the road, or couldn't get out of the garage after spending a night with a younger Volkswagen Polo.

When it came to recording the now iconic vocals for *3AM*, Maxine recalls that she *was* allowed to have some input. "I concentrated on melodies a lot. They had the bare bones of *3AM* and that's my melody - all my melodies, just not my lyrics - (sings) 'It's Three AM' – that's my melody." Harvey is keen to stress that she's not looking to take credit in retrospect, but continues, "They used to do that back in the day, you never got credited for melodies. You know what you're doing is something that you love and you are being creative and you don't mind giving away what you've created if it's going into a shape that's for everyone, which that was."

The original version of the track was issued in 1989, and, like the original version of *What Time Is Love?*, was aimed at dance clubs rather than the charts. Drummond and Cauty had 'played' a version at their appearance at Chipping Norton in September 1989, and although Harvey didn't appear with them that night she does recall another occasion when, "we did it in the middle of a field, way out somewhere. As you know, back in the day they used to have these raves in fields. Everybody just turned up - it was from about ten to four thirty and we were there all night. How can I forget that!"

Drummond and Cauty had no problem with the remix culture of the 12" market, and later in 1989 issued another 12" – *3AM Eternal: The UK Mixes* - that, along with the original version, contained two remixes by Tony Thorpe under his Moody Boys alias as well as a remix by The Orb – *3AM Blue Danube*. This last track was credited to Orbital, which caused some friction between Cauty and Alex Paterson as it should have been credited to The Orb, and there was another emerging dance act called Orbital at this time, hailing from Brighton and just starting to make a name for themselves with their wonderful debut 12", *Chime*.

As with *What Time Is Love?,* it was decided to remake and retool the track for the charts, and the music was re-recorded and beefed up. When it came to putting a rap onto the new *3AM Eternal*, Drummond and Cauty wanted Bello again. "What happened was I was on tour with Outlaw Posse and they called my manager and asked if I could do *3AM* - he told them *we were on tour*. Had I known, would I have done it? *Hell yeah!*" Amazingly, Bello's manager turned down the chance for Bello to appear on the follow up to *What Time Is Love?* "But you know what?" states Bello today, "I'm a true believer that everything happens for a reason, so maybe I was not supposed to do it, and the guy that did it ended up being really cool, and we eventually met and he was a cool guy and everybody liked him." The person who eventually did the rap on *3AM* was Jervis Ricardo Alfonso Lyte, an MC who was out and about on the scene and already featured on records by The Manic MCs and Adamski. It was probably Tony Thorpe (again) who brought him to the attention of Drummond and Cauty.

"I had to redo Ricky's one…" recalls Nick Coler, who worked on the revised version of *3AM Eternal*, "His timing was dreadful, so I had to put it all in the sampler, cut it all up and then re-trigger it into time." Coler also had to redo the kick drum "as it was not loud enough - I had to go through the whole of that and make it bigger. It was full on all the time, going from one thing to another, which I love as that's my whole way of making music."

With regards studios, Drummond, Cauty and their growing team had outgrown The Village, which saw them hiring larger studios like Lillie Yard in Fulham, which had a dedicated programming room and was owned by film composer Hans Zimmer. They also worked in the nearby Marcus Studios, which had two SSL 48-track studios. Mixing the tracks was now a critical part of the process, and Mark 'Spike' Stent was brought onboard - along with J Gordon Hastings, he was responsible for bringing out the full flavor of the KLF sound at the mixing desk, whether at Lillie Yard, Marcus or Townhouse in West London.

As with *What Time Is Love?*, whilst some parts of the new track were taken from the original version others were created from scratch. Others were the result of musical accidents, "We wanted some submarine noises, some asdic (sounds), and were thinking, 'We don't have any samples to do that,'" recalls Coler, "We were at Marcus Studios, and (the film) *The Boat* came on (the TV), so we were like, 'Quick!'" The freshly captured samples made it onto the track.

When the final version of *3AM Eternal* was complete, Drummond and Cauty had – along with their team – constructed a musical fireworks display. For example, the three note musical refrain on the original was memorable but understated, whereas here it was a powerful and arresting force, followed by an infectious chant of

"Ancients of Mu Mu!" Harvey's sweet vocal refrain was perfectly balanced by Lyte's infectious and commanding rap, which, like Bello's before it, celebrated KLF mythology. "Down with the crew crew/talking about the Mu Mu/Justified Ancient Liberation Zulu." His opening line, "KLF's gonna rock ya!" became as memorable to a generation as the "It's 3AM..... Eternal" refrain.

   In a rare interview, given to Richard King for his wonderful book *How Soon Is Now?*, Bill Drummond related that, around this time, he *wanted* The KLF to become an international success, "It was important for me that The KLF was successful worldwide because I hated bands that somehow thought they were big, and really they were big in this fake world of the *NME* and *Melody Maker*. They would have a fan following that could put them into the Top Twenty, but I was thinking, that's not a real Top Twenty record, that's just your cult following all buying it in a week, and I'm not interested in that. *I* want to know that the records we're making are touching a vast amount of people. That's actually plugging into something that – that's what pop music is – that reaches out and people don't care who the fuck these people are: this record makes me feel a certain way, I want it and I want that. And so that was incredibly, incredibly important to me."

   To this end, Drummond not only wanted KLF singles to top the charts in the UK but also to hit the charts in Europe and worldwide. He and Fellowes continued to negotiate additional licensing deals that would eventually see them licensing KLF material to Arista Records, helmed by Clive Davis, in America. Drummond and Cauty even took Cressida and Bello over to Amsterdam in October 1990 to 'perform' at the Paradiso as part of the DMC industry convention. Drummond made sure that the band secured maximum publicity by starting to give away some of the equipment to the audience at the end of their short set, before he was stopped by venue security. There is delicious footage of him sitting backstage in the dressing room afterwards, laughing his head off as Cauty comes into the room equally amused.

   In some respects, although Drummond and Fellowes had some industry experience, there were aspects of these deals that were very much on the job training. Before she left Appearing, Andrew Lee recalls that Fellowes would spend a lot of time on the phone to the manager of The Farm, a band who had also come from nowhere to become one of the biggest selling acts in the UK, with hits like *Groovy Train* and *All Together Now*. Like The KLF, The Farm had co-founded their own Produce label, and so were in a similar position. "He and Sallie used to ring each other up all of the time because both of them were like 'Holy Shit! We're selling truckloads of records with no idea of what we are doing!' They used to try to compare licensing deals – 'how much have you been offered for this?' – because they'd gone from The KLF selling nothing and being a clubland underground act to, with The Farm, becoming the number one selling singles bands in 1991."

The business of licensing tracks onto compilation albums was very lucrative at this time, especially for chart and dance hits, and both major labels and independents worked hard to license hit tracks for these releases. "An independent can expect to pick up around £30,000 in advance fees for licensing a hit single for use on compilations," David Brooker told *Music Week*. Brooker ran the independent Rumour Records, who issued a series of very successful *Warehouse Raves* compilations. Better still, according to Brooker independent labels could have their cake and eat it as, "it does not necessarily kill sales of the single. It can boost sales of the 12" in particular." KLF Communications were to license a number of KLF hits to compilations such as *The Ultimate Rave* LP, and one imagines that they too may have received up to £30,000 a pop. This would have been in addition to money received from sales and income from radio play.

3AM Eternal went straight into the chart at number five upon release in January 1991, and saw The KLF whisked straight into the *Top Of The Pops* studios for another appearance. Rather than be broadcast on its usual day of Thursday 17th January, *Top Of The Pops* was cancelled that week due to coverage of the invasion of Kuwait – Operation Desert Storm – which started with an aerial bombardment of Saddam Hussein's forces on that day, and was instead broadcast on the evening of Saturday 19th January. Dressed in their trademark black weather wear, Drummond and Cauty mimed playing the three note melody on guitars as they flanked Lyte, who was also decked out in a similar black jacket with an *It's Grim Up North* T-shirt beneath it. Maxine Harvey was also there to deliver the "It's 3AM, it's 3AM, it's 3AM Eternal," refrain, alongside Tony Thorpe, who mimed playing electronic percussion with gusto. When asked by *Music Week* if he had any thoughts on the lost sales boost they would have received on Friday and Saturday if the original broadcast had gone ahead, Drummond was not too bothered, "That's life, really, isn't it? We weren't expecting a Number One anyway, let alone a number two." That said, Drummond did arrange – probably on the advice of Scott Piering – to remove the sound of machine guns on a special Radio Edit that was sent out to DJs in order to preclude any slackening of playlist rotation during this martial time.

Whilst *Top Of The Pops* was the most important programme in the UK to showcase chart acts, it was not the only outlet. "Part of my job was taking artists to TV and radio interviews," recalls Andrew Lee,

"I used to go to *The Tube, The Power Station* or MTV with Bill and go out for the day and chat. Sit around, get him a cup of coffee and make sure he wasn't being arsed around." There were several other shows who wanted to feature *3AM Eternal*, and the best way to satisfy this demand was not a physical appearance but a video. Of course, this was all ready to go before the single was released. Crucially, by this time Drummond and Cauty had coined the term 'Stadium House' and the video for *3AM Eternal* was a 70mm affair at which they threw the kitchen sink, and then some.

Whilst footage of Drummond and Cauty driving around London in Ford Timelord with Lyte echoed some of the material shot for *The White Room*, the main 'performance' part of the video presented The KLF on a stage setting that imagined that they were performing in a stadium in front of forty thousand people. Thus, Drummond and Cauty stood in front of a *wall* of Marshall amps in their trademark black rain wear, sawing away on their guitars, whilst Lyte sang not with a microphone but into a large, early mobile phone. There were two drummers (one was Nick Coler), Tony Thorpe on percussion and, along with Maxine Harvey, a number of backing singers arranged on stage in a pyramid shape, all wearing blue silken robes. There were also strobes, two large pyramid ghetto blasters flanking the stage and the first sighting of the Japanese girls who became an obligatory element to future KLF videos.

"They were all brought in by me and Youth," recalls Alex Paterson, "Let that be a myth for the time being. Who were they indeed?! One was called Izumi, and I can't remember what the other one was called. There were quite a lot of Japanese girls going to clubs in the late '80s, they liked DJ'ing - they came to Trancentral and Jimmy and Bill were looking for people to film, and Japanese girls in weird outfits looked very ethereal, especially in the (later) Mu shots. They were very chuffed that they did that." Cut into the video of the 'band' performing was footage of a small city built by Cauty's brother (with assistance from Jimmy and Drummond), who designed and built models for use on TV and film. As well as including a small model of Stonehenge, the city had billboards posted on many of the constructions offering up images of Drummond and Cauty's history, from The JAMs to the *1987* LP, and even the words "sample city" on one skyscraper. All told, it was a stunning video that matched the scope and power of the song.

3AM Eternal went to Number One in the UK on 2nd February 1991, where it clung like a limpet for two weeks, and then took a further three weeks before it slipped out of the top ten. Ironically, the song ended with Scott Piering stating, "Ladies and gentlemen, The KLF have now left the building," an amusing joke that played on the Stadium House idea of The KLF being an internationally successful band - well, now they were! This success extended beyond Drummond and Cauty being feted in the press - Maxine Harvey recalls that she was suddenly recognised in the street. “You had your family, your teacher, your friends, your mates… We were so up there. My kid was famous at school. I had a problem with my eye as I was wearing so much make up, I got a sty on my eye and someone said, ‘you need to get that looked at.’ I went to King’s emergencies (in Camberwell) and said, ‘Can you sort this out for me?’ ‘Nah you can come back?’ I said, ‘I work with The KLF and I’m doing a session next week.’ They had people saying, ‘She works for KLF! She *works with KLF!’* and I was in and done and dusted before I knew it.”

Success also allowed Drummond to climb onto a soapbox and make his feelings known to the industry at large in an opinion piece in *Music Week*. After some opening comments on the Gulf War and having to edit out the machine guns at the beginning of the song for a new radio edit, he went on to state, “At five to seven on Sunday January 27th we won the weekly race. It was only then that I realised we did not have an album to release in the next two weeks. We had no idea how to put a major album campaign together. In my opinion, groups like us should not be allowed to have their own labels and get to Number One without having any notion of how to exploit the situation. The job should be left to professionals and we should be banished to the indie charts where we belong.”

This sentiment was, of course, tongue in cheek. Drummond was really saying that he and Cauty had done it their way *and won*.

BACK SIDE OF THE MOON

Journalist: Have you been aware of acid house?
David Gilmour "No. (then, after receiving explanation).
So it has almost come back round to our time again
(laughs). I hadn't heard about that."
                                   - New Musical Express, 9ᵗʰ July 1989

"So, an album sounding like Pink Floyd without all the
self-indulgent solos. Samples from around the globe and
quite possibly the universe. Is Alex Patterson the Eno of
the '90s?"
          - review of 'The Orb's Adventures Beyond The Ultraworld',
                                   NME, 13ᵗʰ April 1991

I'm standing in the Electric in Brixton bearing witness. The Orb are playing a twenty-fifth anniversary gig to celebrate and commemorate their fabulous debut LP, 1991's *The Orb's Adventures Beyond The Ultraworld*. It all seems a little strange and surreal as Alex Paterson warms up the crowd with a DJ set - whilst I can accept that its around forty years since punk detonated across the consciousness of the nation in 1977, it seems almost *impossible* that twenty-five years have passed since The Orb released their seminal 2-LP set.

As for the gig, after Paterson's set his longtime Orb partner Thomas Felhmann DJs for a while before an Orb super-group amble onto the stage. Youth starts plucking some notes from an upright double bass before strapping on an electric one and the show begins its ascent into the higher musical planes that The Orb are now famous for. As this is a special anniversary show the line-up includes Steve Hillage, Miquette Giraudy, Tom Green, Andy Falconer and Hugh Vickers. To ice the cake and give the party a special kick, Sex Pistol Paul Cook is on drums. So punk and ambient music celebrate an anniversary together.

A couple of weeks later, I'm knocking at Youth's door in South London. When he opens up I get the sort of greeting you want when writing a book, "Hey man, you've caught me in my kimono!" The Kimono in question comes down to just above his knees, but after he makes me an espresso the legendary producer pops upstairs to shower and get dressed. When he comes back down we discuss his time with Killing Joke, Brilliant, his move into production and, of course, Alex Paterson, Jimmy Cauty and The Orb. He hardly needs any prodding to discuss the twenty-fifth anniversary show. "It's great that Alex has managed to keep The Orb going, and that gig was a really wonderful celebration of The Orb, him and everything that we've been through on the way. It was a real family affair. Jimmy wouldn't do it. Jimmy offered to do a show in a matchbox that he could take on tour with his miniatures (ADP Riot Tour installations). Alex really loved the idea but Jimmy said, 'I'm joking!'"

It was a shame Jimmy Cauty chose not take part in the celebration of this classic LP - although he and Paterson had parted ways by the time of its release in 1991, his role in what became The Orb was vital, and *Ultraworld* included a live mix of the seminal Cauty/Paterson track *A Huge Ever Growing Pulsating Brain That Rules From The Centre Of The Ultraworld* that is the cornerstone upon which The Orb's entire journey across the decades was built.

The origins of The Orb extend back to where Paterson and Youth were schoolmates at Kingham Hill Boarding school in Oxfordshire. Paterson was a year older than Youth, and both took part in the ad-hoc bands that played together when students had time to themselves. Youth even recalls Paterson singing a cover version of Mud's *Tiger Feet* in one of them. When punk broke out Paterson formed a band called Kill Bloodsports, who, by 1978 when they played the Roxy in London as a support act, were just billed as Bloodsport. The line-up was Paterson (vocals), Graham Wheelan (guitar), Kenneth Topley (guitar), Wally Walden (bass) and Paul Fergusson (drums). "That was with Wally, the original bass player with the Sex Pistols," recalls Paterson today, "Wally we met in a squat and he introduced us to Cookie and Jones (both former Pistols by this point)." Bloodsport were still mobile when Youth joined Killing Joke in 1978, and Youth and Paterson hooked up again as Paterson was keen to become involved in Killing Joke in some way or other. He was soon serving as drum roadie for his soon-to-be-former Bloodsport bandmate Paul Ferguson.

As Killing Joke built a live reputation and began a recording career, Paterson began to perform encores with the band. At this time he had blond hair, and Killing Joke tour manager Adam Morris, who was also involved in the record label Malicious Damage, who released the first Killing Joke EP, recalls that, "they used to do *Bodies* by the Sex Pistols as an encore and Alex used to sing it. Coleman used to hate him because Alex was a better front-man than Jaz." Frank Jenkinson, who was close to the band took some photographs of Killing Joke during this period, including some of Paterson performing with them, "he was Youth's friend and became the roadie of sorts, he sang *Bodies* now and then." According to Paterson, the real reason he got to sing encores with Killing Joke had more to do with the economics of agreements over the length of shows with the venues they played. "Rehearsals," he cackles, "Singer's disease. Jaz would go home early and the rest of the band were pretty psyched up but did not have any more numbers to do. They had forty minutes (of material) in the first year and Jaz refused to do covers, but the sets sometimes had to be forty five or fifty minutes, so they got me in to do *Bodies*, *No Fun* or both to extend the set time, and then they got paid. I was still on a mattress and one-bar fire wages in those squat days. I didn't understand what money was then, it was more like, 'Can I barter with you, sir?'"

According to Paterson, Bloodsport was still active when Killing Joke began to gain traction, and "they nicked my name and put it on the first album" as the title of an instrumental track. There was supposed to be a Bloodsport record issued by Malicious Damage, and the band even went into the studio to record it, "we had a multi-track done but Malicious Damage didn't pay the bills for the tapes and they recorded over them. The stuff of legend!"

Youth left Killing Joke in 1982 after the band had recorded their third album, and things went a bit strange and Icelandic before they carried on without him and he formed Brilliant. Killing Joke, however, "asked EG (their label) to give Paterson a job, and he became an A&R guy and they had him looking after Editions EG, which was Eno's ambient label," as Adam Morris recalls, "So he started getting into all of the ambient stuff and he started to DJ." Paterson was one of a small number of people who had developed a taste for the output of America's Kiss FM, and anybody visiting New York was told to come back with cassette copies of some of the shows. For Paterson, "'87 was the turning point, when we started getting these Chuck Chillout tapes coming in quite regularly as there was an EG office in New York, so I was getting the (female) A&R scout over there to record Kiss FM tapes, purely for research purposes darling! And personal enjoyment as well. We got an hour of Chuck Chillout, then half an hour of Tony Humphries, who was playing all this weird fucking techno from Detroit and Chicago house, so it changed from hip-hop to this new weird thing, (Roland) 808s and 303s. We were like, 'Wow!' so I phoned her up, or telexed her I think in those days. 'Can you stop recording Chuck Chillout and start recording the whole of the Tony Humphries show - we want to hear what is going on.' (She said) 'I can't do that, I've got to get up in the middle of the night to turn the tape over.' It never did quite come off that bit."

Cauty and Paterson first met in the mid-80s. "I got to know Jimmy when he joined Brilliant as I was a part-time roadie with them and a part-time roadie with Killing Joke. The spy in both camps, basically. I got on really well with Jimmy." Even at this stage, Paterson had already cut his teeth as a DJ, playing before Killing Joke sets, with his own adventurous listening experiences being reflected in what he played. One of the key factors in developments between he and Cauty was not only playing DJ sets at parties held at BENIO but the establishment of Cauty's home studio, where he could work on musical ideas, not only with Drummond but a number of other ad-hoc collaborators, like Tony Thorpe and Paterson. The music he made was inspired by the emerging dance music scene they were all tapping into.

The seminal early acid house club in London was Shoom, which kicked off in late 1987. "I first went to Shoom in order to shut Farley up," Andy Weatherall told *Melody Maker* in 1991 - Terry Farley was the friend and fellow remixer and DJ the now-famous producer had started a football fanzine with. "He'd been going on about it for ages, saying how the music was mad and it was full of football lads, Ibiza lads, and I just thought, 'Fuck off, it sounds terrible.' But as soon as I walked in I knew it was something special - the strobes and the smoke were on from start to finish, and I had to keep touching people to make sure I wasn't alone in there. I had a ball."

Richard Norris, who graduated from being a journalist with his finger on the pulse of the dance scene to forming The Grid with Soft Cell's David Ball, told *Music Week* in 1989, "Yeah, it's a bit like the first Sex Pistols gig – five million people at Shoom. But it's true - you only had to experience that atmosphere once to know that something was going on and a change was taking place. I feel incredibly lucky to have been part of what went on. And it wasn't just Shoom, I went to clubs just as good in Liverpool, with forty people who knew nothing about what was going on in London." This was probably Mardi Gras on Bold Street, or, from 1988 on, The State, which held considerably more and began to hold house and acid house nights on a Monday night under the name *Daisy*. This was run by Cream founder James Barton, who initially approached the resident DJs Mike Knowler and his partner Andy Carroll with the idea. Knowler we've met before – he'd previously run the MVCU recording facility in Liverpool before becoming a DJ.

"We were playing more or less what they were playing at Spectrum, which was at Heaven in London on a Monday night," he recalls, "We were playing the same stuff that Paul Oakenfold was playing. A lot of this stuff was being released in the UK, and I remember some of the stuff was coming in from Italy, like *Airport 89* by Wood

Allen." Later on he began to play a track by The KLF, "I thought *What Time Is Love?* was beyond belief, but we didn't play it (at first). It was big in London at Spectrum, but it didn't go down particularly well in The State at the beginning. But in 1990 they did a remix with a rap, and I think that's an absolute classic. All power to Bill Drummond for doing that."

It was Nancy Noise, the receptionist at Pete Waterman's PWL studios at this time, who was instrumental in steering Youth and Alex Paterson towards Paul Oakenfold and Spectrum. "Yeah, I worked for Pete at the studio and got to know Youth and Jimmy as they were recording the Brilliant album there," she says, "Also, Bill was the A&R man, so he was around a lot too. I used to talk to Youth quite a bit as he was out and about a lot, so we spoke about different clubs and stuff. I thought he was really cool as he was always at the Wag and places like that." Noise was to later leave Waterman, and not only played a part in importing the Amnesia experience from Ibiza to the UK but also became a DJ herself.

"When I got back to London after Ibiza and had started DJ'ing," she recalls, "I rang Youth and invited him down to The Future. Ian St. Paul and Paul Oakenfold, who I'd been hanging out in Ibiza with, had started the night and asked me to play there. I remember ringing him up saying, 'Hi Youth, I'm a DJ now'. Youth came along that Thursday, and I think he kind of liked it and got into the vibe straight away. At that time I really wanted to share what I'd experienced and what was happening with my friends, as it was such a beautiful thing. As Youth had come along, Alex and Jimmy and Cressida started coming to the nights, that's when Spectrum had got going too. I'd probably introduced them all to Paul and Ian at the clubs, so then the connections were made. Everyone was really enjoying the music and the vibes." Among other things, Noise raved about a Paco De Lucia track to Youth, which was sampled and ended up on a on a Wau! Mr. Modo track.

Oakenfold had some ideas of his own for his run of Sunday nights in Heaven. "I think he liked the idea of me and Jimmy," Alex Paterson recalls, and Oakenfold asked them to DJ upstairs at the club in the smaller VIP area. Armed with a set-up of three turntables, a DAT machine, a tape recorder and a mixer, they would serve up sets whose vibe was important, not the beats. "The first night Alex did the VIP bar, I remember him setting up all of his stuff, and when the music stared I was like, whoaaa..." recalls Noise, "there were clocks chiming, sheep noises, voices, along with the music." The music Paterson and Cauty played was wide-ranging, and crucially not just confined to the emerging Chicago house, Detroit techno, Belgian EBM (Electric Body Music) and early acid house records. "It's the sort of music that functions as just being there," Paterson told a journalist during the Land of Oz residency in one of his best summations, "It's a rhythm *of* rather than *for* life, a heartbeat. With The Orb we use

159

house music and whatever else, and then take away the beats, although occasionally in Heaven we throw in a few breakbeats to make sure people are still alive."

Ironically, according to Paterson this now legendary residency was almost ended after one week by the most unlikely of spanners - Ford Timelord! "When we first did Land Of Oz, we nearly lost our gig after the first night. It was around four o'clock on a Monday morning and everyone was coming out of the club - titted as usual. Jimmy goes, 'Watch this!' and starts putting all the lights on on his police car. He opens the bonnet, and it's got shark teeth in there. Everybody starts to fucking worship the car. He puts the sirens on. Wow! It's got sirens! He gets a little bit of smoke coming out of the back. Wow! He's got smoke! He starts up and everyone is following him, and he goes around Trafalgar Square with all these cars following, worshipping this car. The next week we turn up at the club and Oakenfold goes, 'You do that again and I'm gonna have to fire you!'" Suffice to say, Ford Timelord was on his best behavior after that.

As the residency at the Land Of Oz developed, Paterson never kept a set-list of what he played and so the music is lost in the mists and memories of good times, but it may or may not have included suitably spaced out tracks like Virgo's *Do You Know Who You Are*, DTR's *Journey Into A Dream*, Confidential's *Inner Space*, A Split-Second's *Flesh* and Manuel Gotting's *E2=E4*. Adam Morris, who was allowed a VIP pass, recalls, "It was a mixture of everything - Ron Trent's *Altered States* was a favourite, that was a fantastic record - I can also remember him playing *When The Levee Breaks* by Led Zeppelin at one gig, and Mark Moore from S-Express was there and he came flying across the room going, 'What's that? What's that? What's that?' He'd never heard it before. It was right across the board."

Speaking today, Paterson remains bemused as to the impact that Led Zeppelin can have in a club. "I've done it several times with that track and it never ceases to amaze me. I played it at a Primal Scream gig at the Hammersmith Palais and all of these kids came running up going, 'Is this the new Beastie Boys remix?' I'm going, 'This is an original, mate.' They're like, '*Who is this?*' and I'm going, 'Led Zeppelin,' thinking. I don't believe this, am I getting old? That happened twenty years ago!" That said, Mark Moore very much had his finger on the pulse at this time, and was following through what artists like The JAMs and others had started in 1987. "The really big difference between now and ten years ago," he wrote in *Melody Maker* in December 1989, "is that at the start of the eighties people just didn't think you could make a record unless you turned up with loads of drums and guitars and songs that were written. If you'd have said, 'I want to take a bit of an old Rolls

Royce riff and throw in a bit of this and a bit of that with a few voices' no one would have understood it." So hearing a track at a club, be it *Airport 89* or something 'obscure' like Led Zeppelin, was all grist to the mill of the creative process.

The fact that Patterson was mixing something like Led Zeppelin into his sets with vinyl from the EG catalogue, elements of classical music, spoken word and other records shows just how fluid and open things were. The key thing for Cauty, and especially Paterson, was a DJ's ear for what could flow and be mixed together to maintain a musical journey throughout the night. People were coming to their room to take a break from the martial dance beat, and wanted something more suited to a reflective state of mind. Later, there were visuals as well, projected onto screens. "I was there pretty religiously every week to listen to what they were doing," recalls Richard Norris. One night he was there, Paterson even played a record - *Rainbow Dome Musick* - that led to a future collaboration, "I'd heard the name Steve Hillage," Paterson told the *New Musical Express* in September 1991, "but that was as far as it went. Then this bloke comes up whilst I'm DJ'ing and says, 'Hello, I'm Steve Hillage and that's my record you're playing.'" Hillage got *his* VIP pass as he was a friend of the guy who'd actually put the sound system into Heaven, and these two happy accidents - the pass and Paterson playing the record - led to them working together with The Orb and System 7.

Going to clubs and playing sets at Heaven and parties at BENIO was opening a path that was leading forwards, and Paterson's work at EG also meant his ear was always open to new sounds and sonic opportunities. "We would get together once a month, me, Youth and Alex, as we were still mates," recalls Adam Morris, "We kept saying we should start another label based around this acid house and rave culture that's kicking off. It was the new indie DIY." This was soon to become a reality - Youth and Paterson had already decided on a three-point plan, of which two points were to set up a radio station and their own record label. To this end they'd set up a production company called Wau! Morris had also formed a company called Modo, "My partners name was O'Donovan, so it was MO for Morris and DO for O'Donovan - it was Youth who came up with putting it together as Wau! Mr Modo, and we thought, 'Sod it, let's just go for it.'"

Soon records began to be issued on Wau! Mr Modo. The first was *Let Jimi Take Over* by STP 23 (1988), and comprised a number of Jimi Hendrix samples. "Then Youth did a record (under the name Mister E) called *Extasy Express*," recalls Morris, "which used samples of *Trans Europe Express*. He got a vocoder and he just went 'Extasy Express! Extasy Express!' over the top. They were sort of issued as bootlegs as you couldn't get clearance on them. A few years later I met Kraftwerk at Sheffield City Hall. They said, 'Yes! Yes! We've got that record, *Extasy Express*. We think it is very funny!' That was the start of it."

As they were playing DJ sets together and seeing each other socially, it seemed logical that Cauty and Paterson also look to record something together. In fact, the third part of the Youth/Paterson plan was to set up The Orb. "I was always much more into hanging around with Jimmy than Bill," recalls Paterson, "Bill was not my rival in any way. I respected what he was doing (with Jimmy), it was just one of those things that it happened to be that I was an A&R man as well at EG." According to Paterson the personal chemistry was also right. "I think it was just a natural gelling," he recalls "I remember the first day when I walked in and there was a synthesiser he (Jimmy) had bought and he didn't know how to turn it on. It was just a stroke of luck that it was the same keyboard I'd been looking after for Killing Joke for six years, so I certainly did know how to turn it on! Also I knew all of the presets, and that was the day The Orb was born, with me and him. It really was that simple. It was very chaotic."

As to *where* they started, things are unclear as Cauty was also working on other material at Trancentral, at Village Recorders in Dagenham and at other studios with Bill Drummond, but as he had his own home studio it was just a question of finding time to get together with Paterson. The first fruits of their collaboration appeared on the *Eternity Project One* LP on Gee Street, issued in February 1989 and also showcasing some of the earliest output of Youth and Wau! Mr Modo outside of white label 12" records. A track by The Orb called *Tripping On Sunshine* appeared, which was, simply, "*Tripping On Sunshine* with loads of samples all over it," according to Paterson.

This was followed by *The Kiss EP*, which was limited to nine hundred and forty nine copies because, as Paterson later related, "we didn't think we'd sell any more." It was his love of Kiss FM that saw Paterson drive this particular 12" forward. Morris agrees, "*The Kiss EP* was samples that Jimmy and he had put together of Kiss FM, and I pressed that up and put it out for them and everybody told me that I was mad because it was awful (laughs). And it was, but it had an amazing press release written by Bill Drummond."

It was only fitting that Cauty's partner in musical crime penned the first words about this collaboration: "The Orb spend their weekends smashed out of their heads making noises by turning on a drum machine and leaving it running, recording everything, including mistakes. They make no claims that the results of their efforts can be considered music, or has any relevance to the outside world, or contains any elements of a tune, or tracks of anything vaguely memorable. The only positive thing

Bill Drummond with KLF sheep Courtesy of Chris Clunn

Jimmy Cauty with KLF Sheep Courtesy of Chris Clunn

Iconic Pure Trance label Courtesy of Ian Shirley

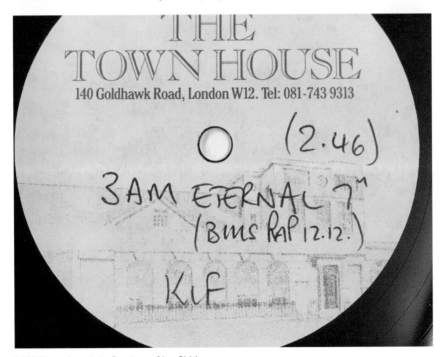

3AM Eternal acetate Courtesy of Ian Shirley

Nick Coler prepared for heavy weather at a KLF video shoot Courtesy of Nick Coler

Tammy Wynette with Blacksteel Courtesy of Errol Nicholson

**'The White Room' gold disc – retrieved from a mast on the 'America What Time Is Love'
shoot** Courtesy of Andrew Swaine

ISSUE NO. 98   MARCH 1991   U.K £1.50   U.S.A $4.95

KLF
TRANSCENTRAL TALES

MIXMAG

RIMINI:EUROPEAN CLUB UNITY
VICTORIA WILSON JAMES
HOLLYWOOD SWINGERS
ANDREW WEATHERALL
RECESSION CLUBBING
ITALO HOUSE '91
FRAZIER CHORUS
DAVE DORRELL
FLYING
P.M DAWN
TAXMAN

COMPUTER GAMES
LOVE AT FIRST BYTE

YUGOTOURS
CROATIAN CLUB CULTURE

ESCAPE TO NEW YORK
BIG APPLE BRAIN-STORM

ESSENTIAL CLUB/DANCE MUSIC NEWS

9 770957 662002   03

Mixmag cover Courtesy of Jerry Perkins

Bill Drummond and Jimmy Cauty Chill Out with some sheep... Courtesy of Chris Clunn

KLF = Kings Live Forever Courtesy of Chris Clunn

I can say about The Orb is, when I'm off my cake on Monday nights I love it. Cross-over potential: Nil."

This first EP didn't have enough weight behind it to suggest that The Orb were going to be anything more a footnote in the growing DIY scene of 12' records that were being made and farmed out to shops across the country. This was a scene where it was the DJs who were emerging as the masters of the dance, and it was a question of playing the right records to enthuse crowds who just wanted to have a good time, whether or not they were taking ecstasy. Many of the musicians were faceless to their audience - just a name on a 12" single - and were hardly going to get coverage in publications like the *New Musical Express, Sounds* or *Melody Maker*, who were hard-wired to associate good music with good band photos, an image and quotable lead singers. Saying that, they did begin to interview the early movers of Chicago house and Detroit techno, like Todd Terry, Derrick May, Kevin Saunderson, Juan Atkins and Frankie Knuckles, as well as UK acts like The Grid, who included Richard Norris and David Ball, formerly of Soft Cell. Norris had secured a record deal on the back of the *Jack The Tab* compilation LP and the fact that they told label executives they were "the new Pink Floyd."

When their debut LP, *Electric Head*, was released in 1989, Norris was keen to stress that The Grid was a duo based around a loose grouping of people, "It was important for us that the label see us like that, rather than as some simple, calculated chart project. And it was important to do it on a major label, because it's something major labels should be able to do now - put out fairly leftfield music and get it into the charts." Whilst The Grid's early singles and debut LP failed to chart, the next Orb single not only became a breakthrough 12" but a musical landmark that helped to establish *them* as the new Pink Floyd.

The track was titled *Loving You* on early Wau! Mr Modo white labels, although it soon became better known as *A Huge Ever Growing Pulsating Brain That Rules From The Centre Of The Ultraworld*. The title actually came from a BBC soundtrack record featuring music from the cult TV series *Blake's 7* called *A Huge Ever Growing Pulsating Core*. "It started off as a synth idea, it started off as a bassline and then it became a synth line," Paterson recalls of the genesis of this remarkable track, which clocked in at around twenty minutes and was a compelling, hypnotic journey. Paterson told the *New Musical Express* in 1989 that *Loving You* was recorded after Cauty and he had attended a rave in Brighton. "We wanted to capture the warmth of the day, the sun and the sea's sound. Initially we started recording the piece with a drumbeat - we built the track around that but it felt wrong. So we took out the drums and it was perfect. It was the chill out music we'd always been trying to find." Today, he believes that one thing that helped them find this music was the state of

Cauty's head at the time. "Jimmy had a really big, heavy headache and I was as bored as shit listening to chaotic drum patterns. I got Jimmy to turn the drums down and the rest, my dear, was history!"

Indeed it was history, and even today Adam Morris recalls the moment he first heard it, "I'd moved up to Sheffield by then but was coming down to London a lot, and I met Youth in the West End. I was in my car, parked up, and Youth got in - he had a cassette and said, "It's Modo, put this on. I think Alex has got a result." We put this cassette on and it was *Loving You*. We were sat there for twenty minutes going "Fuck me! What is this? It's fucking epic!" It was going to be a monster one way or another."

This original version featured a sample of Minnie Ripperton singing her classic, *Loving You*, which had been a big hit in 1975, so that was the obvious title for the early, pre-release white labels. As he knew a certain DJ quite well, Morris made sure one went to the right place. "You put the white label out and got it to John Peel. If John Peel played it - the good ones - he would rave about it, and the others he played even if it wasn't good."

Peel received and played a test pressing of the *Kiss EP*, and not only wrote the name of the tracks on each side - for example, "The Orb Roof 1. *Kiss Your Love 4.25*" - but even gave them his legendary star rating, with all four tracks receiving two stars. As soon as he received it, Peel began playing *Loving You*, and it received the rave treatment. At this point, though, Wau! Mr Modo were on the horns of a dilemma as the sample of Minnie Ripperton was uncleared - "so, a nightmare" according to Morris - especially as she'd died young in 1979 after a battle with cancer. At this time, with the entire issue of sample clearance potentially toxic, trying to secure permission through the estate of a dead artist was hard due to their usually conservative nature. Thus, a new white label pressing without the sample was sent out. "They all came back with the same reaction (on the reaction sheets)," Paterson stated in 1992, "'Where's the *fucking* sample?' So we scrapped that release and did another one with chunks of *Loving You* on it." On 2nd December 1989, *Melody Maker* reviewed a retitled copy, "This is designed specifically for showing off to your mates, none of whom will have the faintest idea of what The Orb are about, but will love it nevertheless. Fasten your seatbelts."

This last comment about fastening seatbelts was apt, as John Peel had asked The Orb to come into the studio to record a session, and a day after the review was printed – 3rd December 1989 - Cauty, Paterson and a friend who helped them with their equipment arrived at Maida Vale studios. They arrived early and worked in the control room rather than the massive main studio, although they had to relocate when the producer allocated for the session turned up late and threw them out. Paterson recalls it was all about ambience, from the setting to the music, "we got some settees from the corridors, a lampshade, some plants, and made a little front room, like we would do at Trancentral. We used to mix things on the floor, we used to put the mixer on the floor if we wanted to do an ambient project, and now we were immersed in ambience with this tune. It was all in different sequences, but we just had to place the samples on the multi-track, it was eight-track and it didn't take that long. We were out of there by seven thirty. You started at two o'clock normally, and the producer turned up about five, pissed, pretended he was producing, gets a credit for it and goes off home. He turned up halfway through when we'd actually done most of the work, like an engineering thing with the sampler and the keyboard going straight into the mixer rather than having to take it outside and patch it through."

When the first Orb session was broadcast it not only made it into Peel's 1990 festive fifty but became the most requested Peel session of all time. It's easy to see why - opening with the crow of a cockerel and gentle ocean waves, a repetitive synth line emerges and acts like an acoustic canvas over which samples and sounds are added. These range from birdsong to spoken word, and even the cunning deployment of a snatch of iconic Pink Floyd guitar from *Shine On You Crazy Diamond*, which, thankfully, was able to be cleared for broadcast through Guy Pratt, a former school friend of Youth and Paterson was now playing bass with Pink Floyd. The mix of *A Huge Ever Growing Pulsating Brain That Rules From The Centre Of The Ultraworld* was crucial as it allowed the music to ebb and flow, and when Minnie Ripperton seeped through for a refrain of *Loving You* it gave the song wonderful warmth, before the repetitive synth part re-emerged to take it back into the ambient rainforest of sound. There was also what Paterson describes as "typical Orb humour," possibly aimed at Peel, with the line, "What, you're a disc jockey. What's that?" mixed in from either a spoken word record or a sample captured from a radio or TV broadcast. Although the track lasted for twenty minutes it felt like ten, such was its compelling and immersive nature.

The exposure by John Peel, as well as positive reviews and music press coverage, led to record company interest in The Orb. Cauty and Paterson were already developing more material, and as early as November 1989 the *New Musical Express*'s Jack Barron reported that, "there are three albums on the way dealing with ambient house. A WAU/MR Modo triple affair which will be one complete track, a KLF special called *Chill Out* and a Jimmy Cauty and Dr Alex bumper on EG called *Space*." There was certainly a particular ambience in the air. "It's obvious that album-based, album orientated bands are going to do really well. Someone just has to come up with *Tubular Bells* and they'll make a fortune," Richard

Norris told the *New Musical Express* around this time, "That's how we got signed in the first place. I said we were going to be Pink Floyd for the house generation and we got signed. It's really funny because I talked to Bill Drummond about that and he said, 'Yeah... I've been going round saying that as well!'"

Of course, Bill Drummond being Bill Drummond, he was not only talking about it but was actually doing something about it with Jimmy Cauty, which would emerge in 1990 as the *Chill Out* album under the name The KLF – so Barron was right on the money, as was Norris, who was hoping it would be The Grid who would serve up their own *Tubular Bells.*

It was at this time, however, that things grew complicated for The Orb. "Big Life had come into the equation," recalls Morris, who was now also managing Paterson. "Youth had made another track for us by that point, which was *Naked In The Rain* by Blue Pearl, and had got Jimmy to do a trance mix of it. So the original *Naked In The Rain* comes out as a four-track white label with these trance mixes that Jimmy had done on the back. Originally that was going to be on BMG, but then Big Life heard about it and decided that they wanted it on their label, and they steamed in and we did a deal on that. They had a sales team going around the shops called Contact, and when they started taking *Naked In The Rain* around the shops and when they saw our logo on the label they said, 'Can you get that other one on that label by The Orb with Minnie Ripperton on it?' so Contact told Big Life that we had this other one." Blue Pearl was, in fact, a collaboration between Youth and Durga McBroom, a backing singer with Pink Floyd who Youth had met through Guy Pratt at their gig in Venice in July 1989. When she came to London, Youth, ducking and diving as a producer at this time, had done a deal with the studio where it was recorded - in return for free time, he would give them a percentage of any profits if it became a hit. He'd done this with a lot of tracks at the time and, "I did that with *Naked In The Rain*," he laughs today, "and it cost me forty grand!"

By this time, Youth had already remixed *The Only Way Is Up* by Yazz for Big Life - that had been a massive hit in 1988 and both he and the label were on a roll. "He said he was going to take our Blue Pearl record, *Naked In The Rain*, into the top five and he did exactly that," Adam Morris told *Music Week* in a profile of Big Life boss Jazz Summers at the time. As Big Life was also a management company, Summers offered to manage Youth and secure him work, telling him he was, "the rarest cat in the jungle," a writer/producer. Summers was now interested in signing The Orb, and Youth was worried that if they didn't sign with Big Life his days as a cat in the jungle might be numbered!

"There was this whole debate over the ownership of The Orb," states Morris, "I remember Bill sending me this sarcastic letter saying, 'Who do you think owns The Orb? Do you think that you own The Orb or does The KLF own the Orb?' I was like, 'well, it's Alex's band and Alex is part of Wau! Mr Modo, so I think that we own The Orb." I never got a reply to that." As for Summers, apparently he also had a meeting with Bill Drummond where he may or may not have discussed the possibility of Drummond not being able to stand on one of his legs for a short period of time.

Summers wanted to sign The Orb to Big Life and develop them into a major act, "We're not interested in one-off twelve inches," he told *Music Week*. "I'm not going to sit here and say I've got the best ears in the business, but I have been right quite a few times. I've been right on Yazz, I've been right on Coldcut, I've been right on Lisa Stansfield. I do rely totally on what I feel." And he felt that The Orb was going to be big.

This certainly seemed to be the case after Cauty and Paterson were asked to remix a track helmed by David Stewart of the Eurythmics, an instrumental called *Lily Was Here* and featuring Candy Dulfer on saxophone. "That was a funny experience," recalls Paterson. "We just dovetailed the beginning and the end, gave it a funny title (and) told and them to send the money on a bike. They sent the money on a bike and we gave them the DAT, and we just thought that we'd got away with it. Suddenly it became a top ten hit and suddenly everyone wanted an Orb remix on that basis." Paterson's work with EG Records also led to an early Cauty/Paterson retooling of a track called *Money $* for a German band called Fischerman's Friend. Although attributed to The KLF on the label when issued in 1989, the Orbital Club Remix was by Cauty and Paterson and must have been worked on around the time of their Peel Session, as two of the same vocal samples – "So you're a disc jockey?" and "The music just turns me on" - were worked into the mix. Whilst this record sold reasonably well under the radar, the Space Centre Medical Unit Hum version of *Lily Was Here* went top ten in March 1990, and gave the profile of The Orb a massive boost. "That did us a lot of good - suddenly we were flavour of the month," states Paterson. "The press, Peel.... at the end of 1989 the press were looking for something to do in the '90s and picked on us for a while."

For his part, Jimmy Cauty was keen for albums with an ambient feel, like *Space*, to appear on KLF Communications, but Paterson - who also had a stake in Wau! Mr Modo - was worried that if he went with KLF Communications The Orb might become a side project to Cauty's main work with Bill Drummond. After all, 1988 had seen the Drummond/Cauty partnership score a Number One hit with The Timelords' single *Doctorin' The Tardis* and, when the money began to roll in from this, start to make

The White Room film and soundtrack album, as well as engaging in other musical projects, including a number of house records as The KLF and spin-off projects like Disco 2000, who they were trying to turn into a two girl Bananarama. So, for Cauty at that time The Orb probably *was* a side project, like some work he did with Tony Thorpe of The Moody Boys at Trancentral that ended up being released on XL Recordings as the *Journey into Dubland*, 12" in 1990. The five tracks – *Dub Me Right*, *Free*, *Lion Dance*, *Pumpin Dumpin* and *A.U.N.* – clocked in at nearly thirty minutes and remain a lost gem.

"I was always into multi-track EPs and liked the way that labels like Nu Groove and those releasing Frankie Bones stuff in the USA would just say, Yo, here are some cool track rather than just offering up one cut per side," recalls Nick Halkes of XL, who decided to put the record out. "Obviously Jimmy Cauty co-produced and it's a slight regret that I didn't manage to get to know him during that process as The KLF obviously exploded in subsequent years and I wouldn't have minded signing them to XL too actually. But maybe signing The KLF and The Prodigy would have been plain greedy (laughs). Like Jimmy and Liam though, Tony (Thorpe) understood the potential and power of the underground scene, and it was a pleasure to work with him."

Whilst all of this was going on The KLF released their first LP in February 1990 - *Chill Out*. The record was, in effect, Drummond and Cauty's take on what became known as 'ambient house', and, in true Drummond fashion, review copies came with a photocopied, hand-written sheet headed: *Ambient House - The Facts*. What followed were eighteen points that ranged from the amusing – "Ambient House is just a Monday night clique in the VIP Lounge in Heaven" via the very amusing – "Ambient House is what the angels chill out to after the Christmas rush" – to the profoundly true – "Ambient House celebrates the sounds we have heard all our lives but never listened to."

As well as dealing with the basics – "*Chill Out* is The KLF's first complete LP. The music it contains is that 'the media' have already dubbed 'ambient house'. For those that need a handle it's as good as any" - the press release for broadcast media issued by Appearing also put its tongue firmly in cheek by extending enthusiastic credit to one of the vocalists on the album, "The KLF have discovered, through working with the guest vocalist Sheep on *Chill Out*, that sheep, far from being the lazy, mindless animals of easy virtue that is their stereotype, are spiritually highly-evolved creatures who are totally at one with their universe. If you doubt this, just gaze at the cover of *Chill Out* whilst listening to it and share the serenity."

The album cover depicted a number of sheep in a field, and

captured perfectly the music contained on the LP. Drummond had given each track a very detailed and specific title too – *Brownsville Turnaround On The Tex-Mex Border*; *A Melody From A Past Life Keeps Pulling Me Back* – which were probably intended as coat hangers on which to drape the music as some kind of soundtrack to an imaginary film. But each side of the LP, or the whole thing played continuously on a CD, really didn't need titles as the music took the listener on a journey only limited by their own imagination. Opening with running water, birdsong, snatches of radio and the brief refrain, "We're justified and we're ancient, and we like to roam the land". We then hear passing trains and soft country guitar before a relaxing synth theme emerges and the first track ends with another train passing. The entire album manages to convey a sense of tranquility and relaxation, especially when elements like the sound of sheep are deployed and synth themes and country and western guitars rise up again. Then there are the Tuvan throat singers, who give the impression at one point that one is listening to an updated version of the Residents *Eskimo* LP, whilst the introduction of a radio preacher gives a strong sense of Americana.

One of the most imaginative elements of *Chill Out* was how Drummond and Cauty worked in a few well known songs, such as Elvis Presley's *In The Ghetto* and Acker Bilk's *Stranger On The Shore*, which give the impression of cross-faded radio broadcasts coming together. All told, it was a stunning album – a classic that has stood the test of time amazingly well.

Upon release, the reviews ranged from the positive to the positively baffled. Crucially, however, Drummond and Cauty had staked a claim in the territory of ambient house with one of the first albums in the genre to be released. As to how it was recorded at Trancentral, Cauty later told *Record Collector,* "Well, *Chill Out* was done with two DAT machines and a cassette recorder!" Drummond added, "*Chill Out* was a live album that took two days to put together from bits and pieces. It was like jamming with bits from LPs and stuff we had lying around. We'd run around having to put an album on here, a cassette on there, and then press something else to get a flow." Cauty was keen to stress that, "There's no edits on it. Quite a few times we'd get near the end and make a mistake and so we'd have to go back to the beginning and set it all up again. The two DAT players, the couple of cassette players, a record player, and a twelve-track were feeding into a mixer and back out to one of the DATs."

The cover of *Chill Out*, with its pastoral setting featuring a number of sheep, provided a visual motif that Drummond and Cauty were quick to use as capital for publicity. Drummond struck a deal with a local sheep farmer near his Aylesbury home in Hertfordshire to arrange for a photo shoot that was also attended by freelance journalist Ian McCann. "I'm not sure why these creatures were chosen," states McCann, "it was doubtless some comment on the flock mentality of music fans, but as ever with The KLF, you were left to work it out. The sheep were duly sprayed with the band brand – it was like creating your merchandise before it had even been knitted! By the time it came to the photos, the sheep had had enough and wanted to go back to being fans of Lamb or whatever it is they do, and it took a bit of time to shepherd them into position to be shot – with a camera that is. The farmer was surprisingly agreeable to the whole palaver – perhaps there was an Art Council grant involved, or some payment under the EU's agricultural policy/rave music commissioning division. Considering what a farce it was – the weather was grey and it was getting dark and doomy, and it was by no means clear that these photos would ever be usable - Bill was particularly earnest about it all, and determined to get it done. Which proved correct, as the photos were excellent in the end. What did we learn? That art, however ridiculous, requires commitment."

Cauty and Paterson stopped working together in April 1990, having come to an agreement that Paterson could retain the name 'The Orb' whilst Cauty would issue the material they had been recording that was intended to be their debut LP. "There was a split in that one person had one record label and the other person had another, and he also had The KLF as well," Paterson told the *New Musical Express* in 1993 when the battleground was three years older. This allowed Paterson to sign The Orb, via Modo, to Big Life. He would eventually be able to move out of A&R and become a full-time Eno himself.

As for the Paterson and Cauty recordings that were intended to be the first Orb LP, "Jimmy went back to the Space recordings," stated Adam Morris, "and took all of Alex's bits of it and changed the name of it to *Space* and put it on - I'm not sure it was on KLF or not (it was) - but he put it out through their network. Through Rough Trade."

Thus, on 16th July 1990, Cauty's *Space* LP was issued, and advance copies contained another Drummond-penned press release that waxed lyrical about a mythical figure in the KLF canon - Distribution Girl. "She picks up the unopened album mailer. She already knows what's inside. Can she be bothered opening it? She knows. A KLF Communications Promo LP and press release. She shuffles off to bed. Lying there she attempts to read the press release."

Crucially, the press release made sure that it hammered home the fact that *Space* was the work of one man:

FORTY MINUTE ROLLERCOASTER RIDE
AROUND THE SOLAR SYSTEM. WRITTEN AND

PRODUCED BY J. CAUTY - ORIGINALLY
INTENDED TO BE THE ORB'S DEBUT ALBUM.
NOW SIMPLY "SPACE" BY SPACE, FOLLOWING
THE SPLIT OF THE ORB IN APRIL 1990.

Whether it was intended or not, the *Space* LP could have killed the career of Alex Paterson and The Orb stone dead. There is probably no disputing that Cauty was the musician of the two, with Paterson serving as a kind of vinyl Eno who had a unique sense of knowing just what to add to a recording to give it a wonderful sonic flavour. Youth, who was close to both at this time, speculates that one reason for the split – apart from the label tug of war – was possibly that Cauty, "came up with some lame excuse over publishing – DJs don't write music, they're just DJs – and they fell out."

Looking back, Paterson muses that the fact that the version of *Space* he recorded with Cauty wasn't issued may have been a *good* thing for his career. "We were trying to do the planets, the different planets, and rather than call it *The Planets* we would call it *Space*. *Pluto* is really cool as Pluto doesn't exist on (Gustav) Holst's *Planets*. So we were taking references from there and putting it on the *Space* album as a DJ sample thing. We could have ended up like Beats International, getting sued really heavily by a whole orchestra for using a piece of music on there, so in retrospect it wasn't such a bad thing that we didn't put it out, and *Ultraworld* was definitely a statement of intent by myself because I had to prove to Jimmy - I didn't have to prove anything to Youth – that the impetus that I had drove me to make a double album that still stands out today."

Taken on its own merits, the *Space* album is a fantastic record and still holds up today. Although divided into eight different tracks – *Mercury*, *Venus*, *Mars*, *Jupiter*, *Saturn*, *Uranus*, *Neptune* and *Pluto* – it is best enjoyed as either two short vinyl suites or one continuous play. Like *A Huge Ever Growing Pulsating Brain That Rules From The Centre Of The Ultraworld* it has a wonderful organic flow, and is dominated by sequencer rhythms and sensitive samples, ranging from classical voices to an excerpt from *Twinkle Twinkle Little Star*. *Jupiter*, for example, blends elements of classical music, spoken word, ice crystal piano and gamelan.

Whilst reviews were positive and strong - "This is head music for the '90s, a possible soundtrack to altered druggy states, and it is immaculately and intelligently crafted" - it didn't chart, but became, as intended, a perfect album to relax and chill out to. It was, in effect, one of the new *Tubular Bells* that Norris had spoken about – just without the platinum sales. When Cauty spoke about the recording of *Space* there was no mention of Patterson, "I had nothing written," he told one interviewer, "It was just a jam all done on Oberheim keyboards. Loads of samples and different bits and pieces were chucked in there as well. I started on a Monday morning and by Friday it was all done. It was basically a record for 14-year old space cadets to go and take acid to for the first time."

Whilst *Chill Out* and *Space* were amazing ambient house soundscapes, Drummond and Cauty also took the genre into the visual realm when, some time in 1990, they decamped to the island of Jura in the Inner Hebrides with Bill Butt in tow and set up part of Cauty's Trancentral studio on a convenient beach. Journalist Ian McCann was on hand to bear witness and recalls, "There was much talk of burning a wicker man beforehand, but it didn't happen while I was there. Instead, I was flown to Glasgow, then another short flight to Islay, followed by a ferry to the south of Jura. Installed in a country house, it was not clear what The KLF's plan was. The following morning Bill took me out in a jeep, driven by the owner of the house, to get a decent look at the island, which was beautiful and unspoilt. Bill seemed comfortable in this environment, while I found it forbiddingly wild. When we to back to the house, some of the band's gear was being taken to a nearby beach where Bill Butt, The KLF's cinematographer-director in residence, was preparing to film what became *Waiting*. By mid-afternoon filming started. The few music business related people who were present sat around the gear; Hendrix played through a small PA, joined by house beats: two forms of acid music melded. Bill Butt was dashing around with a hand-held camera, creating his own action I guess. It struck me how out of place I was. Most people present were chilled, looking like they'd be happy at a rave. I was wearing a jacket and shirt and looked way too smart. I was waiting for the real business to start, but it already had: this was just a part of it, some blokes on a beach, some plastic foil flapping in the wind, music playing over and over. Waiting for something that was already there."

The resulting forty-minute short film, *Waiting*, was not a concert, or even a Jura travelogue, but a kind of visual and aural wallpaper. The soundtrack was not culled from *Chill Out* or *Space* but made up of a wide range of musical sources, from various chants to elements of *What Time Is Love*? Sold on VHS by mail order (for £9.99 plus 95p postage and packing), it received some baffling reviews, with *Sounds* being right on the money when, after praising elements of Jura's natural beauty, Tim Peacock stated, "you're unlikely to miss anything important should you decide to take five and do that washing-up halfway through."

As for Paterson, despite a report in the *New Musical Express* that he was going to use his EG connection to re-tool some Brian Eno tracks, he next began to work with Youth on a tape recording he'd received containing some female spoken word. "They'd already done

Loving You, which was just seminal," recalls Youth, "and I just followed through with Alex after they'd fallen out with *Little Fluffy Clouds*."

Little Fluffy Clouds was also a seminal record, and unlike *A Huge Ever Growing Pulsating Brain That Rules From The Centre Of The Ultraworld* had a dance engine, partially moulded from slowed down drums purloined from Harry Nilsson's *Jump In The Fire*, beneath elements of Steve Reich's composition *Electric Counterpoint*, played by guitarist Pat Metheney. This acted as a wonderful base to the spoken word part taken from a Rickie Lee Jones interview disc – "We lived in Arizona and the skies all had little fluffy clouds." An opening cockerel crow was followed by a purloined sample of a mouth organ part taken Ennio Morricone's famous spaghetti western soundtrack *Once Upon A Time In The West*.

"We got in touch with him and he said, "Give us £500. End of,"" recalls Morris, "No royalties. Give us £500. Easy." Both Rickie Lee Jones and Reich were flattered by the imaginative use of their material, although Big Life did later make payments to them. Youth, Paterson and Kris 'Thrash' Weston, who mixed the track, artfully blended a classic, and *Little Fluffy Clouds* received rave reviews upon release in November 1990 and sold strongly, whetting the appetite of listeners for an Orb LP. "It took a long time for me to appreciate *Little Fluffy Clouds* without my pop head on," states Paterson today, "Pop head works perfect, but to me *Huge Ever Growing Brain* is to lay down a marker of any intent of what you intend to do in the world. And what a perfect record to start, or nearly start, with."

When it came to recording an Orb LP, Paterson had told Jazz Summers at Big Life that he wanted to release a triple album, but it was eventually agreed that he would record a double album set. Paterson knew what and who he wanted, and collaborated with a number of people, including Youth, Thomas Fehlmann, Thrash, Steve Hillage and even Paul Ferguson, over a number of sessions.

Due to the peaks and troughs in the music, where some parts would be quiet whilst others exploded sonically, and the sheer length of some of the sides, there was some difficulty in cutting the LP, and a number of test pressings were made before sonic satisfaction was achieved. Indeed, the initial pressing was made to the standard of a 'classical' record, using new rather than recycled vinyl, which was usually the norm for the rock and pop market. Review copies came with a "track by track visual talk over by Dr Alex Paterson." This was a typed sheet of his thoughts - very clever marketing and a nice personal touch. "So begins an amazing trip into little fluffy clouds that cover a third of the planet Earth, growing into a rhythm of colours, to taste the universe, for most of us the furthest we will climb," ran the opening passage, before ending with something that could have been penned by Bill Drummond himself, "We float over colourless massive stars until at last we fade into a flyby and many left over ideas and pictures – and rest sleepily - and take the kettle off as it has burnt dry as you forgot that you were making tea."

Of course, the words that mattered were those penned by reviewers, and when released on 25th March 1991, *The Orb's Adventures Beyond The Ultraworld* received rave reviews, and became the ambient equivalent of *Tubular Bells* and *Dark Side Of The Moon* rolled into one. Matters were helped by cleverly use of an image of Battersea Power Station on the front cover, visually riffing off the Floyd's *Animals* LP. "I felt sorry for Richard Norris in that sense," Paterson states today, "I kind of saw what he was doing but I wasn't in any way copying him. I wasn't copying anyone. It was a different ballgame and we were never in a thousand years intending to be the new Pink Floyd - that was a label the press put on us and that was a thing that we couldn't get out of." That said, The Grid later went on to score a hit singles in 1993 and a hit album in 1994, so Norris also put himself on the map. Better still for Paterson, he eventually got a triple album version of *Ultraworld* into the shops. "We did the mix album as I said, 'Can I get all of the artists to do their own interpretations of the tracks on *Ultraworld* and see what it sounds like?'" The album was released and deleted on the same day, but got into the charts and earned Paterson a gold record into the bargain.

After the release of *Ultraworld,* The Orb were soon flying, especially as they became a touring act, and Paterson set the controls for the heart of the sun on a journey that still continues to this day. Although, like many creative artists Paterson is always looking forward towards his next recording project or his busy schedule as an international DJ, he does reflect that the link between The Orb and The KLF was mutually beneficial. "All press is good press, so just the words The Orb mentioned with The KLF for many years has always been a good thing. I know a lot of KLF people pick up on things by The Orb due to the Jimmy connection and become immersed in The Orb. It's not, 'Oh I listen to them because Jimmy is in them.' No, it's, 'The Orb is actually quite good. I like what they are doing.'"

With The Orb in their third decade in the field, there are many people around the world who share the same sentiments, and in 2016 Canadian filmmaker Patrick Buchanan premiered a documentary called *Lunar Orbits* about their history and the recording of the album *Moonbuilding.* When it came to the section that dealt with the genesis of The Orb, although Jimmy Cauty was contacted and asked for an interview he declined to take part. "The first email I ever got back from him was a no thanks to being interviewed on camera, he just didn't want to appear," Buchanan told me, "he seems to have moved on in life and his focus is his artwork and models."

THE WHITE ROOM

"I think if we wanted to make it easy for ourselves we'd sign to a major company, sign a deal for a million quid and make all the compromises. Because, whatever bands say, you're always completely compromised when you sign to a major label. I know that, if we signed a band, we wouldn't let them behave like us, doing what the hell they wanted, that's for sure."
- Jimmy Cauty to Melody Maker, 16ᵗʰ February 1991

"We hardly ever saw Jimmy. He used to be, well, I don't think 'intimidating' is the right word but he just used to be there with his hood up, hair and sunglasses and just didn't say anything. Whether it was shyness I don't know, but he came across as a more aggressive Pet Shop Boy. He used to come into the office, sit down and put his feet up on the desk and smoke whoever's cigarettes were hanging around. But I rarely ever saw him. Two or three times maybe. I think he was in the studio and Bill enjoyed being the self-employed Record Executive."
- Andrew Lee, former Appearing employee, to the author

By the time *3AM Eternal* hit Number One in the charts in February 1991, another piece of The KLF's musical jigsaw was already in place. Enter Errol Nicholson, better known as Black Steel. "I was known as Steel as I chop like stainless steel on the guitar," he tells me today, "That's how they do it when they're playing the Jamaican style of reggae music. It was a guitarist by the name of Jerry Lyons who first called me Steel. I thought, 'Steel. Hmmm. OK, I'll stick with that,' but it was a bit too lonely. So I said, 'Shall I put Black with that?' Ah, Black Steel - it worked! That was in 1979." At this time, Nicholson was making his way as a musician and developed as a multi-talented instrumentalist who could play bass, drums, keyboards and sing, both inside and out of the studio. As well as recording and playing live with a large number of reggae artists, he soon became a fixture at Mad Professor's Ariwa studio in South London, where his talents were much in demand, and he was to appear on many of the records that Mad Professor issued on his own label, also called Ariwa.

It was his link to Mad Professor that saw Nicholson introduced to The KLF. "Professor called me to ask, was I interested in doing a session for this guy called Tony Thorpe? I said, 'cool, no problem.' I came up and that was the first time I heard *Eternal*. Tony asked me, 'Blacksteel, can you sing?' I said, 'Of Course. What would you like me to do for you?' He asked me, 'Can you sing 'Justified Ancients Of Mu Mu?'" So I did and he loved it. He liked what I sang."

Drummond and Cauty were building up a talented team similar to that which served Pete Waterman so well, and it wasn't long before Nicholson was asked to come down to Lille Yard Studios in Fulham to meet them. "They said, 'You've got a nice voice.' I said, 'Thank you very much,' then Bill said, 'Would you like to sing some lines for me?'" This led to Blacksteel recording some backing vocals with Maxine Harvey around the *Justified and Ancient* theme.

With the chart success of *3AM Eternal*, Nicholson was also drafted into the presentational line-up of The KLF, "I said, 'Mum and Dad, I'm going to be on *Top Of The Pops*!' They went, 'Really?' 'Yeah, so watch out for your son,' and that was my very first time going to the BBC television studios. We were new in the charts then and it just went up and up until it hit the Number One spot. I appeared three times, and it was a good performance - they (Bill and Jimmy) liked my performance."

There was a lot to like about Blacksteel playing bass and flashing his dreadlocks for the camera, and he also got to do the same thing in the promotional video for the song. According to Nicholson, he was also responsible for an iconic KLF visual moment, "When we was Number One and appeared (on *Top Of The Pops*) in red (robes), Bill was saying, 'We have to have something different rather than holding a microphone. I said try my phone.' This saw rapper Ricardo De La Force appear to be dialing out the opening tones of the song on what, at this time, was one of the first, and very brick-like, mobile phones 'So they (then) went 'KLF is gonna rock you' – BOOM! Yes, oh yes. That was my idea."

As well as working on what was becoming an assembly line of singles, Drummond and Cauty were at last completing *The White Room*. This would not only be used for the film, which, at that stage, was still being edited into its final form, but also issued as the next LP by The KLF. After the success of *What Time Is Love?* and *3AM Eternal* a KLF LP would be, on a financial level, like side footing a football into an open goal from two yards out again. It was classic Pete Waterman, but they didn't have the album ready!

A core group of Drummond, Cauty and Nick Coler were working hard on a number of tracks at Lillie Yard and Marcus Studios, and whilst the album would feature slightly revised versions of *What Time Is Love?* and *3AM Eternal* there were a number of other tracks that had to be completed or recorded from scratch. Thus session musicians like Blacksteel and Maxine Harvey were added to the mix, along with long-term collaborator Tony Thorpe, who was providing breaks, and no doubt Cressida and some other session singers, who were laying down backing vocals. A number of other vocal refrains, like the "Mu Mu" chant, had been laid down some time ago at Village Recorders in Dagenham and, as they were stored on disc, could also be added to songs when required.

Tony Thorpe's musical knowledge was an important tool in The KLF's armory. Whilst Drummond and Cauty might be filmed for in Trancentral demonstrating to the TV cameras how they would capture a break from a record – "There's a good groove in this one," states Cauty in one, "Everybody's using it, but it's good." "We're going to find a bass drum beat on this record that we can sample and clean up," adds Drummond – when the cameras weren't there it was Thorpe who was also providing them. "How he knew people like Pete Tong and all that was because he had been part of the Caister (soul) thing, and they all knew each other from years before," recalls Nigel Laybourne, "so he knew about that whole jazz funk thing. He knew all about the old records and so that was that. You can usually trace his basslines and things like that to old jazz funk records."

Of course, many people were also sourcing old records, but Thorpe's ear for a bassline or drum break was very helpful to The KLF when building up the ideas for some of their tracks, or giving them that little bit of additional spice other records didn't have. Thorpe would also do a number of remixes of KLF singles, as well as taking his own Moody Boys into more expansive territory, ranging from reggae to African rhythms, "It's taken me a while to separate all those influences," he told *Melody Maker* in 1991, "there was a time when everything was mixed into one and some of the ideas didn't work. It was like trying to mix oil and water, impossible. But now I've sussed out where I want to take The Moody Boys." This was evident in a track like *What Is Dub?*, issued in 1991 and featuring the vocal talents of Screamer. Errol Nicholson, Nick Coler and Jimmy Cauty were also part of this session, but, according to Coler, as Cauty had flu he spent most of the time asleep on the sofa in the studio!

Last Train To Trancentral (Live From The Lost Continent) would become The KLF's third top five single when it was released in May 1991. Drummond and Cauty were very much a team in the studio, and in an interview with *Record Mirror* they related how their different skill sets perfectly complemented each other. "Jimmy's far better at time-keeping on the percussion side," stated Drummond, "I usually come up with the basic chords. I think I've got more of a pop mentality whereas Jimmy's got more of a groove mentality." As for Cauty, "Bill has a more analytical brain, so he's good at structuring the stuff, and I'm better at just jamming. But there's no set pattern."

Saying that, they were more than open to input from those working with them. "The part I created was, 'All aboard, all aboard, Wooah' recalls Nicholson, speaking about *Last Train To Trancentral*, "but the rest of the lyrics were written by Bill." As well as programming and playing keyboards on this, and many other tracks, Nick Coler remembers that, "on *Last Train To Trancentral* they wanted to put some vocoder onto it. They used to always go to me, 'You do it,' and I would say, 'I don't want to do it but I'll show you how to do it.' They did it and said, 'That's it.' I said, 'It's not in time,' but they said, 'That's it!' So.... That's it then!"

Some of the other tracks on the LP were probably inspired by the footage that they were intended to accompany in the abandoned *The White Room* film, and may have even been refreshed material from earlier *White Room* sessions in Dagenham. The atmospheric *Build A Fire* not only had lovely slide guitar but saw Drummond acting as a film narrator, his spoken word lyrics including, among other things, a reference to Lee Marvin's *Wandering Star* playing on the jukebox - a nod to his love of country music. With regards to her vocal contributions, Maxine Harvey recalls that, "some had more work than others, but *Build A Fire* was about two takes."

The track *The White Room*, although propelled by a dance beat, also had an atmospheric vibe and another short Drummond narration, as well as a Nicholson scat-like vocal that he originally did as a joke. "I did some funny voice style that sounds like (reggae legend) Eek-A-Mouse," he says, "and I wasn't expecting that. I said, 'Bill, that's not my style, that's Eek-A-Mouse! I don't know if he's gonna like that!' But he (Bill) loved it, so I said, 'OK, I'll do it, no problem.'"

In many respects, studio work on singles and the album all blended into one, and Nick Coler recalls that, at times, different people were working on different tracks that were at different stages of development. "At one point when we were making *Last Train To Trancentral* we were in Townhouse four," he says, "and there was this great snake of keyboards going out of the door, running live and everything. Jeremy Wheatley, who is now a big remixer, was Spike (Stent's) tape operator and Pro Tools had just come out, so it was a four-track system you were able to edit and then stick it all on tape. He would be in the live room editing the track that was going to go out, which might have been *3AM* or something, and they (Bill and Jimmy) would be working on *Last Train To Trancentral*. (Meanwhile) I was in the drum room with a great heap of sequencers and samplers programming the orchestra for *It's Grim Up North*."

In the midst of all this, in early February 1991 Drummond and Cauty lost a day working in the studio when the long arm of a paintbrush saw them encounter the long arm of the law. Scheduled to be interviewed by David Stubbs of the *Melody Maker*, the pair planned to deface a billboard near Battersea Power Station. They must have driven past it on the way to Lillie Yard in Fulham at some point and seen it advertising coverage of the Gulf War - "THE GULF - The coverage, the analysis, the facts." Cauty and Drummond cleverly decided to paint a large K over the GU, thus changing the message of the poster to "THE KLF - The Coverage, the analysis, the facts."

It was absolute heaven for *Melody Maker* photographer Kevin Westenberg, and although Stubbs was a little nervous due to his own flyposting past the copy wrote itself - "Jimmy in particular displays a steady hand, considering he's painting fifteen feet up from ground level using two extensions. Nice brushwork." With their defacement complete, painting tools dumped and photos snapped, it was the perfect raid. Now, back to the studio. But Drummond and Cauty decided that they should be photographed holding up their brushes in front of their handiwork, and it was at this point they were approached and arrested by three plainclothes officers. Ironically, one of them actually knew who they were, "You're KLF? Yeah, I know you." He then proceeded to comment on Cauty's fashion sense, "I dunno why you wear those sunglasses. They're crap!"

Drummond and Cauty were taken down to the police station and held in separate cells before eventually being let off with a "stern reprimand" by the Chief Inspector, who realised it was a publicity stunt of some kind. It was, and was gleefully reported as an exclusive in the next edition of the *Melody Maker*. Meanwhile, back at the studio Nick Coler was scratching his head and wondering where they were as they were all supposed to be working on a track together. "I was in there all day. They went off and said, 'We'll see you in a bit.' I was just programming and they came back around seven o'clock. I said, 'Where the hell have you two been?' They went, 'We've been in jail all day.' 'Oh, alright then.' Then they went, 'By the way, all that's shit.' I said 'OK, Thanks for that!'"

The defacing of the Gulf poster, as well as serving to boost the image of Drummond and Cauty, was also noticed by another electronic duo. "I like the way they changed Gulf to KLF on that hoarding," Chris Lowe of the Pet Shop Boys told the *New Musical Express* in May 1991. "Also, they had an incredibly recognisable sound," added Neil Tennant, "I liked it when they said that EMF nicked the F from KLF. They're in a different tradition to us in that they're pranksters and we've never been pranksters." By this point, the two acts had collaborated when the Pet Shop Boys asked The KLF to remix their track *So Hard* in 1990. But things hadn't turned out how Tennant had expected, "When they did the remix of *So Hard* they didn't do a remix at all, they re-wrote the record and that's why I had to go in and sing the vocals again. They did it in a different way. I was impressed that Bill Drummond had written all the chords out and played it on an acoustic guitar. Very thorough." Of course, there was no acoustic guitar on the final version of the song, which was a fantastic electronic powerhouse of a track.

Publicity aside, with regards to tracks that were still being laid down for *The White Room, No More Tears* added a wonderful dub reggae feel, with Blacksteel also playing bass and piano and adding vocals. "I obey everything they say," recalls Nicholson, who played his bass part along to an existing drum pattern, "I obey. It's not my thing, it's their thing, so we have to listen to them. When they tell me what to do and what to sing I sing it." He was glad, however, to add sweet harmonies on this track with Maxine Harvey – "she is so good, she is fantastic" – although when he thought it would be a good idea to try the same thing on the LP version of *Justified And Ancient*, on which he again contributed vocals, "Bill said it would be a little *too* sweet, and I understood that."

One of the crucial aspects of The KLF's sound, both on the singles and the subsequent LP, was the mixing, which was handled by Julian Gordon Hastings and Mark 'Spike' Stent. "He's always had amazing ears," Nick Coler recalls when talking about Stent, who cut his teeth on bands like The Cult and The Mission, "His hearing is so great. They just got in there and did what had to be done, with him editing. Jimmy would just say, 'No! No! We need more – turn that up louder!' They were pushing him to make what was the sound of the time."

The sound of the time was very much what The KLF were creating, with deep, wide-angled sonics that had depth, space and clarity as well as some grit. Nick Coler recalls that he and Cauty used to have a lot of fun when making tracks by adding the sort of things that professional studio engineers hated, such as a drum stool or chair squeaking, or the sound of a spring on a kick drum. Actually, when it came to the kick drum sounds used on a lot of KLF records, "we would put two kick drums on there, and then there would be a high one as well - that was unusual for Spike. Jimmy *really* made him EQ. There were engineers who used to get a nice sound, (but) it wasn't until dance music and digital stuff came along that everybody began to crank it up and distortion became fashionable."

The KLF were one of the first acts to crank up this particular volume. At one point, Drummond and Cauty even decided that they wanted to overdub something onto one track at the cut. The cut of a record is the last stage in the process and is usually only used to do a last bit of EQing to a finished track, rather than any further work on it. "I've never seen a man so frightened," laughs Coler, "The (cutting) engineer was like, 'I haven't got any inputs!' They said, 'You must have something.' He said, 'I've got one input!' But he was just freaking out. There was always something mad going on."

One such mad thing, according to Coler, was that Drummond and Cauty usually liked most tracks they recorded to run for around eight minutes. "On *Make It Rain* there was a (Yamaha) DX7 and a Cheetah MX-6, and we would turn the lights out and I would play two or three chords. And yeah, eight minutes of that and then you would listen back for eight minutes, and in about an hour you've done an overdub. That was the way it was." In some respects, this probably had something to do with the fact that dance tracks at the time could run for six or seven minutes, but it did mean that mixers like Mark Stent had to work really hard to pare down tracks for final edits, which might only run for three or four minutes. Of course, when it came to remixes and different versions that appeared on B-sides of singles, the lengthy running times of the original tracks meant that there was *plenty* of material to work with.

With the huge success of *What Time Is Love?* and *3AM Eternal*, it was obvious that a KLF LP was going to sell strongly, and the ground was laid by Sallie Fellowes to ensure that it was pre-sold by the Rough Trade sales team to retailers. But she left someone out of the loop. "He really loved The KLF, and the only time I ever saw him cross and hurt was when *The White Room* came out," recalls Andrew Lee of Scott Piering, "I was living with this guy called Martin Carghill, who had got me my job at Rough Trade, and he went on to work in the sales team at the new Rough Trade in Seven Sisters Road. I got to hear *The White Room* before Scott because Sallie went and gave all the sales people, the telephone sales people, a copy of the album on cassette to pre-sell it. Scott came in and I said, 'Have you heard the album? It's great!' He went 'No.' I said, 'Have you not got a copy? Sallie has been giving them out, surely you've got one as well?' No? *Oh shit!* 'I've brought it with me, you can have it if you like.' (He went) *'FUCKING HELL!* I'm selling this thing, if it's promotion you want we're your rocket to the moon. Sell all you like, but you won't without us!'"

When it was finally released in March 1991, *The White Room* really was the sound of the time. Crucially, the first side of the album was sequenced like a concert, complete with crowd noise, and was a KLF greatest hits, kicking off with *What Time Is Love, Make It Rain, 3AM Eternal* and *Church of The KLF* and ending with *Justified And Ancient*. Reviews were positive, with Tim Nicholson of *Record Mirror* hitting the nail firmly on the head when stating, "Anyone whose introduction to the JAMMS-Disco 2000-Timelords-KLF saga was via the Stadium House reworking of *What Time Is Love?* last year will be ever so pleased with this strong and cohesive LP."

The White Room crashed into the album charts at number three on 16th March 1991, and although it never got any higher than that it spent a total of forty-six weeks in the album charts, of which twenty-two were in the top thirty. The album sold in the region of two million copies in the UK alone, and was also issued in Europe and America, where sales were strong.

Behind the scenes at this time, there had been some interesting developments. As related earlier, Drummond and Cauty had sampled the voice of Wanda Dee from the *To The Bone* 12" on *What Time Is Love?* and, whilst the original versions of the song had enjoyed a low profile, the interstellar success of the definitive Stadium House version eventually came to the attention of Dee's husband and manager Eric Floyd. According to Dee, in an interview with Werner Von Wallenrod's *Humble Little Hip Hop Blog* in 2006, he went on a, "one man warpath that night, calling Wax Trax Records in Chicago, KLF Communications in London and so on and so forth." Although the specific details of the agreement are unknown, Dee also revealed that her husband/manager got her a six figure settlement, as well as "featured credits on the *White Room* album, starring roles in the music videos and a lucrative co-publishing deal with them (as I wrote the hooks to their biggest worldwide hits)." Whilst she acknowledged that Drummond and Cauty, as producers, were, "light years ahead of their time," claims that they would not have enjoyed success without her contributions were, to put it diplomatically, not entirely accurate. Whilst the, "I wanna make you sweat" refrain was a vital and memorable part of the final version of *What Time Is Love?* it was hardly the genesis of the song. Indeed, if you stripped this vocal line out the basic, beautiful sequenced engine would remain.

According the Nick Coler, everyone was amused by Eric Floyd's initial attempts to contact The KLF when they were working at Lillie Yard Studios. "This guy Eric, every night on Hanzi's (Hans Zimmer's) answering machine there used to be this, 'Wild dogs will come and grab you if you do not reply to this... I will so and so.' I recorded some of them but – unfortunately – I don't have them anymore. I was going to chop them all up and make a song out of it and put beats all over it." This went on for some time, "Every night there would be another one. We used to crowd around the answer machine and have a good laugh. Obviously they (Bill and Jimmy) had to do something because they'd had the problem with the MCPS before with the original record (*1987...*) and everybody was getting really hot on samples at that time." Not preclearing the sample and agreeing to pay a flat fee upfront left Drummond and Cauty open to challenge. This cost them money, and Dee and Floyd were to cause a totally different kind of headache in the future.

Of course, once a deal had been done it was all smiles, and Dee and her husband flew over for her to take part in the video shoot for the single edit of *Last Train To Trancentral*. Ironically, Dee's one repeated lyrical refrain on this track was, "Come on boy, do you wanna ride?" which was *also* taken from the *To The Bone* single. The performance part of the video was intercut with scenes of a model of Ford Timelord flying through a mythical model city of Mu, which had been built by Cauty's brother who did this for a living. Drummond and Cauty helped out and cleverly conductied magazine and TV interviews on the set during construction, which was great publicity and also gave magazines and TV shows great visuals to use in their features or brief broadcast spots.

Although Dee appeared in this lush video wearing a sexy white outfit, Errol Nicholson, who had contributed the "All Aboard!" line, did not. He was unavoidably delayed on that day and only arrived at the studio after filming was completed. "I would have stayed around Jimmy's house, but because it was so crowded I'd rather sleep in my own bed." As with *3AM Eternal*, *Last Train To Trancentral* was a lushly staged affair, with Cressida handling most of the aspects of the choreography and costume design, although she likely steered clear of Drummond and Cauty as they deployed sparking circular saws.

Whilst the Wanda Dee issue was, and would remain, costly, it was, in some respects, a price Drummond and Cauty had to swallow for the uncleared sample, in a similar way that Black Box had been legally clobbered by Loleatta Holloway for the unauthorised use of her voice on the *Ride On Time* single. Even when Drummond and Cauty used '60s soul singer P.P. Arnold for session work, she later took legal action against them, stating that she should receive royalties for her contribution at the beginning of *3AM Eternal* – "KLF! Uhuuhuuhu." Arnold also refused to appear in KLF videos wearing a blue robe over her head as she thought it made everyone look like relations of the Ku Klux Klan, which was not the case at all. The matter with Arnold was settled, but around the corner was another disaster that was to cost Drummond and Cauty much more money that any sampling issue…

By 1991 Rough Trade had come a long way from the day in 1976 when Geoff Travis had opened a record shop in Ladbroke Grove, having expanded into a record label, a publishing company and a powerhouse of an independent distribution company. The tipping point had been The Smiths and the ability of Rough Trade's Cartel of distributors to get their records into every shop across the country, and also into the charts. From the mid '80s onwards, independent records became big business as bands like Yazoo, Depeche Mode and New Order sold millions in the UK through independent distribution. As the decade progressed, the definition of an 'independent record' became fuzzy. For example, many records issued by Pete Waterman's PLW team were on their own Supreme and PWL labels and distributed through Rough Trade's major independent rival Pinnacle, so a label that generated major chart topping singles and albums by artists like Jason Donovan and Kylie Minogue were, technically, as 'indie' as The Fall, Spacemen 3, The Cocteau Twins, My Bloody Valentine and the early output of The Stone Roses.

Initially run as a collective, with The Smiths' success Rough Trade had grown, like the Orb track, into a huge pulsating brain that ruled from their offices and warehouse in Collier Street, Kings Cross. Although Geoff Travis helmed the record label, the distribution arm became the main engine for generating cashflow. Rough Trade even offered a service that would take care of vinyl pressing, sleeve printing and overall manufacture, and by 1989 the distribution turnover was £22 million. By 1990 this had shot up to £40 million. These were serious numbers and extraordinary growth, suggestive of robust health, but sadly these figures papered over massive cracks - in truth, Rough Trade Distribution was not being run as well as it could have been. For example, when Parkfield Video collapsed in 1990 it was revealed that Rough Trade's credit control department, (responsible for collecting monies owed for distributing Parkfield product) were owed £500,000. This was very lax indeed. And after running down the regional Cartel distribution network to work from a new and larger central warehouse in North London, the upgrade was botched to the extent that when they moved into their new premises the lease on the old Collier Street office still had some time to run, so the company were paying rent on two large warehouses.

Rough Trade also famously invested over £600,000 in a computer system that was supposed to streamline orders and distribution but ended up being described as the most expensive computer catalogue ever built in the music business. The system simply could not complete the task it was created for. There was also *another* warehouse in Camley Street, Islington, full of unsold stock that continued to occupy space on which rent, light, heating and staff costs had to be paid.

Rough Trade Distribution had encountered financial difficulties before and managed to solve these problems and carry on trading, but by 1991 they were approaching a perfect storm that would shipwreck all aspects of the business, from the record company to the publishing arm. Matters were not helped by the fact that the management structure - from Rough Trade Records to Rough Trade Distribution - was run partially by committee rather than senior or middle management.

Also, a decision to try to focus on becoming the top independent distributor led to some crystal ball gazing wherein money was advanced to some new labels - including some in the dance sphere, where Rough Trade Distribution was making good money – in exchange for exclusive future distribution rights, all in the hope that one of these labels would become the new Mute, Factory, 4AD or Creation. Several of these labels served up duds, whilst in some cases no records appeared at all, despite their receiving, allegedly, five or six figure advances.

But what really moved Rough Trade towards the rocks was their decision to expand into America. Not only did they underestimate how large the country was when it came to distributing records across a continent, but also the business was underfunded, and the £3 million allocated for a five year roll out was swallowed up in nine months. Whilst Rough Trade distributed Mute records in the UK and Europe, their records were licensed to Sire/Reprise in America, and so the coffers of Rough Trade America couldn't be bolstered by an earned percentage on shipping millions of copies of albums like Depeche Mode's *Violator*.

Ultimately, Rough Trade America required regular cash infusions, and rather than go to a bank to fund a business that should have financially remained in its own silo, it was decided to funnel money into this black hole from profitable operations in Germany and the Benelux. Attempts were made to try to square the circle and head off disaster, and George Kimpton-Howe was poached from rivals Pinnacle to try to add some business rigor to Rough Trade's Distribution operations, but he was drinking from a poisoned chalice from day one. Redundancies, streamlining, and attempts to run the collective-like consciousness like a normal business met with resistance from staff ingrained in the Rough Trade culture.

By 1991, with record sales down across the entire industry, word was beginning to leak out that Rough Trade was in trouble, "We are not in danger of going under," Kimpton-Howe was quick to tell industry publication *Music Week* in February 1991, "we are currently waiting to finalise a very big financial deal." Talk of £1 million was bandied around to fill the hole in the accounts of the distribution arm, although as Rough Trade owed no money to the bank one wonders why they didn't try to negotiate a loan to float them over their current financial sandbar. But being wise after the event doesn't change history, and at the time labels like Mute – who'd been here before with Rough Trade - were confident that matters would be resolved, and even provided *Music Week* with a statement of support," We are aware that Rough Trade have had serious financial problems and we are committed to help them resolve their difficulties."

The horizon grew dark and ominous when labels like Revolver moved their distribution elsewhere, and rival distributors Pinnacle and Charly began to receive enquiries from worried labels also looking to move, especially when forty staff were laid off when accountants from KPMG were summoned in February 1991 to try to save the company from collapse. David Murrell, head of KPMG's Entertainment and Media division was appointed as acting Managing Director and shot from the hip, "While I greatly regret what has had to be done, if we had kept these jobs there would be no future for Rough Trade." Murrell went on to state that the company had been losing money every week for the last year as revenues went down and overheads - especially for the new distribution warehouse - had increased.

Rough Trade was also in the position of not paying its creditors, many of which were the independent labels that it distributed. They were owed money for records already distributed and sold, but were told that under the new regime Rough Trade wanted to pay them all at once. However, although there was money in the bank there wasn't enough to pay them all. A new financial model was therefore established whereby all monies received for records shipped out after 8th February would be held in trust and then paid out immediately to the labels concerned.

Murrell was optimistic about Rough Trade's prospects and stressed that it was not in receivership. Although there was no immediate sign of cash injection there was talk of drafting a prospectus to send out to prospective buyers, such as Geffen records. A statement like this showed that Rough Trade Distribution was, for all intents and purposes, on the auction block. More staff were then laid off and *The Catalogue* magazine was shut down as a cost cutting exercise as Rough Trade was slimmed down to make it more attractive for potential investors.

Jazz Summers, Head of Big Life, gave words of support - "We are going make sure Rough Trade is not going to the wall. The future of the music industry depends upon the independents." Neither Geoff Travis or George Kimpton-Howe were willing – or perhaps allowed – to comment to *Music Week*, or any other publication for that matter, on the state of play inside the crumbling Rough Trade empire. It was no wonder Jazz Summers wanted Rough Trade to find their way out of the woods - Big Life had enjoyed massive hit singles and album, all of which had been distributed through Rough Trade, and so he was a major creditor at this point, along with labels like Mute, 4AD, Situation 2, Rhythm King, and, crucially, KLF Communications. There was soon a meeting called that included around seventy labels Rough Trade distributed, to appraise them of the situation and probably explain why only interim rather than full payments had been made since February. These labels needed this cash to pay out royalties to their artists as well as meet the running costs of their own businesses.

By May, things had deteriorated further, with Pinnacle looking to take over distribution of a number of labels, and ranks were breaking as Jazz Summers took the distribution of Big Life through Polygram and stated, "I am angry with Geoff Travis. He is Mr. Rough trade, and although they enabled a lot of us to start up they strangled us with complete inefficiency and gross incompetence."

As all KLF Communications records were distributed by Rough Trade, Drummond, Cauty, Fellowes and Cressida followed events closely. After all, by May 1991 they'd scored two top five singles and a top five album and were owed in the region of £750,000. Worse still, *Last Train To Trancentral* and *The White Room* were still in the charts, so not only was there the issue of the money still being generated by these massive selling records but also the strong possibility that, if Rough Trade collapsed, they would simply stop appearing in the shops, and thus the charts. The KLF were riding the top of a huge wave with the prospect of their surfboard vanishing into thin air.

When it came to dealing with the issue, it was Bill Drummond and Sallie Fellowes who went in to bat for KLF Communications. They attended the meeting held for the seventy labels, as well as subsequent meetings that were only held to address the biggest creditors. KLF Communications, it was calculated, were owed in the region of thirteen percent of the total debt.

Cauty told Richard King in an interview for his *How Soon Is Now* book that "Bill and Sally (sic) would be there working out how much money we were owed and I'd be in the studio trying to finish the track (*Justified And Ancient*) and trying not to think about the studio bill." According to Mute's John Dyer, who was at these meetings, Drummond rose to the challenge, and managed not only to contribute to the discussion but to take the time to book Pinewood Studios for a video shoot, as well as phone Cauty in the studio and listen in on mixes of *Justified And Ancient*, "Yeah, bit more bombastic Jimmy, bit more bombastic."

It was *pure* Ken Campbell.

MAKE MINE A 99

"I think 'Justified And Ancient' cost a quarter of a million quid to make. Studios were so expensive, and there was a lot of time spent on it. Then there were the sets at the James Bond sound stage."

- Nick Coler

"When we were doing the video shoot with Tammy, to see some of the African dancers..... oohhh! That kick off rumpus! To me, I can now see where Bill and Jimmy and Cressida were coming from. Having various cultural people in The KLF sessions and doing the African drums, I loved that!"

- Errol Nicholson

"They looked like they had no money and they acted like they had no money, so even when they asked the world press to come to Glasgow and get on a boat (to Jura), filmed 'Justified And Ancient' at the weekend and flew back from the island they still looked like living tramps, Jimmy especially. Jimmy looked bedraggled."

- Maxine Harvey

After *Last Train To Trancentral* went to number two in the UK in May 1991, it would be another six months before the next KLF single, *Justified And Ancient (Stand By The JAMS),* was released early in December. The reasons for this were probably more mechanical than artistic - not only were Drummond and Fellowes dealing with the administrators of Rough Trade Distribution in order to extricate some of the monies owed, but out of the ruins a new company emerged called RTD that would, from this point, handle KLF Communications releases, as well as the output of other labels. Establishing this company and getting everything in place to ensure smooth distribution of product across the country took time.

In the meantime, however, The Justified Ancients Of Mu Mu were resurrected in November 1991 when they finally unleashed the *It's Grim Up North* single. As we've seen, a version of this track (with Pete Wylie providing the narrative vocal line) had been sent out as a promo a year previously, but the track had since been retooled with Bill Drummond providing the vocal, a spoken word run through of a shopping list of northern cities and towns that was the main thrust of the song, over a throbbing and pounding industrial beat.

Typically inventive in the studio, one of the musical parts on the record was supplied by one of the most common items - "That's Hans Zimmer's (door)bell along with the orchestral sample," reveals Nick Coler, "Gimpo turned up there (Lillie Yard Studios) and there was a buzzer bell. It went – GRRRRRRR – and we went, 'That's a good sound, lets sample that!' So we stuck in it." The bell sound was then replayed on a keyboard. According to Coler, the industrial whooshing sound that ran throughout the track was more organically generated, with Cauty or Cressida bellowing into a microphone and then electronically treating the results.

When it came to filming the video for *It's Grim Up North*, Drummond and Cauty reverted back to their guerilla days, when they'd spray painted the National Theatre and enjoyed defacing billboards. "They went and found the people building a road, who lived in caravans, and said, 'Can we use the motorway?'" recalls Coler, "They went, 'Yeah, sure,' and charged – I can't remember – a couple of thousand quid. They didn't have the jurisdiction to give permission to use the motorway as they'd just tarmacked it!" Whatever, at night it provided a stunning backdrop for a video, and Drummond stood beneath, one assumes, a rain machine in trademark black, hooded waterproof, announcing the names of towns into a microphone connected to a loud hailer held by one of the Japanese girls, whilst Cauty stood to his left miming out the thunderous low- end on the song on a bass guitar. Behind them were a drummer and a wall of amplifiers. It was an arresting image for an arresting song.

"I took my son down there," recalls Nick Coler, "you could see these huge spotlights going into the sky, and they were just pumping water over Bill. He didn't have a spare pair of clothes and it was also freezing cold." An attempt to dry his shoes out in a microwave didn't meet with success, and Drummond had to return home to Aylesbury literally bare-footed. One of the first people to see the completed video was actually John Hollingsworth, who bumped into Drummond in Soho and was dragged into an editing studio where it was being finished. They also went for a drink and a catch up, and Drummond told him about the ongoing problems with trying to extricate KLF money from the ruins of

Rough Trade Distribution. According to Hollingsworth, at one point KLF Communications were offered the Rough Trade warehouse with all the stock in it as a possible settlement, although Drummond told Hollingsworth that, "I just want a cheque!"

As for *It's Grim Up North*, by this point press releases and reviews – "A hell of a record. Literally." according to the *Melody Maker* - hardly mattered as Drummond and Cauty were now chart royalty. Matters were best summed up by a teasing, hand-written note on copies of Appearing's mail out to radio, which stated, "We're shipping 40,000 of this little gem – you've seen the DJ reaction sheets – you've heard the shop reports – all signs point to a top twenty entry – but why should your boy want to play it?"

It's Grim Up North went into the charts at number eighteen on 9th November 1991, and once again the KLF team appeared on *Top Of The Pops*. Such was the fame of Drummond and Cauty now that there was no confusion in the mind of the public over the brand names of their musical vehicles, but it appears there *was* some confusion in the House Of Commons, where the Labour MP Joseph Ashton put down an early day motion on the 21st October 1991, "That this House calls on the Secretary of State for Transport to remove the huge, white painted graffiti on the bridge over the M1 on the northbound carriageway just north of the M25 junction, which reads 'Its Grim Up North', or alternately arrange to add the words, 'Gruesome in the Midlands, and Nowt but Homeless Folk in Cardboard Boxes in London' to restore a fair regional balance during the next election." When the magazine *Select* informed Ashton that the JAMs/ KLF were a pop group and that *It's Grim Up North* was the title of their latest single, he took it in good grace, "Theses lads have far to go, and not just up the motorway. I think Saatchi & Saatchi ought to sign them up right now."

A better response to *It's Grim Up North* - which went top ten on 16th November - was actually a piss-take white label 12" record by a band who called themselves KYJ, entitled *It's Great Down South*. The 12" even included a version called *They Play Down South* that listed London football teams, "Barnet, Wimbledon, Millwall, Crystal Palace..."

In the studio, Drummond and Cauty were driving themselves and their team to finish recording further singles. The next KLF release would once again be the reworking of an existing song that was not only pumped full of musical steroids but also given a new element - star power.

Musically and lyrically, *Justified And Ancient* was another old warhorse that had first seen service on the *1987* LP. There had also been an updated version on *The White Room* that featured Errol Nicholson on bass, piano and vocals and was sweet, laid back and soulful. Drummond and Cauty now updated it once again to release as the next KLF single. Although recording sessions were constant throughout 1991, Nick Coler, who was at most of them, gives an interesting insight into The KLF's working process at the time around *Justified and Ancient*. "He (Bill Drummond) came in and he had the chords, and we talked about whether it should be a major or a minor, how long that bar should be - should it be a two or a four - and we would get like that. Then I might play some very rough chords, then Tony (Thorpe) would come in with his deck, or there'd be a deck there, and he'd bring a load of records. He's amazing with rhythm and everything, he would come in and go, 'What about this?' He had all these obscure records, but they all sounded amazing and were so well recorded.

"So we would select all of the stuff like that and then add the kick drum. We had a kick drum sound we'd made over time that was a sample that just had this really high (sound) in it. I think Jim and Spike did that. Then we would put that on. One day we couldn't find that and we were all like 'Where has the sample gone? What are we going to do?' We were looking all over the studio for it and we found it stuck to Jimmy's shoe. The floppy disk was stuck to his foot!"

When it came to this new version, Maxine Harvey initially recorded the main vocal at Lillie Yard. But there was a problem, "It was about ice cream. An ice cream van! I said, 'I'm not singing it.' It was about ice cream and at that time I was very much getting into my culture, because I had a strict upbringing and black parents, but at that time I was working with Papa Levi on an album called *The Lion Ain't Sleeping* and the songs we set down in the studio, a lot of them were quite deep, so I was going through a natural phase. Even though I was working with different people I'd always been conscious about lyrics and I weren't singing about ice cream! So that was it really, and they just got Tammy - she just sang over the top of my harmonies."

In his book *45*, Drummond rather cruelly wrote, I assume about Harvey, that, "The singer we had been using sounded uninspired, doing a job, watching the clock." Whether there was a discussion about the merits of ice cream went unreported, but crucially Drummond did recall that Cauty, sitting beside him, suddenly had a musical vision, "What this song needs, Bill, is Tammy Wynette."

If this was indeed the case, it didn't take much for Drummond to agree. He was, after all, a big country music fan and responsible for those elements that infected parts of the *Chill Out* and *White Room* albums. He rose to the challenge, later stating that twenty minutes after the suggestion he was speaking to the famed country singer as she stood backstage in a concert hall in Tennessee. Drummond played *Justified And Ancient* down the phone and suggested that she do a real life

Whitney Houston and join the JAMs.

Drummond had been able to contact Wynette due to his vision of worldwide domination for The KLF that would see singles and albums riding high in the charts in other countries around the world, particularly in Europe, where singles had charted powerfully from The Timelords onwards. But America was the big prize, and in order to penetrate that market he had licensed The KLF to Arista Records, who were headed by the famed music business executive Clive Davis. According to an interview that Drummond gave to an American magazine called *X* in late 1991, when *America: What Time Is Love?* was in the American charts, Davis had lured The KLF with the possibility of working with Whitney Houston, who was signed to Arista, but Drummond was keener to work with Aretha Franklin. He stated that they would sign with Arista "if you let us do a track with Aretha Franklin." Once they'd signed on the dotted line, however, "I find out that she's not on the label anymore!" That said that, Davis was a consummate deal-maker and this likely wouldn't have stopped him brokering a studio marriage of Franklin and The KLF in the future, especially if the fruits of the collaboration would have been issued Stateside on his Arista label. Anyway, a call to Davis apparently smoothed the path for Drummond's phone call to Tammy Wynette.

Did all of this magic really take place in the time it took to play one side of a long-playing vinyl LP as Bill Drummond Said? Who knows, but a week later he was on a plane to America to meet Wynette in Tennessee, where he was picked up at the airport by George Richey, Wynette's fifth husband and manager, who drove him down to meet Tammy at her large home. She was, at this time, forty-nine years old and, although a country music icon, had not had a hit single for three years. But, although she was certainly more Justified And Ancient that Drummond and Cauty, she still constantly roamed the land on a never-ending touring treadmill that was part of the life of a successful country music artist.

After Wynette heard *Justified And Ancient* it was arranged for them to go into a local studio to synch her vocals with the backing track that Drummond had taken with him on a DAT. But once in the studio there were problems, as Wynette would speed up or slow down and could not keep in time with the machine-honed track. Richey told Drummond that part of the problem was that, when Wynette recorded she usually laid down a guide vocal with her band as they played the backing track, and they took their timing from her. Even when Richey went into the studio so that Wynette could stand by her man, "things didn't get much better," as Drummond later recalled. "I felt truly ashamed hearing her voice, the voice of poor white American womanhood, struggling to find some emotional content in our banal, self-referential lyrics."

When he returned to London with what he though was a busted vocal flush, Drummond was informed by Cauty that there was a new machine in their studio arsenal that allowed them to sample Wynette's vocals and fit them perfectly into the machine honed KLF vision of ice cream nirvana. This was probably an update of Pro Tools, or the program Cubase, which allowed blocks of musical tracks to be moved around on a computer screen, edited and synched together. Errol Nicholson, who'd sung on the *White Room* version of the track, was called in to add some backing vocals. "I heard this vocal and I didn't know who it was. 'Don't you know, Steel?' (said Bill). I was like, 'Hold on – 'They called me up in Tennessee' – Oh, Tammy Wynette! She doesn't sing this type of music, she only sings country and western.' I did not know. That was amazing."

Although this new version of *Justified And Ancient* was a kitchen sink affair, as always there was element of improvisation as to how some parts were added. As well as working with The KLF, Nick Coler was also collaborating with Tony Thorpe on some of his recordings, and the pair had gone into an East London studio run by a friend of Cauty's to record some Zulu singers. "It was such a shit studio," recalls Coler, "everything was sort of home-made. There was an electric two kilowatt fire and Tony put a cup of coffee on it. Somebody – him actually – bumped into it and knocked it over, short circuited the whole thing and blew all of the fuses in the studio!" When power and light had been restored they recorded the Zulu vocals, that were probably intended for a Moody Boys track - Thorpe had already explored some African elements on the amazing *Funky Zulu (You're So Fresh)*, released on XL in 1990. That track sounded like Kraftwerk riffing with an African percussionist and a TB-303 acid bassline, and the vocal line over the top was just *killer*. When Thorpe and Coler had finished recording their East End Zulus, "we took it back to Bill and Jimmy and they said, 'That's really good. Let's put that into the track.' Thus these new Zulu vocals were added to *Justified And Ancient*.

The success of KLF singles had seen their press officer Mick Houghton deluged with interview requests from journalists and TV companies across Europe. Whilst in the past Drummond and Cauty had been happy to speak to anybody, with The KLF now an international success they had to pick and choose in order to allow time to continue working. Even at this stage, however, they were clever enough to stage encounters that burnished their myth as accidental pop stars. Ian McCann recalls one interview at BENIO with Cauty, "He was relaxed and reflective and sat on the sofa, where he later found an un-cashed £25,000 cheque stuffed down the back of it – possibly as a prank." This cleverly gave the impression that making money from their music was not central to what they were doing. During the same interview, "Jimmy spoke of how weird it was when he drew his legendary *Lord Of The Rings* poster as a teenager, sent it to Athena, and soon after a helicopter landed in the field next to his Devon family home and the boss of the wall art company got out, in a hurry to sign Jimmy up."

Unlike many other successful chart artists, there was not only a self-created mythology surrounding The KLF that begged interrogation but a broad raft of other multi-media projects, from the *Waiting* video to the *White Room* film. Although this still had not been released, a cut *was* screened in Germany in 1991, and both Drummond and Cauty flew out to bear witness as, according to Houghton, "They've never seen it before in a proper cinema and they're really excited about it."

Drummond and Cauty also received a large number of offers to make personal appearances. These ranged from European TV stations wanting The KLF to fly out and mime to hit singles like *What Time Is Love?*, *3AM Eternal* or *Last Train To Trancentral* to tour promoters enquiring about the possibility of putting The KLF on the road. After all, their lush videos gave the impression that The KLF was a band, complete with a stage set ready to rival the Parliament-Funkadelic mothership! "We were supposed to be guests for Prince in the United States," recalls Errol Nicholson, "They refused. They didn't want to do it. That would have given me the chance to meet Mr. Purple Rain himself – I would have looked forward to that. Tony Thorpe, everybody was looking forward to it, but they weren't interested." Even when they refused, this was still not good enough for some people. "They got offered loads and loads of money for adverts and for appearances and they just decided that they would never do it," recalls Nick Coler, "That just drove people on and on and on to get them. That was the first thing I was in that was really super successful, and you get to experience what it's like when everybody wants a chunk. It's like being in a volcano as you're being pushed to the tip of this thing. Everybody wants it and it almost gets out of control."

At this point, though, Drummond and Cauty were very much in control, and the fact that they were successful allowed them to indulge themselves in a way that would also give journalists something to write about and add more blocks to the growing KLF mythology. "They just had these brainstormed ideas," states Coler, "Whereas most people would go down to the pub and talk about it and never do it, we would go down to the pub or just talk about it and they *would* do it."

One of these ideas was to hold a special event on the isle of Jura, off the coast of Scotland in the Inner Hebrides, to coincide with the summer solstice on June 21st 1991. This harked back to what Drummond had done with Echo And The Bunnymen previously, when he had got them to play in unusual places that included the Outer Hebrides. Of course, as The KLF didn't play live Drummond and Cauty came up with the idea of staging an event they called *The Rites Of Mu*. They would not only invite a load of journalists to report on it but also get Bill Butt to film it.

Whereas it was standard industry practice to invite writers and photographers down to gigs to meet a band backstage or conduct an interview or photoshoot, this was something totally different. Firstly, only one publication per country got an invite – *ID* was the UK representative – and pleasure was mixed with business as those invited included a number of European distributors and licensees. Part of the invitation read, "The KLF require your presence. You'll be transported to the lost continent Mu. Bring your passports."

Once again, it was the Bunnymen routine in action, with the journalists being left to find their way to Jura. When they arrived by ferry they were met by a passport control officer - none other than Bill Drummond - who stamped every passport with The JAMs' pyramid blaster logo. This was a nice touch of detail, although he refused to answer questions or give interviews when going about his *official* duties. Drummond and Cauty had spent a lot of time planning and preparing the event, which was staged over an entire weekend, and attendees were given a one-page sheet that mixed philosophy with fact and ended thus:

AS WELL AS ASKING YOU TO ACCEPT THE CONTRADICTIONS OF THE ABOVE WE HOPE THAT YOU WILL GIVE YOURSELF FULLY TO THESE THREE DAYS, ACCEPTING WHATEVER THE ELEMENTS TIP OUR WAY, WHATEVER MILD PHYSICAL STRAINS MAY BE PLACED UPON OUR BODIES, AND SAVOUR THE UNDERVALUED QUALITIES OF WAITING, AND MAYBE AFTER IT IS ALL OVER WE WILL UNDERSTAND THAT THERE IS FAR LESS TO UNDERSTAND THAN WE EVER KNEW.

The event was very much a celebration, and collaborators like Errol Nicholson and Maxine Harvey were also in attendance, although Nick Coler didn't get an invite. "They didn't take me as I was working with Ian (Richardson) - he was my writing partner and they did not want to take him as they knew he would be taking the piss out of them. They came (into the studio) with all the ropes and lanterns and things and we went, 'Where are you going?' (They went) *'Nowhere!'*"

Up on Jura, at some point on the Friday everybody was decked out in ceremonial robes and led by Drummond and Cauty – sporting large tusks on their foreheads beneath the hoods of their robes - along a pre-planned route that included passing an artful arrangement of sheep bones. Soon they ended up in a clearing before the sea, where Drummond, Cauty and probably some friends had constructed a large wicker man. The Angels of Mu – Japanese girls in blonde wigs and white gowns – asked each attendee to give them a personal item that was put at the base, and then Drummond gave a speech in a made-up language.

"All of a sudden you saw the wicker man blow up, which transfixed you," recalls Maxine Harvey, "and the next thing you knew bottles of champagne were being popped and it was party weekend." It was a mixture of symbolism and theatre all rolled into one, along with something that hardened music journalists all understood – the ritual flowing of free alcohol!

Most of the Saturday was given over to "waiting" which conveniently allowed everybody to sleep in and maybe take in the sights of the island, although there may have been some additional filming. Errol Nicholson recalls that he was, "doing my part, singing *Justified And Ancient* from right to left and left to right, and when I finished I kept on walking, but I did not want to keep walking into the seawater as there were a lot of stinging jellyfish in there. Even some of the Japanese (girls), they were very scared as the water was freezing and it was low temperature, like one degree. It was damned cold. If they had a special wellington boot or (some)thing that went up to here (indicates stomach) we would have walked in - slowly, slowly, slowly - and then cut." Four Japanese girls in blonde wigs were actually filmed and photographed in shallow water on a beach as the four Angels Of Mu, footage that was later edited into the *Rites of Mu* video. The soundtrack, though, was crafted in the studio, and Nick Coler recalls that, "when the ferry comes in that's us (Cauty and Coler) running up and down the drive with a trolley jack and a big piece of metal."

On the Sunday - June 23rd - everyone was transported to the Liverpool Festival of Comedy, where, during the interval in comedian Emo Phillips' show at the Royal Court, a number of people went on stage in their robes and were joined by some members of the audience for a brief rendition of *Justified and Ancient*. There was also an ice cream van parked onstage, and after *Justified and Ancient* was completed members of the audience were invited up to buy ice cream, served by Drummond and Cauty.

It is estimated that the *Rites Of Mu* event cost Drummond and Cauty in the region of £70,000 to stage. The amount of publicity they received across Europe, however, was extensive, and they also had the experience filmed by Bill Butt, which would not only end up as a short film that would be broadcast on *MTV* but was also diced up and used in upcoming promotional videos. Of course, Drummond and Cauty also had the satisfaction of taking yet another bold and imaginative idea from discussion to stunning execution.

The only downside of the Jura trip was that the attendance of Scott Piering lost him a client. "We did a lot of stuff for Creation as well," recalls Andrew Lee, who was working for Appearing at this time. "I think it was when (Primal Scream's) *Higher Than The Sun* came out as a single, that was the same weekend that the Isle of Jura thing was on. Alan (McGee) rang up and was like, 'Where is Scott?' I said, 'He's away.' 'What do you fucking mean he's away?' 'He's away with The KLF.' 'Why is he not working my fucking record?' He (McGee) wanted radio playlist. Alan went off on one and I had to ring Scott in Jura - Scott had a mobile phone at this time, in 1991 - and I could not get hold of him to tell him that Alan McGee was going off on one. They had a big falling out and we lost all of the Creation stuff to the detriment of us supporting The KLF."

Piering was very much part of the inner circle around The KLF at the time, and Nick Coler recalls that he would always come down to the various studios where tracks were either being recorded or mixed, "He was always around, we spent a lot of time together." As well as wearing his professional hat, listening to tracks as a radio plugger and even suggesting edits for radio, "He would also come down with his latest invention. I remember one was a see through carrier bag with a speaker in it. Bill went, 'What use is that?' and just stuck it over his head and said, 'Is this how you do it?'"

The *Rites Of Mu* event showed that Drummond and Cauty were now looking to stage and create visual counterparts that were as equally impressive and imaginative as their singles, and when the time arrived to film a video for their next release they literally pushed the boat out.

When it came to the staging of *Justified and Ancient*, the plan was to film the band performing the song in a representation of Mu Mu Land. To this end, Drummond and Cauty not only tasked Bill Butt to direct the video but to do so on an epic scale. This not only saw the hiring of the largest sound stage at Pinewood Studios, where films like the James Bond series were shot, but also the construction of an elaborate set that resembled an ancient temple, complete with columns. At the time, *Alien 3* was also being filmed there, and Gimpo, now part of the small and tight-knit KLF family, managed to sneak onto the set with a video camera before he was caught by their security team, who arranged for everything on his tape to be erased before escorting him back to The KLF's set. When it was time for cameras to roll, not only was this Mu Mu Land populated by the band but there were singing and dancing male and female Zulus, warriors, dancers, Japanese girls and, of course, Tammy Wynette.

On the day of shooting, one person who made sure they got to the studio on time was Errol Nicholson, who was a huge fan of the county music star and went straight up to her. "I said, 'You're Tammy Wynette!' 'Yes.' I sang her a verse from *Stand By Your Man* and told her, 'Tammy, every time I hear that at a family party - and they always play it - everybody goes crazy and they pull the one they love (close) to dance to your biggest ever multi-million selling classic. It is forever a classic. *Stand By Your Man* is forever a classic!' She said. 'Thank you' and kissed me. I nearly choked when she kissed me on the cheek, and luckily someone filmed that. Wow. I was excited because we, as musicians, we like to meet the legends. We don't care where you come from or who you are, it doesn't matter because we see you on TV and we watch them. When she gave me that kiss it was something to treasure for always and forever."

When not kissing Nicholson or performing in a tight blue dress that she said made her "feel Like Madonna," Wynette was interviewed by the *New Musical Express* and told them, "I really don't know why they chose me, there's dozen of people they could have gone for. I was a little apprehensive at first, but I'm really excited about the way it turned out." She continued, "It's the first time I've ever been on a rap record, although I'm glad they got someone else to do that part, because I didn't think I could get the words out fast enough. As it was, I didn't understand what some of the words meant. I know about ice cream vans, but I'd never heard of a ninety-nine before. Bill explained it to me, and now it makes perfectly good sense. I'm not sure about justified and ancient though.'"

With the shoot complete and the video edited into its final form, press releases were written and pre-releases pressed and sent out to journalists - everything was ready for another assault on the charts. By this point The KLF were so mainstream that bookmakers William Hill were offering odds of 16-1 that *Justified And Ancient* would be the Christmas Number One. Those odds would have probably lengthened considerably if they'd known that, at one point, one of The KLF's more outlandish ideas involved hiring an ice-cream van and handing out ice-cream, but anyone who said, "Make mine a ninety-nine" would also receive a dose of ecstasy. Thankfully, in this instance it was talk rather than action, although it was a signpost to some of the more outlandish behavior that was to come from Drummond and Cauty. A *Melody Maker* review stated that, "There's a gutsy, galloping dance beat to hold the whole cracked edifice together, and it ends up feeling like somebody slipped something hallucinogenic into the Christmas sherry. Merry madness." If only they knew!

When released in the first week of December 1991, *Justified And Ancient* went straight into the UK Charts at number five, and anyone who'd placed a bet with William Hill must have been confident at that time that it would get to the top of the charts, especially as it went up to number three the following week. But it remained at that position and, over the Christmas period, slipped down to number four whilst the Queen medley *Bohemian Rhapsody/These Are The Days Of Our Lives* stayed riveted to the Number One spot. A late surge in sales saw *Justified And Ancient* climb back up to number two for two weeks before it slowly began to slip down the charts as January 1992 progressed. It was also a massive international hit single, and charted in a number of countries - its chart placing ranged from Number One in a small territory like Sweden to number eleven in the Billboard Chart in America, where it had been released earlier in 1991. Drummond's call to Clive Davis at Arista had paid out a dividend for both of them.

This being The KLF, there was a bizarre coda when, in January 1992, *Music Week* asked a number of industry figures what, in their opinion, was the best and worst moment of 1991. David Murrell, at accountants KPMG, obviously stated that the collapse of Rough Trade Distribution was the worst, but the best probably took a number of people by surprise - "*3AM Eternal* by The KLF was a great new sound - from time to time, something completely different comes along. I'm a former country and western singer – twenty-five years ago I was playing the Camden Palais on a Friday night, so I love what The KLF did with Tammy Wynette on *Justified Ancients Of Mu Mu*."

THE KINGS OF TECHNO METAL

*KELLY: "Er, no... I've seen them before though. Cor,
I didn't know The KLF looked like that."
SUSAN: "Er, I don't know. Blimey, I thought The KLF
were young."*
**- Two Smash Hits readers after being shown a photo of
Drummond and Cauty and asked to identify them**

Early in January 1992, *Music Week* took its annual look at the most
successful bands, artists and record companies of 1991. The most
remarkable figure appeared on a bar chart that gave the breakdown for
total singles sales in the UK for the year by company. Polygram were at
the top with a 21.3 per cent share, followed by EMI at 16.7 per cent. The
most interesting figures, though, were at the bottom of this top ten chart,
where KLF Communications accounted for 1.9 per cent of the total
number of singles sold in the UK in 1991. Just above them with 3.5 per
cent of the total market were Peter Waterman's PWL. The most interesting
fact was that The KLF only released a total of four singles in 1991 – *3AM
Eternal, Last Train To Trancentral, It's Grim Up North* and *Justified And
Ancient* – whereas companies like Phonogram and EMI would have,
through their own labels or subsidiaries, released hundreds. The chart also
showed that Warner Brothers only had 8.8 per cent of the singles market,
which was only around 3 per cent more that KLF Communications and
PWL combined. Another chart showed that, in 1991, The KLF were the
third biggest selling singles artist in the country after Bryan Adams and
Queen, whose sales were bolstered at the end of the year by the death of
their singer, Freddie Mercury.

Considering that KLF Communications was not a big corporation
with hundreds of staff, marketing, A&R and publicity departments, this
was an amazing performance. The British Phonographic Industry (BPI)
couldn't fail to take notice of these achievements, so The KLF was asked
to appear in the annual Brit Awards that celebrated the successes of the
industry, to be held at the Hammersmith Odeon in February 1992. "The
Brit Awards are going European in an attempt to make them compatible to
the Grammy Awards," stated a news report in *Melody Maker* in late 1991,
"Organiser Lisa Anderson says that, as 1992 approaches, Europe will be

treated more and more as a single market by the record industry, rather than as a number of different countries." Crucially, this meant that the show would be broadcast on prime time TV in the UK to showcase British musical talent, who would not only receive awards but also perform some of the best-selling songs from 1991. The KLF were not only on the shortlist for three awards – Best Album, Best British Group and Best Single - but were also asked to perform. Remarkably, they agreed to serve up a live version of *3AM Eternal*.

Typically, Drummond and Cauty decided to do something unique and perform the song with hardcore band Extreme Noise Terror. As to how this collaboration came about, Dean Jones, lead singer of the Norfolk band, later told the *New Musical Express* that, "Bill heard us on Peel when he was in the bath and got in touch. They wanted to do rock versions of their songs with Motörhead but something fell through, so he rang us."

At this time, Extreme Noise Terror was one of the pre-eminent hardcore bands in the UK. They'd formed in 1985 in Ipswich, and became part of a scene, along with bands like Napalm Death, whose music was brutally loud, powerful and well-known for its remarkable brevity. *System Shit*, on their first release – a split LP with fellow grinders Chaos UK called *Earslaugher* – clocked in at just over a minute. John Peel quickly became besotted with Extreme Noise Terror, especially after they recorded a session for him in November 1987. When this was issued on Strange Fruit in 1988, he gave six of the seven tracks three stars – his ultimate seal of approval – with only *Use Your Mind* – ironically the longest track, clocking in at 2m 10s – getting two stars.

"I like the sons of Hüsker Dü bands," he told the *New Musical Express* in July 1988, "and I play them a lot, but once you get beyond two and a half minutes I think you're on dangerous ground. I like the idea of doing ludicrous tracks that are only half a second long, although I realise there's more to life than that. I find brevity really attractive." As for Extreme Noise Terror, "sooner or later I knew Peel would catch on to hardcore and he has," drummer Mick Harris said in the same feature "It's great. He treats it seriously, whereas that pillock Steve Wright's just using it as a piss-take." After another LP, shared with Filthkick - *In It For Life,* issued in 1989 - Extreme Noise Terror released their debut *LP, A Holocaust In Your Head*, later that year.

Whether Drummond and Cauty did contact Motörhead is a delicious unknown, but hearing Extreme Noise Terror on Peel in his bath chimed with Drummond (and Cauty's) plan to record metal versions of KLF material - this was *The Black Room* project, which they had first talked about when *It's Grim Up North* had first been sent out to DJs as a one-sided 12" promo. Sessions with Extreme Noise Terror must have started in late 1991 as there was a version of *3AM Eternal* in the can that Drummond and Cauty wanted to perform on the Christmas Day edition of *Top Of The Pops* at the end of the year, but the BBC turned it down as it was so radically different from the original version that had been in the charts. Instead, this Extreme Noise Terror recording was pressed up as a limited edition 7" early in 1992 and sold via mail order (for £2, including P&P) via the KLF Communications PO box in Aylesbury.

With the idea of performing with Extreme Noise Terror rekindled for the Brits performance, Drummond and Cauty decided to deploy some extreme terror themselves, and discussed a number of ideas as to how to make the performance memorable. At one point, Drummond was going to cut up a dead sheep live on stage and, at the end of the performance, throw buckets of blood over the front rows of the audience. To this end, he got up very early on the day of the performance and drove to an abattoir in Northampton to collect a dead sheep he'd pre-ordered, as well as the blood.

Although there were some misgivings amongst the organisers during rehearsals over a rendition of *3AM Eternal* several nautical miles removed from the version that had stormed the charts, it was agreed that Extreme Noise Terror would be allowed to perform it with Drummond and Cauty. The master of ceremonies that night was, ironically, Jonathan King, who had form after accusing Bello of being a white man blacked up and wearing a wig, and he introduced Extreme Noise Terror/KLF. Drummond performed wearing a kilt and brandishing a crutch as the band sawed and growled through the song. Cauty, for his part, planned on doing a Jimmy Page, "I've always had this rock star fantasy, ever since I was young, that I'd have this massive guitar solo," he later told writer Richard King, "I'd been rehearsing it and rehearsing it. This was it. Hammersmith Odeon – I'm gonna do my guitar solo at last, then I'm finished. So of course, I come up to the front of the stage and go "wram" and my lead gets pulled out of my guitar. I've only got, like, twenty seconds to do my solo and I spend the whole time just finding the end of the lead to plug it back in and that was it – that was the last thing I ever did in the music business." Drummond was probably unaware of Cauty's impression of an ambient Jimmy Page as he disappeared off stage, returned with a machine gun and, with a cigar clenched between his teeth, proceeded to fire blanks out into the auditorium. This was fifty shades of Sid Vicious in the *Great Rock N Roll Swindle*. At that point King picked up the baton, and it was on with the show.

Once the performance was over, Scott Piering announced that, "The KLF have left the music business." They'd also left the Hammersmith Odeon, and sent a friend dressed as a motorcycle despatch rider to collect the Best Group award that they shared with Simply Red – which must have made Rob Dickens at Warner Brothers, their label, very happy.

But Drummond and Cauty were not done. They had abandoned the plan to cut up the sheep onstage due to protests from Extreme Noise Terror, who were all vegetarians, and plans to throw the blood out into the audience were thankfully headed off by publicist Mick Houghton. Instead, the sheep was dumped on the steps of the Royal Lancaster Hotel, where the post Brits party was to be held, with a note attached which read, "I died for you. Bon appetite."

"It was awful - really terrible," the manager of the hotel told the *Daily Star* the following day, "Police were called after our duty manager saw a man leap out of a van and roll the dead sheep onto the red carpet. There was blood coming from its mouth. It was one of the saddest things I have ever seen. But it did not ruin the party because the police managed to move the carcass." Amazingly, *The Sun* missed out on the dead sheep scoop but ran with a story that stated, "The KLF proved pop's biggest wallies by 'firing' a realistic machine gun at the star studded audience."

The biggest question about the Brit Awards performance was, what were Drummond and Cauty hoping to achieve? The KLF had dominated the single charts and scored a massive selling hit album, and had done this on their own terms with their own company and with independent distribution. It's ironic that the biggest problem they'd encountered in 1991 had not been from the establishment but from their independent distributor, Rough Trade, who had gone out of business and probably cost them hundreds thousands of pounds after the company had gone into administration. If the former credit control department of Rough Trade and some of the management had been given seats in the front row at the Brits, one might grasp the logic behind the plan to throw the blood, but they were not. Was it really a loathing for the business that had contributed to their success that drove them to take their ideas about self-promotion to such an extreme? Or was it a case of trying to defenestrate their reputation with an act of outrage? To self-destruct like a *Mission Impossible* recording, live on TV? Or was it simply the result of sheer mental exhaustion brought on by the heavy workload of maintaining creative forward momentum for the last five years?

The Brits performance was pre-taped and, when aired that evening, probably confused readers of *Smash Hits* and a broader range of KLF fans used to their more lavish theatrical TV performances, chart-tooled music and expansive videos. But as The KLF had, by now, obtained a reputation as "pranksters" and "master media manipulators" it was probably seen by most as just their latest, attention seeking publicity stunt in a business that was all about self-promotion. Many probably thought the sight of Drummond firing a gun whilst dressed like some kind of kilt-wearing Arnold Schwarzenegger was quite cool.

A journalist and photographer from the *New Musical Express* had been with the band all day at the Brits, and had even gone back to BENIO after the show, where, after members of Extreme Noise Terror had called their parents to make sure they watched them appear on TV that night, he received an urgent phone call from Bill Drummond asking, "Where are you guys? You should be with us... *we're doing stuff....*" This stuff specifically involved the placing of a dead sheep at a hotel entrance, which was, of course, snapped for the readership of the *New Musical Express.*

The next day, Drummond spoke to the magazine, "There is humour in what we do, and in the records, but I really hate it when people go on about us being "schemers" and "scammers". We do all of this stuff from the very depths of our soul, and people make out that it's some kind of game. It depresses me." Drummond expanded about entering the dark side of the soul, and even stated that he and Cauty had mentally gone to a similar place to Charles Manson and "that bloke who shot up Hungerford". When questioned as to whether he was serious about this and believed it, he fired back, "I do actually. Yes I do. It is the same area. Someone recently used the phrase 'corporate rebels' - about the Manic Street Preachers I think – and both Jimmy and I did not want just to be corporate rebels, because there's just so much of that, shameless, in the music business. We felt that we were head butting.... head butting, trying to push at what's acceptable. It was completely pointless, and you don't know why you are doing it, but it has to be done."

Drummond confessed that the plans for the performance kept changing, with options ranging from cutting his age – 38 - "Manics style" into his chest with a knife to the more romantic image of snogging Cauty onstage. He also stated that well before the Brits he'd bought all of the tools required to cut the sheep up on stage, "But of course in the end Extreme Noise Terror made it blatantly known that they were totally against the idea."

Whatever the intention or the perception of what happened at, and after, the Brits, The KLF remained at the top of the tree. When former Bunnyman Ian McCulloch was asked to review the singles for the *New Musical Express* in February, he was dismissive of the Art Of Noise's *Paranormia*, "That was just nowt. Have they been dropped from their record company? It sounded puny, cheap and weak, like they were back on the eight-track or something. The question is, why did they bother when The KLF do that kind of thing so much better?" It was a good job McCulloch hadn't heard *The Ambient Collection* issued by Art Of Noise in 1990, which showed that even Youth couldn't polish a turd.

Laurence Colbert, from Ride, also told the *New Musical Express* around this time that, "We want to be the ultimate pop band. That's what we're most keen on. At one point it was considered cool to not go on *TOTP*. Now it's cool to go on, everyone wants to be invited. Which is how it should be. Get on there and make it better. I think The KLF handle it really well. There's this slight sense of outrage in the midst of all this tepid stuff." Saying that, some of the outrage had been in the North Lambeth Housing co-op, as Cauty later related to Bo Franklin, "Co-op meetings were a bit weird, because people would say 'I just saw you on *Top Of The Pops*, what's going on? You're not supposed to use the co-op van for things like that, you're supposed to use it for picking up materials...' We were earning a huge amount of money, which you could in music in those days. So in the end, in about 1992, I just had to move out and buy a house. It was becoming ridiculous."

The same week that Drummond was baring his dark soul, all of the music papers contained a full page advertisement showing a two speaker stack covered in an American flag, with text beneath it which read, "In the year of our lord 992, The Justified Ancients of Mu Mu set sail in their longboats on a voyage to rediscover the lost continent. After many months on perilous stormy seas, their search was fruitless. Just when all seemed lost they discovered... America!"

For all the talk of *The Black Room* with Extreme Noise Terror – which was to include a track called *38* - there would not be, at this point, anything other than the limited edition 7" released. Indeed, Extreme Noise Terror issued *Phonophobia* in March 1992, their own mini-LP containing eight tracks clocking in at a total of seventeen minutes. The record received fulsome and positive reviews, as well as obligatory KLF references, "After the BPI fiasco I would forgive them almost anything. Stand aside Fruitbat! Some spikier heroes of the anti-crap jihad deserve a place on your podium." But by that time The KLF were back in the top five with *America – What Time Is Love?*

Ironically, this new single *was* a somewhat spikey affair, being a heavy rock version of an old KLF warhorse. *America - What Time Is Love?* had probably been recorded and mixed at the end of the summer in 1991 when the dust was still settling from the collapse of Rough Trade Distribution, and, crucially, it was first issued in America in October 1991, where it went top twenty and, one imagines, gave the KLF finances a positive boost, especially as *The White Room* album also sold strongly Stateside.

In the studio, Drummond, Cauty and their team had pulled out all the stops to give the song a hard rock edge. This not only saw Cauty playfully adding *Ace Of Spades* guitar riffs, but they also drafted in former Deep Purple vocalist Glenn Hughes to bellow out the main chorus lyric. Nick Coler recalls that, on coming into Olympic Studios in Barnes to lay down his parts, "he blew the mike up as his voice was so loud." Hughes seized the chance to get his career back on track, and told *Select*, "I mean, the KLF guys were aware of my previous record of drug-induced unreliability, but were willing to give me a chance... I did ten vocal tracks for them in just twenty-five minutes and realised that *America* would be huge, and probably my last chance to make a go of my career again."

Azat Bello also had to take time out from his work with Outlaw Posse to retool his original rap. "That was all fresh," adds Coler, "It was a completely different tempo, around 140 or 150 beats per minute. Most rock stuff is around 145." Bello remembers that, "I came in, Jimmy started the track and I started rocking to the beat. He gave me a piece of A4 paper and said, 'That room over there that is the writing room, so go and do your thing.' So I got a pen, and twenty minutes later I came out thinking, 'what's going to happen now?' I tell him I'm ready, so I go in the booth and I put it down one time. I'm thinking, that will be a good guide (vocal). I walk into the studio from the booth and say, 'What do you think?' They said, 'That's it.' I'm like, 'Do we need to do it another time?' but they were, 'Nah, nah, nah, nah. That is it. Trust me – it's banging.' Well, he didn't say it was banging, but whatever banging means (in Cauty-speak). So I said, 'You mean I'm done?' He says, 'Yeah, man. You can bust out now, we're going to mix the tune.' I was like, 'Wow!'"

When it came to finishing off the track, Nick Coler recalls that, once again, they added the "Mu Mu" chants recorded so long ago at Dagenham, "that one in particular, we thought, someone is going to come around and kill us soon, as we were just (re)using 'Mu Mu' or 'KLF' on every track. We thought, surely someone is going to turn around and go, 'Fuck off.' The submarine noises sampled from the film *The Boat* and used on *3AM Eternal* were also recycled. "All of the drums at the end were played by hand on the drum machine. It was all machines, except for Jimmy playing the guitars." The cherry was added to the cake at the mixing stage by Spike Stent, who, having previously worked with The Mission, knew how to break a heavy rock.

America – What Time Is Love? was another kitchen sink production affair, and when it came to the video Drummond and Cauty used the largest kitchen sink in England. Bello remembers walking into Pinewood Studios, "That was crazy. They had all of these extras, and they had *the ship*. It was proper, like we are going into a movie, with 'Take one! Take Two!' It was not like a normal video shoot."

The ship in question was actually a full size replica Viking longboat, one of two made for the 1989 film *Eric The Viking*. The Pinewood stage had been filled with water to accommodate the ship, which was actually set on hydraulic rollers and would be stationary in the water for filming. The impression of a raging open sea would be provided by huge hydraulic wave and rain machines that also sucked up water and sprayed in onto the boat. To help the musicians and extras mime their parts in time to the music, there was a 10,000 Watt PA system to one side that would play *America - What Time Is Love?* once Director Bill Butt screamed, "Action!"

Bello performed his rap in a black waterproof and was literally sheeted in water, "My memories of it are Jimmy's wife (who was on the stern dancing with just tape over her nipples and a machete in one of her hands) and the singer, the rock singer (Glen Hughes). He was pretty crazy because he was going for it! He was going for it like he was actually in the studio. I though, mate, this is a video - you don't have to, but he was on full throttle! He was going for it! He was going for it, man, and it *made* the video."

As well as Cressida's brother gyrating in the rigging and Zodiac Mindwarp's drummer hammering a sodden kit, somebody else who appeared in the video was Andrew Swaine. He was a student in St Albans, and in his spare time was a member of a society called Regia Anglorun, which was basically a Viking re-enactment society. Regia had been asked to provide rowers dressed in authentic Viking clothing to act as extras in the longboat, and in return not only would each person be paid but at the end of the shoot Regia Anglorum would be given the boat to take away and use for their re-enactments. Whether Drummond and Cauty had bought the boat or the prop manager at Pinewood decided to give away this rather large item is unknown, but it was good news for Regia Anglorum.

According to Swaine there were two days of shooting, "the guys who had been involved in the first day didn't show up again on the second day as it had been such a miserable experience, so they put the call out again to get more people in. I was involved in the second day and spent that day in the studio." As with all film and video shoots, there was a lot of standing around, although it appears that the band had their own trailers to rest up in. As for Swaine, "I can't remember how many takes there were, but we would jump in the ship and you could hear the beat and some music playing over it and we would row like crazy. But we weren't going anywhere - the oars were just splashing around and these rain machines were sucking water out of the pool and blowing it onto us and it was really, really cold. Our kit was genuine Viking stuff, made out of wool, and just became heavier and heavier as we got colder and colder. Then we would stop and the crane would pull the ship back to the side and we would jump off and stand around these heater things to dry off. Just as we got comfortable again it would be back in the ship and we would be off again. We would repeat that throughout the day."

The worst thing for Swaine was that the set for the *Justified and*

Ancient video was still standing on the edge of the water - he could see it from where he was sitting at his oar, and it looked like a tropical paradise compared to his rain and windswept position.

The rowing Vikings were supposed to get £30 each for oaring themselves out, but as they'd worked so hard and suffered so much were actually given £60. Swaine also received a special bonus, "I was standing to the side having a cigarette, and I became aware that somebody was standing beside me. He was fairly distinctive, with the hunched shoulders and the hair – I thought, 'Hello, I'm in the presence of royalty here,' – and I just said "'Hello,' (to Jimmy Cauty). We had a few words about this and that. He said, 'I appreciate that it was rotten out there, and it was very cold. I could see it was unpleasant out there. Thanks very much, and good luck with the ship when we're done with it.'

"I said, 'I don't want to be cheeky but that gold disc (screwed to the mast) that's warped. I suppose no-one is going to want that now?' He said, 'Do you want it?' I said, 'If you don't mind,' and he said, 'No. No problem at all,' and called someone to get the crane driver and pull the ship in, then called someone else over with a screwdriver and said, 'Can you go and get that for me please?' The man gave it to him and he said, 'Do you want me to sign it for you?' and he did. I said, 'Thanks very much - it was a pleasure working with you.' And that was it, my brush with pop stardom was pretty much over."

Of course, when the shooting was over Pinewood studios had to strip down the sound stage in preparation for the next production company that wanted to use it. "It took five days to fill it up with four feet of water," laughs Nick Coler, who took his young daughter down to watch the shoot, "and at the end of it they just pulled out a plug and it ran off across the car park!"

The resulting video was as stunning as the music was powerful. Drummond and Cauty had even worked a chorus of *America* from *West Side Story* into the music as an operatic refrain – recorded by one male opera singer doing loads of overdubs. Nobody knew, but this was a song Cauty had rehearsed with Angels One 5 nearly a decade before!

Again, press releases and reviews – "the tusk-wearing terrorists have gone full-tilt trouser-exploding metal, with Deep Purple's Glen Hughes bursting his lungs over massed choirs and screaming guitars and crackling thunderclouds and walloping skyscraper-sized disco beats!" – were almost superfluous. Not only did the record go top five in the UK in March 1992, but it also charted in Europe. The KLF were on top of the world.

As ever, rather than resting on their laurels Drummond and Cauty drove themselves on. They were soon back in the studio, not only working on another single but also with Extreme Noise Terror on the *Black Album*. "The most awesome track for me was one called *The Black Room And Terminator 10*," Spike Stent later stated, "which was like a very slow tempo thrash. It was mad. It was brilliant, absolutely brilliant, and it would have shown a lot of people up because it was ballsy as hell. Guitars screaming all over the place, Bill doing his vocals and Dean doing his. There was such a raw power to it. It was so different from anything anyone had ever heard. This was really heavy."

But at this point things began to unravel. Part of the problem was expectation - how they could top what they'd already done? "Bill and Jimmy started to get more and more carried away and wanted to do a Swingle (Singers) type thing," recalls Nick Coler, "(then) they got two Mexican guys in, they came in and sang *Make It Rain* in Spanish. They had sombreros on as they played their guitars. I think Bill and Jimmy made them wear the sombreros. It was getting madder and madder. There had been so many ideas that I suppose were trying to be fresh and original." Ideas ranged across the cosmos, from having a stonemason chip out statues of themselves to laying down real grass in a recording studio, bringing in a load of sheep and recording the consequences. Spike Stent later related to *Select* magazine how their success in using Tammy Wynette and Glen Hughes led to a veritable deluge of calls from potential collaborators, "I was in the studio and we had Neil Sedaka phoning up, we had Sweet phoning up, we had all kinds phoning up. I mean, that's just when I've been there."

According to Nick Coler, the end came when thoughts turned to recording a single with one of the greatest soul singers of all time. "We were all in Marcus (studio) and Spike was making the (*Black Room*) album with Jimmy on one side, and Bill and I were on the other side making another single, and he wanted to get Barry White. By this time, I had a huge pile of stuff, and all of these things were going on. We were going, 'Yeah, Barry White!' Then Jimmy walked in and said, 'It's shit. It's all over.' And that was it. That was the end of it. It was like someone pulling the rug from under you - there was no more making or doing what you wanted to do for the hell of doing what you wanted to do – that's what appealed to me about it. Bill and I sat around the piano for a bit, then we all went home."

In many respects, Drummond and Cauty were burnt out. They were not musicians signed to a major label with management to sort out their affairs and take care of everything, from arranging photo shoots to making sure records were mastered and cut properly - the main burden of running the business that was The KLF fell upon their shoulders. The fact that Drummond had driven up to collect the dead sheep himself on the day of the Brits was symbolic of how much hard work he put into oiling the wheels of the KLF machine. The core of The KLF who got things done involved Cressida – very much a power behind the Cauty throne - Sallie Fellowes, Mick Houghton and Scott Piering. Gimpo was also involved to some degree, but apart from a few other friends that was it. There had also been the stress and uncertainly surrounding the collapse of Rough Trade Distribution, which led to worries as to exactly how much of the money owed they would eventually receive, as well as the basic day-to-day administration involved in booking recording studios, paying musicians, making sure that records were pressed and sleeves printed, as well as the logistics involved in setting up and editing expansive video shoots. At the end of the day, whilst Bill Butt would direct the videos, Drummond and Cauty still had to view and approve the final edit as it was their label, as well as listen to and approve final mixes of songs and remixes.

In addition to this, success in America led to another problem with Wanda Dee, whose husband Eric Floyd arranged a club tour of the US in late 1991 which included the name The KLF in the billing. Whilst the settlement with Dee over the use of her sampled voice on *What Time Is Love?* and *Last Train To Trancentral* had given her songwriting credits – which also applied to the tracks appearing on *The White Room* LP – there was certainly no permission asked for or given to Dee to tour as The KLF, or use their music as backing tracks for performance. Drummond and Cauty contacted Clive Davis at Arista in America in an attempt to stop Dee touring, and may have put the matter into the hands of their solicitor, but she would continue to tour America, and worldwide, deploying the KLF name, which, in the world that she and Eric Floyd inhabited, meant, at that time, the Kinky Love Force. Of course, Drummond and Cauty could have solved this particular problem by taking The KLF out onto the road themselves, but, despite having a willing core company of players – Nick Coler, Errol Nicholson, Maxine Harvey, Azat Bello, Ricardo Lyte, Tony Thorpe and Cressida – and a number of lucrative offers, this was simply something that they had no appetite for.

After Cauty had drawn a line under that final session at Marcus Studio, he and Drummond probably got together to discuss the present situation, as well as their future together. As a two-man partnership there had never been – it is believed – any great tension or artistic differences between them. Both stated in interviews that they enjoyed working together, and when they were not working together they did their own thing with partners, family and friends, rather than go to clubs and gigs or hoover up mountains of cocaine. They were, after all, both married men in their late thirties, although the unravelling of Drummond's marriage at this time must have contributed to the amount of stress and pressure that he was under. Lyrics from the unreleased track *38*, concerned with losing control among other things, probably summed up his feelings at the time.

"The KLF have left the music business," stated Scott Piering at the end of the Brits performance, and Drummond and Cauty now decided to make this official. To this effect they sat down and drafted a statement, then Drummond rang Mick Houghton. "When he actually told me, he read the statement out, it was quite a shock, because even though I could see it coming I thought it was just that they were both mentally and physically exhausted," Houghton told *Select* magazine, "and to hear that statement… Bill told me that was it, we're not going to exist anymore, we're deleting the records. There's a finality to it."

The statement was not just released to the press but placed in full-page advertisements in the major music weeklies. It was, in some respects, a harking back to the letter Drummond had written when leaving Warner Brothers, when he had started out on this journey, "There is a mountain to climb the hard way, and I want to see the world from the top." He'd certainly achieved his aim, but now it was time to descend from the summit.

"We have been following a wild and wounded, glum and glorious, shit but shining path these past five years. The last two of which have led us up onto the commercial high ground - we are at a point now where the path is about to take a sharp turn from these sunny uplands down into a netherworld of we know not what. For the foreseeable future there will be no further record releases from The Justified Ancients Of Mu Mu, The Timelords, The JAMs, The KLF and any other past, present and future name attached to our activities. As of now all our past releases are deleted. Our P.O. Box will be open for correspondence. Our fax machine will remain switched on and our answerphone ready to record. From time to time these may be responded to. We would like to thank everybody (Friends and enemies alike) that have played a part on our journey (so far). If we meet further along be prepared… our disguise may be complete. In the meantime, the dark dip beckons. There is no further information. Rockman Rock and Kingboy D."

Fittingly it was Scott Piering who went into the KLF office to change the answerphone message to "This is the last recorded announcement from KLF Communications. Listen carefully, because it's the only and the last statement that will be made. Bill Drummond and Jimmy Cauty have left the music business. This answering machine and the KLF fax number will be operative for one month only from 13th May 1992. Do not expect a response, but all essential matters will be responded to. That's it."

It's the nature of the music business that bands split up, but no band had announced their departure in such a high profile manner at the peak of their commercial success, and stated that they were going to delete their back catalogue into the bargain. This was a bit of a jolt to Extreme Noise Terror, who were awaiting a call to go back into the studio to carry on with *The Black Room*. A few days later they began to worry about the £7,500 owed to them by The KLF. Presumably this payment would have been one of the "essential matters" that would be dealt with, one assumes, by Sallie Fellowes.

The news was widely reported in the music and mainstream press, and even got into *The Sun*. Beginning to establish a solo career, and working in Denmark on a track with Dr. Baker, Ricardo Lyte was even asked for his opinion on the demise of The KLF by a local journalist, although he had no real insight, "You never know. People can just believe what they want." Drummond and Cauty wisely removed themselves from the equation and flew off to Mexico. They did not announce whether it was to check out ancient Mayan temples or just drink lots and lots of tequila.

The KLF were no more.

WHAT THE K IS GOING ON?

> *"Public NME can exclusively reveal that BILL DRUMMOND and JIMMY CAUTY have already reformed. Holidaying together in Mexico, Bill 'n' Jim were sighted by a vacationing NME reader in a cantina in Tijuana, where they hopped on stage with a traditional conjunto band to run through a few Latin American favourites. Blimey, it's grim south of the border."*
>
> **- New Musical Express, May 1992**

> *"I think Bill invited me because I'm skint – I tried to tap him for some money at Reading – and when I saw the million pounds I just thought, Me debts! You bastard!"*
>
> **- Pete Wylie to Select, 1993**

Leaving the music business meant getting their affairs in order. When Drummond and Cauty deleted their entire catalogue in the UK, this meant there would be no further pressings of singles or albums on vinyl or CD to fulfil back catalogue orders from shops. There would be no *Greatest Hits – Now That's What I Call The KLF!* compilation either. What records were left in the warehouse of their distributor may have simply been liquidated or allowed to sell out. Matters may have been a little more complicated in other territories like Europe, America or further afield, where KLF Communications had licensed their material for a number of years, but as Drummond and Cauty intended to issue no more singles or albums this would dampen future demand. Those who wanted JAMs, Timelords, Disco 2000 or KLF records could now only buy them second-hand or on import.

Like any business, KLF Communications had legal representation and accountants, and Drummond and Cauty ensured that, as well as meeting any outstanding financial obligations, they recouped all monies due from record sales, radio play and overseas licensing. With over four million singles and two million albums sold in the UK alone, these sales had generated a lot of money, later estimated to be in the region of £6 million. Once expenses, professional fees and tax was taken into account and set aside for payment, Drummond and Cauty were probably millionaires.

Although they were both practical and bought houses, they also ordered a couple of matching, ultimate boys' toys. These were Humber Pigs, the armoured personnel carriers best known for being used by the British army in Northern Ireland. Once received, Drummond and Cauty employed a company called Powerhouse Design and Engineering Ltd in Kew to make them roadworthy. "The Pigs had to have three tons stripped off them to make them usable on the roads here," the company's Kevin McEvoy told *The Daily Mail,* who did a profile on them in July 1993. "The group just wanted to drive around in them. We had the police around the other day – they thought they were being prepared as ram-raiders." One assumes the vehicles were then taxed and insured, and the first time one was seen by the public was probably when Cauty took part in a charity car race with a number of other pop stars in an American Police car - a Pig was brought along, and even made it onto the racetrack at one point.

Despite leaving the music business, the next venture that Drummond and Cauty conceived was epic enough to deem a theme tune. "One day, Bill and Jim called me up," recalls Nick Coler, "They said, 'What are you doing?' I said, 'I'm going to a session.' They said, 'Could you just pop by Olympic (studios) and give us a hand?' I said, 'Alright,' as I had an hour or something. So I went down to Olympic as it was on the way to where I was going, and there were coaches outside - three great big fucking coaches - and all these guys walking around with sandwich bags. I went in and they said, 'We've got the Red Army Choir here. (laughs). We're doing a song but it's all wrong, so could you give us a hand?' They had all these guys walking around and they didn't have a translator with them - some guy with broken English was doing his best to get it all over. They had the orchestra and all the balalaikas set up and they couldn't play to a click track or anything, so I got the tempo and then left and went off to where I was really going."

Coler later went back to help Drummond and Cauty finish the track, which featured the Red Army Choir warbling the famous track *Que Sera Sera,* which had first been recorded in 1958 and was originally associated with Doris Day. Over time it had become something of a football anthem in the UK, sung by fans during FA cup runs, where they inserted a "we're going to Wembley" refrain, usually when they were 2-0 up with five minutes to go. The Red Army Choir version segued into the "War is over" chant from the 1972 song *Merry Xmas (War Is Over),* by John Lennon and Yoko Ono.

K Cera Cera (War Is Over If You Want It) was the first manifestation of Cauty and Drummond's new vehicle of expression - The K Foundation. Indeed, the Pigs were like enormous company cars, and would later be garishly painted and have a massive K daubed on their side. It was soon made clear to all that The K Foundation was not, however, the next musical station along the JAMs-Timelords-KLF mainline. "The K Foundation is not just the latest guise of The KLF," a spokesman told a music press desperate for news on Drummond and Cauty's activities. "Basically they're planning to release information through ads in the press over the next few weeks, and I'm not allowed to tell you much now. But one thing that I *can* tell you is that there will definitely not be pop records – or at least, not any that will be available."

This last cryptic statement made sense when banner adverts for *K Cera Cera* appeared and stated, "This recording will only ever be made commercially available once world peace has been firmly established. The responsibility is yours. Until then it will be heard only at selected state occasions, sporting events, music festivals or mass rallies." One of the music festivals that Drummond and Cauty hoped would play the song was the annual summer festival at Glastonbury in Somerset – they wanted the song to be played at the opening and closing of all three days like some rock 'n' roll Olympic anthem. "They sent a copy down to me and I listened to it three times, but it was absolutely appalling," stated organiser Michael Eavis, "It didn't sound at all 'rave'. It was just no good." So no Glastonbury. The Football Association also rejected *K Cera Cera* when Drummond and Cauty approached them to have it played before the annual Charity Shield match, between Champions Manchester United and FA cup winners Arsenal, at Wembley on 7th August 1993. Sadly, there were also no convenient mass rallies scheduled.

Although the full-page adverts stated that *K Cera Cera* was, "available nowhere" on "no formats," it was soon made available in a limited edition of three thousand copies as a CD single via mail order in Israel. "Only a few days after the production (of the single) was finished, I turned on the TV and saw Yitzhak Rabin (Israeli Prime Minister) and Yasser Arafat (leader of the Palestine Liberation Organisation) standing next to each other in front of the White House," Drummond told a journalist *from Yediot Ahronoet*, Israel's leading newspaper, "I was very moved. It was like something you never dreamt would happen suddenly being realised. I phoned Jimmy and we decided to release the limited edition. For us, it's a sort of tribute."

This was Drummond's first pronouncement to any media organisation for some time as he and Cauty would not even make themselves available to promote the work of The K Foundation through interview. It was Mick Houghton, their press officer, who'd been their spokesman to the press, and as trustees of The K Foundation the only way Drummond and Cauty would communicate was through further adverts in the music press and nationwide newspapers. That said, Drummond did state in his interview with *Yediot* that The K Foundation had higher aims than topping the charts, "Our idea was to create awareness of peace in the world. Because we were worried it would be interpreted by the public as an attempt by The KLF to return to the music world on the back of a humanist gimmick, we decided to hide behind the Foundation."

What Drummond and Cauty were now doing as The K Foundation was slowly but cryptically spelt out in their adverts. "TIME IS RUNNING OUT. SWITCH TO K TIME NOW" read one, and "ABANDON ALL ART NOW. AWAIT FURTHER INSTRUCTIONS" another. "MAJOR RETHINK IN PROGRESS" stated a third. Both adverts featured a PO Box address, from which further information could be requested.

It was soon being reported that The K Foundation's initial "situationist ads" had cost Drummond and Cauty in the region of £47,000, ranging from a reasonable £3,000 in the *New Musical Express* to a whopping £28,000 in *The Sun*. These figures were, of course, provided as a press release.

The next stage in the development of The K Foundation was soon announced, "IT HAS BEEN BROUGHT TO OUR ATTENTION THAT YOU DID NOT ABANDON ALL ART. SERIOUS DIRECT ACTION IS THEREFORE NECESSARY." This was the establishment of The K Foundation Award, which would be handed out on the 23rd November 1993 to the artist, "who, in the opinion of the jury, has produced the worst body of work in the preceding twelve months." The prize was £40,000 in cash, and the shortlisted artists were Hannah Collins, Vong Phaophanit, Sean Scully and Rachel Whiteread.

Drummond and Cauty hadn't chosen those four artists at random or engaged in extensive research on the merits of the UK art scene, but had simply listed the four artists who'd been nominated on the shortlist for the Turner Prize, which had been established in 1984 and was awarded by the Tate Gallery in London to rising British artists. Previous winners had included Gilbert and George, although in 1991 there was no award due to the bankruptcy of the sponsors (an investment bank, not Rough Trade). The following year Channel 4 stepped in and doubled the prize money to £20,000. Thus the K Foundation had doubled the existing prize money to £40,000.

The advert generated a glut of articles across the press spectrum on The K Foundation and the Turner award. Even Tate Gallery director Nicholas Serote told the *Evening Standard* that, "The K Foundation advertisements will help stimulate discussion of contemporary art, one of the main purposes of the Turner Prize." A number of opinion pieces on Drummond and Cauty's possible intentions were also penned, with Robert Sandall stating that, "Either way, this year's Turner prize is guaranteed to attract a far wider audience than usual – which fulfils one of The KLF's old maxims: making the unthinkable happen." As for the artist's work, David Lillington wrote in *Time Out,* "They're all different. This year the absurdity of the choice has been given a kind of formal structure, which drives it home with extra force. The judges have to compare a painter, an installation artist, a photographer and a sculptor. It's crazy. Still it gives us something to talk about."

The jury selected by The K Foundation was the public at large - anybody could write in and state who, in their opinion, was the worst of the four artists. The K Foundation even printed a large ballot paper in further adverts. They also cleverly pointed out that an overview of the work of the four artists was opening at the Tate Gallery in a special exhibition on the 3rd November, so that people who wanted to vote could, "flex your artistic critical facilities or just stay at home and use your innate prejudices." As for voting, the ballot could be ticked and then posted to The K Foundation's PO Box, "to arrive no later than 13th of November 1993."

When it came to the day of the award on 23rd November, Drummond and Cauty pulled out all the stops - the winner of the K Foundation award was to be announced on a short advert on Channel 4. In addition, "To keep pace with global events, The K Foundation is forced to bring forward the private view of its first major body of work on the evening of the 23rd of November 1993." Forty people would be selected and transported to a secret location near London, where they would be able to "witness and document the amending of Art History."

One hundred invitations were sent out, and those who were lucky enough to be invited were advised to, "Respond now to guarantee a place." Although Drummond and Cauthy were no longer operating in the music business, those who could be contacted to secure a seat at this rather unusual table included the usual suspects - Scott Piering and Mick Houghton - as well as The K Foundation's legal and financial advisors. The final guest list included a number of journalists, photographers, artists and people from the music business. As for what The K Foundation's first art exhibition would be called, this was soon revealed to be *MONEY: A Major Body Of Cash.* The most arresting item in the list of several works featured in the catalogue was the first, "*Nailed To the Wall* – £1,000,000 (one million pounds sterling) in mint fifty pound notes nailed to a wall constructed of skip pine. To be auctioned. Reserve Price £500,000."

On the day, those selected were picked up outside the Gloucester Hotel by a fleet of white, stretched limousines at six thirty in the evening. The cars were fully stocked with "protective clothing" and champagne, and the first pit stop was the Heston Service Station on the M4. At this point, twenty-five people were handed a pack that contained £1650 in £50 notes. The £1600 formed part of the £40,000 that would be awarded to the winner of The K Foundation Award and would be hammered to a convenient frame later that evening. As for the additional £50, "THIS IS FOR YOU TO TAKE AND HAVE VERIFIED FOR ITS NON-COUNTERFEIT STATUS AND THEN SPEND ON WHATEVER YOU WANT."

At this point, everybody was going to be transported to the final assembly point by helicopter, but due to the very cold conditions this was cancelled, so it was back into the white limos and onto the road, where they were driven to a snow-covered field somewhere in Surrey. When they arrived there was music being played on PA systems attached to the K Foundation Pigs - in keeping with the theme of the evening, the short playlist comprised of *Money Money Money* by ABBA, *K Sera Sera* and the Greenwich Mean Time pips, which were probably intended to serve as K Time for the evening.

In many respects, the event contained elements of the previous KLF outing to the Isle Of Jura, except that in this instance Drummond and Cauty kept a low profile. It had been Drummond who had stamped passports when people had disembarked from the ferry on Jura and had officiated in the ceremony prior to the wicker man being ceremoniously burnt, but on this cold night, apart from driving the Pigs, he and Cauty were nowhere to be seen. Everything was being run on a strict timetable, with the role of master of ceremonies being handled by "Mr Ball" who was part of the security team for the evening.

Those in attendance – wearing protective clothing bearing the K logo and hard hats - were led down a marked track to view *Nailed To The Wall*, which was protected by two security guards in bow ties and illuminated by arc lights. Those filing past were instructed by loudhailer that, "You may look, but you may not touch the exhibit!"

The guests *were* eventually allowed to get their hands on some cash as participants were invited to step forward and, using a hammer, nail £1600 to a pre-prepared frame containing twenty-five white crosses showing where the money should be placed and affixed. When this was complete, an announcement was made stating that four people had not come forward to nail the £1600 they'd received to the frame, and, despite requests for them to step forward, no-one did so. So the total sum nailed to the frame was in the region of £33,600. After soup and bread rolls were served, the frame containing the prize money was put in the boot of one of the limousines in preparation for the drive back to London. In the meantime, Rachel Whiteread had been announced as the winner of The K Foundation Award through the medium of a TV advert on Channel 4 - it appears that three thousand votes had been cast. "She was a fairly convincing winner," stated Mick Houghton, "Whiteread seems to have captured their imagination. Maybe people just liked the sound of her name, or rather didn't." Whiteread had also won the Turner Prize.

When the limos arrived outside the Tate Gallery at around ten forty-five and everybody piled out, it was discovered – one assumes the money was either counted at this point or on the drive back from Surrey – that the "exhibit' actually totalled £2,000 less than £33,600, so in the region of £31,600. Some of the participants had pocketed a number of £50 notes at some point in the proceedings. Neither Drummond or Cauty were in attendance outside the Tate – they were sitting in a car parked around the corner – but it was announced that the missing money would be made good at a later date to ensure that Whitread received the full £40,00 due to her. At first, Whiteread – enjoying the post-Turner party inside the Tate - stated that she would not accept The K Foundation Award as it was an, "absurd joke and publicity stunt." When, however, she was informed that if she did not accept the prize it would be burned, she relented. Filmed and photographed, she declared it, "a great honour" as she received the award.

The night ended with the limos ferrying everyone to Islington, where The K Foundation funded a free bar into the early hours of the morning. The usually verbose Drummond was so tight-lipped that when he encountered a journalist from *Q* magazine in the toilet and was asked for a quote he ended up, "running from the Gents, finger to lip and head shaking wildly." He returned to a private room where he was supping with Cauty and other close associates of the foundation.

Once the dust had settled, The K Foundation were quick to provide facts and figures concerning all of the steps relating to the events leading up The K Foundation Award, and even photos of the construction of *Nailed To A Wall*. It was revealed that the million pounds collected from the Basingstoke Bullion Centre was the largest cash withdrawal that the National Westminister Bank had authorised at that time, that it was collected in person by Jimmy Cauty and that it cost £7,000 to insure the money for the few minutes it was in his possession before he handed it over to Ratedale Ltd, the security firm entrusted with looking after it whilst it was on day release from the bullion centre. One assumes Ratedate officials were also on hand later that afternoon when Drummond and Cauty nailed the million to a board to create *Nailed To A Wall*. Finally, The Bank of England stated that they were unhappy that the notes had been "defaced" by having a nail driven through them, but although there was talk no further action was taken.

Even Peter Chater, director of the Karsten Schubert Agency who represented Whiteread, got in on the act, "They're basically cowards. When I spoke to Bill Drummond, he said he wasn't going to be there because he is shy of publicity, which was a joke. It was obviously a publicity stunt. What sort of statement they were trying to make I don't know. If it was anything to do with the relationship between art and money, it was pretty crass. The KLF made a fortune from a couple of successful singles. Artists' aren't in that position. Threatening to set light to £40,000 is pretty obscene."

The affair generated a number of reports across the entire media spectrum, including radio, TV, the music press and mainstream newspapers. The *New Musical Express* and *Q* magazine, for example, went to town with extensive features and lashings of photographs, as well as a number of quotes from those in attendance, like sculptor Andy Elton – "I've put an offer in of £700,000 for the million. It's not art, it's a million" – and Tony Wilson, former head of Factory Records, who had gone bankrupt in November 1992, "The K Foundation is a very peculiar avant-garde group whose ideas are as valid as anything the Turner people do." *Select* journalist Miranda Sawyer did touch upon the truth when she stated, "no one really minded when The K Foundation spent their money on something concrete like adverts. People got upset when cash was flaunted for the sake of an idea." Ironically, Rachel Whiteread's art at this time was all about covering everyday objects, from the humble mattress to a small house, in concrete, but rather than do the same to the £40,000 she distributed it amongst a number of other artists less successful than herself.

At the end of the day, however, when it came to Drummond and Cauty many questions were not answered. What did it all mean and what was it all for? Was it a prank? Was it a comment upon modern art? Was it a comment on money? A way to offset tax through the enormous cost – estimated in the region of £250,000 – of the whole exercise?

In light of subsequent events, *Q* posed the most pertinent question, "Does it simply mean that Drummond and Cauty have got money to burn?"

CODA - BUILD A FIRE

"Is no more to say now, is no more to say… is no more to say now, is no more to say… is no more to say now, is no more today…"

- The Residents' 'Tourniquet Of Roses'

On 22nd August 1994, Bill Drummond and Jimmy Cauty were preparing to fly up to Scotland. They were returning once again to the isle of Jura.

They'd tried to use The K Foundation Award to springboard themselves into the art world, and in early 1994 had tried to get a number of galleries interested in displaying their million pound installation, in a number of permutations, without success. They'd even offered *Nailed To A Wall* to the Tate Gallery with the sole condition that it be on permanent display for a decade. They were turned down. So, what to do next?

Their next step started as a joke by Cauty, but it took on form and substance and had been agreed between them in a café some six weeks previously. On the 22nd August, Drummond and Cauty were to fly up to Jura with a journalist, Jim Reid, and Gimpo in tow to put their plan into effect.

They left London normal men, albeit with something of a reputation and some rather unique and valuable luggage. But when they returned they would no longer be mere men - what they did in Jura ferried them across more water than they probably intended to cross.

On 23rd August 1994, Bill Drummond and Jimmy Cauty became *media immortal*.

ELVIS ON THE RADIO, STEEL GUITAR IN MY SOUL

As the editor of *Record Collector's Rare Record Price Guide* there is nothing I like more than a good discography. However, rather than serve up a list of The JAMs, The Timelords, Disco 2000, The Orb, Space and The KLF recordings I thought I would provide a playlist that might act as a suitable soundtrack to this book. It goes without saying that you should listen to everything Bill Drummond and Jimmy Cauty served up, as well as every other track by every artist mentioned in this book, but here are thirty-one to get you started...

BIG IN JAPAN	Big In Japan
ECHO & THE BUNNYMEN	The Picture On My Wall
THE TEARDROP EXPLODES	Treason
THE WILD SWANS	The Revolutionary Spirit
WHIPPETS FROM NOWHERE	Last Bench In Dieppe
BIG HAIR	Puppet On A String
ANGELS ONE 5	Countdown
SPOON FAZER	Ballad Of Insect Man
JULIAN COPE	Bill Drummond Said
BILL DRUMMOND	Julian Cope Is Dead
BRILLIANT	Love Is War
THE JAMs	All You Need Is Love
THE JAMs	Hey Hey We Are Not The Monkees
THE JAMs	The Queen And I
THE JAMs	Burn The Bastards
THE TIMELORDS	Doctorin' The Tardis
MR. FINGERS	Washing Machine
PHUTURE	Acid Tracks
RON TRENT	Altered States

MOODY BOYS	Acid Heaven
MOODY BOYS	Funky Zulu
	(You're So Fresh)
DISCO 2000	Mr Hotty Loves You
THE ORB	Loving You
THE ORB	Little Fluffy Clouds
A SPLIT SECOND	Flesh
THE KLF	What Time Is Love?
THE KLF	3AM Eternal
THE KLF	Madrugada Eterna
THE KLF	Justified and Ancient
	(LP version)
THE KLF	The White Room
SPACE	Jupiter

Ian Shirley

Other titles available from

A Plugged In State Of Mind: The
History of Electronic Music
Dave Henderson

All The Young Dudes: Mott The Hoople
& Ian Hunter
Campbell Devine

Arguments Yard – 35 Years Of Ranting
Verse And Thrash Mandola
Atilla The Stockbroker

Best Seat In The House: A Cock
Sparrer Story
Steve Bruce

Bittersweet: The Clifford T Ward Story
David Cartwright

Block Buster! – The True Story of The
Sweet
Dave Thompson

Burning Britain: A History Of UK Punk
1980 To 1984
Ian Glasper

Celebration Day: A Led Zeppelin
Encyclopedia
Malcolm Dome and Jerry Ewing

Children of the Revolution: The Glam
Rock Encyclopedia
Dave Thompson

Death To Trad Rock: The Post-Punk
fanzine scene 1982-87
John Robb

Deathrow: The Chronicles Of
Psychobilly
Alan Wilson

Embryo:- A Pink Floyd Chronology
1966-1971
Nick Hodges And Ian Priston

Fucked By Rock (Revised and
Expanded)
**Mark Manning (aka Zodiac
Mindwarp)**

Goodnight Jim Bob: On The Road With
Carter USM
Jim Bob

Good Times Bad Times - The Rolling
Stones 1960-69
Terry Rawlings and Keith Badman

Hells Bent On Rockin: A History Of
Psychobilly
Craig Brackenbridge

Independence Days - The Story Of UK
Independent Record Labels
Alex Ogg

Indie Hits 1980 – 1989
Barry Lazell

Irish Folk, Trad And Blues: A Secret
History
Colin Harper and Trevor Hodgett

Johnny Thunders: In Cold Blood
Nina Antonia

Kiss Me Neck – A Lee 'Scratch' Perry Discography
Jeremy Collingwood

Music To Die For: The International Guide To Goth, Goth Metal, Horror Punk, Psychobilly Etc
Mick Mercer

Never Known Questions – Five Decades Of The Residents
Ian Shirley

No More Heroes: A Complete History Of UK Punk From 1976 To 1980
Alex Ogg

Number One Songs In Heaven - The Sparks Story
Dave Thompson

Our Music Is Red - With Purple Flashes: The Story Of The Creation
Sean Egan

Prophets and Sages: The 101 Greatest Progressive Rock Albums
Mark Powell

PWL: From The Factory Floor (Expanded Edition)
Phil Harding

Quite Naturally - The Small Faces
Keith Badman and Terry Rawlings

Random Precision - Recording The Music Of Syd Barrett 1965-1974
David Parker

Rockdetector: A To Zs of '80s Rock / Black Metal / Death Metal / Doom, Gothic & Stoner Metal / Power Metal and Thrash Metal
Garry Sharpe-Young

Rockdetector: Black Sabbath - Never Say Die
Garry Sharpe-Young

Rockdetector: Ozzy Osbourne
Garry Sharpe-Young

Tamla Motown - The Stories Behind The Singles
Terry Wilson

The Day The Country Died: A History Of Anarcho Punk 1980 To 1984
Ian Glasper

The Legendary Joe Meek - The Telstar Man
John Repsch

The Motorhead Collector's Guide
Mick Stevenson

The Rolling Stones' Complete Recording Sessions 1962-2002
Martin Elliott

The Secret Life Of A Teenage Punk Rocker: The Andy Blade Chronicles
Andy Blade

Those Were The Days - The Beatles' Apple Organization
Stefan Grenados

Trapped In A Scene: UK Hardcore 1985-89
Ian Glasper

Truth... Rod Steward, Ron Wood And The Jeff Beck Group
Dave Thompson

You're Wondering Now - The Specials from Conception to Reunion
Paul Williams

Please visit **www.cherryredbooks.co.uk** for further info and mail order

Here at Cherry Red Books we're always interested to hear of interesting
titles looking for a publisher. Whether it's a new manuscript or an out
of print or deleted title, please feel free to get in touch if you have
something you think we should know about.

books@cherryred.co.uk

www.cherryredbooks.co.uk
www.cherryred.co.uk

CHERRY RED BOOKS
A division of Cherry Red Records Ltd,
Power Road Studios
114 Power Road
London
W4 5PY